PSALMS 90-150

Eric Lane

PSALMS 90-150

The Lord reigns

Eric Lane

CHRISTIAN FOCUS

ISBN 1-84550-202-7
ISBN 978-1-84550-202-7

10 9 8 7 6 5 4 3 2 1

Published in 2006
in the
Focus on the Bible Commentary Series
by
Christian Focus Publications Ltd.,
Geanies House ,Fearn, Ross-shire,
IV20 1TW, Scotland, UK

www.christianfocus.com

Cover design by Danie Van Straaten

Printed and bound by
J. H. Haynes, Sparkford

Contents

Foreword

This second volume covers Books IV and V of the Psalms, and begins with what is probably the earliest Psalm of all – Psalm 90, since it is attributed to Moses. Psalm 91 probably comes from the same author and refers to the same incident. These are followed by several psalms of praise and thanksgiving addressed to 'the Lord as King'. The long psalms which close Book IV (104–106) give historical proof that 'the Lord is King', as they recall the great works of God in creation and providence and more particularly in the history of Israel. The first few psalms of Book V take up the theme of redemption suggested by the historical psalms at the end of Book IV. Then comes the mighty 119th psalm glorying in the law or word of God, the instrument through which he exercises his Kingship. This is followed by the 'Songs of Ascent' (120–134) the pilgrim songs composed for travellers to sing as they approached Jerusalem to celebrate one of its festivals. Praise and thanksgiving are mingled with prayer and heart-searching in the psalms which follow, but from 144 praise completely takes over and mounts to a glorious climax in the final psalm. In the Appendix you will find a suggested possible chronological order for the composition of the Psalms, which will enable you, if you so desire, to link them with events in the Old Testament. For further introductory matters please refer to the beginning of my Focus on the Bible Commentary on Psalms 1–89.

Eric Lane

Notes

Abbreviations:

f   the following verse
cf   compare
MT   Masoretic Text, i.e. the Hebrew text of the Old Testament
LXX   Septuagint, i.e. the Greek translation of the Old Testament, from the 3rd century BC
OT   Old Testament
NT   New Testament
Mg   Margin, i.e. the notes at the bottom of the page in the NIV
KJV   The King James Version of 1611
NKJV   The New King James Version of 1982
GNB   The Good News Bible of 1971
ESV   The English Standard Version of 2001

Books consulted:

J. A. Alexander: *The Psalms Translated and Explained* (Zondervan)
C. C. Broyles: *The Psalms: New International Biblical Commentary* (Hendriksen/Paternoster)
J. M. Good: *Historical Outline of the Book of Psalms* (London: W. H. Dalton, 1842). Out of print
Allan Harman: *The Psalms – a Mentor Commentary* (Mentor/ Christian Focus)
G. W. Grogan: *Prayer, Praise and Prophecy* (Mentor/Christian Focus)
F. D. Kidner: *The Psalms* (IVP)
H. C. Leupold: *Exposition of the Psalms* (Evangelical Press)
C. S. Lewis: *Reflections on the Psalms* (Collins Fontana)
W. S. Plumer: *The Psalms* (Banner of Truth)

Psalm 90

Consumed by God's Anger

The subtitle *a prayer of Moses the man of God* makes this the earliest psalm in the Psalter. It was not the only poem or song to come from his hand. The triumphal ode recorded in Exodus 15 is called 'The Song of Moses'. He wrote a further song to accompany the housing of the book of the Law in the ark of the Covenant (Deut. 31:30–32:44). His blessing of the tribes of Israel before his death (Deut. 33) is also in verse. There are other poetical fragments: the song they sang as they left their camp carrying the ark (Num. 10:35-16), the ode to the well at Beer (Num. 21:17-18), and the curse on Heshbon and Moab (Num. 21:26-30). Even parts of the Law itself take on a verse form (Deut. 27:14-26; 28:3-6, 16-19).

The psalm is entitled *a prayer* because it is all addressed to God. While many psalms are songs of praise, many are prayers. It was composed at a time when numbers of the people were being struck dead as a judgment on their sin (vv. 5-8). Occasions when this happened include the people's complaint about their diet of manna (Num. 11:33) and their discouragement over the report of the spies (Num. 14:26-45). The one that fits best however, is Numbers 21:4-7, when further murmuring over food provoked a plague of venomous snakes from God.

In Numbers 21:7 the people request Moses to pray for them, which he does. Psalm 90 is probably the prayer he prayed. Verses 3 and 5 refer to sudden death overtaking them; verse 7 indicates this was a visitation on the whole nation, and verse 8 speaks of (literally) *secret lustings*, referring to their discontent with the manna and longing for the food of Egypt (Num. 21:4-5).

It may be objected that the average life span of 70 to 80 years mentioned in verse 10 was not in force at that time. But the longevity of such as Moses, Aaron, Caleb and Joshua was exceptional and no doubt due to the nation's need of these great leaders for a long time, not to speak of it as a reward for the outstanding godliness of some of them (cf. Ps. 91:16). Most of the people must have lived less than 100 years. The probable meaning is that this average life span was brought in during the desert period and soon became universal. Later leaders such as Samuel, David and Solomon lived only 60 to 70 years.

Verses 1-2: The eternal God (v. 2) as the dwelling place of his people
Verse 1 anticipates Moses' words at the end of the plague: 'If you make the Most High your dwelling' (91:9) and his blessing at the end of his life: 'The eternal God is your refuge' (Deut. 33:27). It shows how God's people in all ages should face calamity, even when it is deserved and from God:

(1) We should turn our thoughts to God who is *everlasting* (v. 2), not limited like us to a few short years, and above and beyond all change. In this way we will feel our dependence upon him and, as we know from our 'parenting' lessons, nothing 'bonds' a child to a parent more closely than a sense of dependence. In this way disaster, instead of distancing us from God, can draw us closer to him.

(2) We should look on this God, not as some far-off Being, but as our home, now and hereafter (v. 1). For the fact that God is eternal and we are temporal, that he is holy and we are sinful, does not mean he is not open to receive us. The sense of dependence, which actually comprises faith and repentance, is not merely a comfort but a means of access

to his heart. *We* should know this better than Moses, for the promise of Christ is that through his ministry and the coming of the Holy Spirit, not only does he become our *dwelling place*, but we actually become his (John 14:20, 23)! At the same time he is preparing us a home in which to dwell with him for ever (John 14:1).

Verses 3-6 : Human frailty and helplessness

Realising this increases our sense of dependence. We are subject to death (v. 3; Gen. 3:19; Eccles. 12:7), whereas God is totally unaffected by the passage of time (v. 4). *Death* can overtake us suddenly and without warning (vv. 5-6). This shows that contemplating God's eternal being and dwelling in him (vv. 1-2) does not reduce the realities of life and the starkness of death, but it does show us how to face them – by finding a permanent home, not in our body or the world, but in God.

Verses 7-11: God's sentence on sinful beings

Death is not part of a natural process but is a divine judgment. We need to accept this, for it produces that repentance and faith which will lead us home to God. But not all see it that way (v. 11a) and must be taught how to do so. The right response (v. 11b) is to let our *fear* of God (that is, our acquiescence in his right to judge and destroy) correspond to the reality of *his wrath* (his righteous anger that sends such judgments). In other words, God's righteous judgment should be an over-powering reality to us – enough to cause us to repent of our sin and then fly to him for salvation. Disasters do not naturally affect us like this (Rev. 9:20) – they need his special grace.

Verses 12-17: Calling on God

These verses form the specific request of the prayer, yet occupy only about a third of the psalm. This is a lesson in itself: preparation for prayer is as important as prayer itself. What Moses prays for is also instructive:

- **Verse 12**: that we take seriously the fact that our *days* are *numbered* so that we make wiser use of them. If

disaster and death teach us this they have some value
(cf. Luke 13:1-5).

- **Verses 13-15**: that God will curtail his judgment (v. 13)
  and restore us to his favour (v. 14a) so that we may
  recover our *joy* (vv. 14b-15).
- **Verses 16-17**: that God will *work* in us and also show his
  glory to the rising generation (v. 16), and bring this about
  by blessing us and our *work* for him (v. 17).

Questions:

(1) What is our 'work' for God as Christians? How does it
relate to God as 'everlasting'? (See Rom. 16:25-26.)

(2) Turn to John 3:14-16 and consider how Jesus used the
incident of the brazen serpent to portray his Gospel.

Psalm 91

Healed by God's Touch

Although anonymous, there are good reasons for attributing this psalm also to Moses. The Rabbis did so, although on the doubtful principle that no other author is stipulated until 101, which means that 92–100 are also from Moses! The Septuagint and Vulgate ascribe it to David on the occasion of his numbering the people (2 Sam. 24). However, the atmosphere of the psalm is that of a nomadic life rather than the more settled times of David's kingdom.

The most likely occasion is the ending of the plague of venomous snakes, which occasioned Psalm 90. The spirit of murmuring had been put away and God was again leading them on their journey (Num. 21:10-15). Eventually they arrived at the well 'Beer' (Num. 21:16-18) where Moses composed an ode. There is good evidence for believing he wrote this psalm at that time:

- The spirit of murmuring had given way to the spirit of faith (vv. 1-2); Moses had prayed they would look to God as their *refuge and ... fortress* and now they were doing so.
- The memory of the *pestilence* was still vivid (vv. 3, 6) and possibly they feared its recurrence.
- They were exposed to the dangers of that area: fierce desert tribes like Amalek, Moab and Midian, who might

raid by *night* or fire *arrows* from behind rocks *by day* (v. 5).

- They had seen *thousands* of their friends fall prey to *the plague* (v. 7).
- Other rigours of the nomadic life were continuing: *snares* and traps (v. 3), disease (v. 6), *disaster* (v. 10), boulders and rough ground (v. 12) and wild beasts (v. 13).

As well as these incidentals there is the lesson Moses is trying to instill into them from their recent experience: to repent of their discontent and replace it with a spirit of confidence in God as the one who protects his people from all dangers – the note he strikes at the very outset (vv. 1-2).

Verses 1-2: Words of encouragement

These verses take up the words of 90:1, which he there had addressed to God, and turns them into an encouragement to the people, now that the judgment has passed. Rather than inflict trouble on us, God wants to protect us from it (v. 1). But we must trust him ourselves (v. 2): *I will say ... he is my refuge ... my fortress ... my God*. While we are complaining about the way he treats us we cannot feel relaxed with him – at peace and in safety. We move out of his *shadow* and are exposed to dangers. If we swallow our pride and rebelliousness and trust him, we will enjoy this relationship.

Verses 3-13: Promises of protection

These verses spell out the particular dangers which God's promise of protection covers. They read like an insurance policy! It covers *snares* (v. 3a), *pestilence* (v. 3b), violent attacks from enemies (vv. 5-8), safety both for your person and your home (vv. 9-10) and *angelic* protection from the rigours of the journey and from wild beasts (vv. 11-13). We Christians with our relatively settled life in peaceful communities may not find some of these particularly relevant, but our Christian pathway through the world is beset with difficulties: from the people of the world, from false teachers, from the devil and from our own sinful natures. God's protection covers these equally and verse 4 certainly applies directly to us.

Verses 14-16: Means of enjoying these promises

These verses summarize all this by returning to generalities, in which he balances God's promises along with our use of the means of enjoying them.

His promises are:

1. To *rescue* us from danger (v. 14) by 'setting us on high' (as the KJV correctly translates the word rendered *protect* in the NIV) – that is, by putting us above and beyond the reach of trouble.
2. To answer our cries for help (v. 15), which might not mean instant deliverance, but a period in which he will share our trouble with us until the time for deliverance and restoration comes.
3. To give us a fulfilled *life* (*satisfy*, v. 16), which under the old covenant meant length of days (Prov. 3:1, 2, 16) and under the new covenant the 'full life' Jesus promised (John 10:10) – life in him and the Spirit.
4. To give us continual proofs of his power and willingness to save (v. 1).

Our means are:

1. Loving him (v. 14), that is, deliberately choosing and cleaving to him.
2. Acknowledging his *name* (v. 14), that is, his attributes and person, so that, when we do not understand what is happening, we still believe it is consistent with God's character.
3. Calling on him in prayer (v. 15), which is the outward expression of our inward feeling of trust in him. Prayer brings specific situations to him and expects him to fulfill his promises (cf. John 14:12-14).

Questions:
Consider verses 11-12.

(1) Can we expect angels to minister to us today? If so, in what ways?

(2) When Satan quoted these words to Jesus (Matt. 4:5-7) why did the Lord refuse them as 'putting God to the test'?

Psalm 92

Praise the LORD

Although this *psalm* is entitled *A song for the Sabbath day*, it is clearly not any *Sabbath* but one following a recent victory (11). *The Sabbath* was not only a rest day but 'a day of sacred assembly' (Lev. 23:3), to be used not just for the praise of God in general terms but for celebrating special deliverances, such as this recent defeat of their enemies.

Verses 1-3: Objective Worship
This is a useful summary of what worship is and is for. It is not merely right but *good*, that is, in God's estimation. We should think first, not of how we feel but whether we are pleasing God and honouring the *name (of the) Most High*. We should be preoccupied, not with our enjoyment, but with his *love ... and ... faithfulness. Music* is a useful means of doing this: partly because a *melody* with its regular rhythm enables people to keep together, and partly because it helps to express our emotions. To do this a musician and an instrument are needed. The Hebrew simply reads 'upon the ten' and may therefore refer simply to *the harp* rather than to two instruments.

Verses 4-7: Subjective enjoyment
While the primary aim of worship is ascribing to God his glory, it is impossible to separate the worshippers' feelings from this. If they are truly thankful for his *love ... and ... faithfulness* they

will feel *glad* and *sing for joy* (v. 4). This will be particularly so when something has happened to demonstrate God's *love ... and ... faithfulness,* as it had with the defeat of Israel's enemies at this time. So here the people are moved by God's *deeds ... the work of your hands. How great* these are (v. 5)! This leads to a further consideration. If God's *works* are *great* how much more *profound* must be the *thoughts* which gave them birth! The works of God reveal the wisdom of God: 'O the depths of the riches of the wisdom and knowledge of God!' says Paul, after his in-depth survey of the greatest of all God's works – our salvation in Christ (Rom. 11:33).

But not everybody knows this: *the senseless man does not know* (v. 6) – not because he is mentally deficient, but because he is spiritually dead. He lacks the primary feature of his original image of God – the spiritual faculty. Nor does this just mean that he misses out on the best in life; it means he has no hope for the future. He lives only for the present, when he is alive, growing *like grass* and flourishing (v. 7). But he does *not understand* that *like grass* he will become 'dry and withered' (90:6), then cut down and burnt (Isa. 40:6-8). Worship of God is not merely *good* and enjoyable – it is an expression of life from the dead.

Verses 8-11: Shared Victory
But (v. 8) indicates a contrast with the preceding. *The wicked* are soon *destroyed,* but God is *for ever.* He is also *exalted* over them and over all. So the reason *(his) enemies will perish* and *evil-doers will be scattered* (v. 9) is not due so much to the ordinary course of nature as to his activity. They have exalted themselves against him. Although *senseless* they took it on themselves to refuse him his place. Now they are no more but he continues *exalted.*

But God's *enemies* are his people's enemies. So God's victory is their victory, and whoever may be king at the time can claim that he too is *exalted* (v. 10). *Horn* probably has a double meaning. The mention of *the wild ox* means that *horn* has the usual sense of strength (cf. 75:10; 89:17). But a *horn* when cut off and hollowed out was filled with oil and used in an anointing ceremony. Line 2 of verse 10 shows that this meaning is also in mind. By giving the king a share in his victory God has demonstrated he is truly called and equipped for the office. So he can speak of God's *enemies* as *my adversaries*, and their *defeat* (v. 11) as *the rout of my wicked foes*.

Verses 12-15: Fruitful Life

The contrast between God's people and his enemies continues. The latter are like *the grass* with its short life: it grows quickly but is soon cut down, either by the cattle's teeth or the mower's blade. But *the righteous ... flourish like a palm tree* (v. 12), which outlasts many generations of people, *like a cedar of Lebanon* which does not remain static but grows. This is because God has *planted* them in his *house ... and ... courts* (v. 13), that is, he has taken them from the world and brought them to himself, so that they share his nature and have eternal life. So, however long they last, even to *old age*, they *still bear fruit* and *stay fresh and green* (v. 14): their relationship with God deepens, they become more like him and are 'inwardly renewed day by day' (2 Cor. 4:16). Above all, they never cease to give God the glory (v. 15). If they have continued faithful, strong and fruitful, it is because *the LORD is upright ... my Rock*, free from all *wickedness*.

Such are the thoughts that occupy God's people on *the Sabbath day*.

Questions:

(1) Can there be subjective enjoyment of worship without objective concentration on God's being, and vice versa? Does this describe your personal worship and that of your church?

(2) How is your spiritual life coping with the ageing process? Is it running down like your physical life or is 2 Corinthians 4:16 true for you?

(3) Do you keep 'Sabbaths' – not merely by 'going to church on Sunday' but having times of rest from activity, when you can contemplate God and the progress of his kingdom in yourself and the wider sphere?

Psalm 93

The King Returns Victorious

Although Israel had a King, both they and he were always conscious that the real King was the Lord (see Isa. 33:22) So, just as the church composes hymns to Christ as King, so did Israel compose psalms in honour of the Lord's reign.

Verses 1-2: The King of the World
At times the king would parade before the people in his royal robes and armour, but only to symbolise *the LORD ... robed in majesty* (a phrase which is duplicated to place him high over the king) and *armed with strength* – not with the sword, spear and shield that the king carried, but with the creating, upholding power that made *the world* and *firmly established (it)* so that *it cannot be moved.* For God did not come to his throne at a particular point in time like the king; his *throne was established long ago ... from all eternity.* Thoughts of the king are being left far behind and the Lord alone is taking centre stage.

Verses 3-4: Lord of the Seas
The poetry is graphic – its crescendo expresses a storm raging more and more fiercely and *pounding* against the shore. No doubt the constant attacks of their enemies are symbolised here. But *the LORD on high* rides out the storm and by his *might* he crushes it, as he has done their enemies.

Verse 5: The Lord for ever

Why has the Lord crushed their enemies? Who is the king and what is Israel that this mighty God should take their side? This verse tells us: he is the One who has entered into a covenant with Israel and David – *statutes* is often translated 'testimonies', referring to God's covenant promises to his people. These he will keep because he is *holy*, without flaw, and as the Holy One he dwells among them in his *house*, which has been set up for him on Zion, and where he will dwell *for endless days*.

Question:

Since Christ said **he** was David's 'Lord' (Matt. 22:41-45), this psalm should increase our vision of Christ's present reign. How does it help yours?

Psalm 94

The God Who Avenges

The majestic, sovereign God of the previous psalm will not allow his honour to be impugned. Since it is connected with the fortunes of his covenant people, what is done to them is done to him, and he will swiftly intervene to deliver them. Possibly the psalm was written when Israel was under threat and the writer is appealing to God for his justice to come into operation.

Verses 1-3: The opening call to God
As long as *the wicked* are getting away with their crimes God is hidden from general view; he is not seen as *Judge of the earth*. This has been his office from ancient times (Gen. 18:25) and the writer appeals to him to shine forth and show himself as the *God who avenges*. He himself has claimed this prerogative too from early times (Deut. 32:35). That he will act is not in doubt, the only question is when: *how long*? For all the time he is tolerating them, *the wicked (are) jubilant*.

Verses 4-7: Justifying his call
The Psalmist has good reason for this appeal: the things *the wicked* are doing strike at what God holds most precious. God 'gives grace to (that is, favours) the humble' (Prov. 3:34), but these men are *arrogant ... full of boasting*. Also, the ones they *crush* are God's own chosen, beloved *people*, those they

oppress are his *inheritance*, his sons and heirs, to whom he has bequeathed his riches. Moreover, he has special regard for *the widow ... the alien ... (and) the fatherless* (Deut. 10:18; Ps. 68:5), but these men *slay and murder* them. Worst of all, they blaspheme God himself, charging him with blindness: *the LORD does not see*, or if he does he *pays no heed*. This is the one they call LORD, *the God* of their fathers, of *Jacob* himself. How can he put up with this and still maintain his own honour?

Verses 8-11: Exposing the wicked's folly

They had concluded that since they are being allowed to continue, God does not know about them. Their reasoning is *senseless*, they are thinking like *fools* (v. 8). Since they are Israelites the psalmist can speak to them as those who had at least a basic belief in God. So he appeals to three great truths about God.

(1) He is *the God of Creation* (v. 9), who gave to man the power to *hear* and *see*. Is it reasonable to think that God can give others a power he does not have himself, as they assumed?

(2) He is *the God of Providence*, who *disciplines nations* (v. 10a). Even at that early date there was plenty of evidence that God punished and even destroyed whole nations which became excessively wicked. The story of the Flood and the destruction of the Amorites was well known. He can easily deal with a handful of rebels in his own nation.

(3) He is *the God of Knowledge* (vv. 10b-11). Most of what Israel knew had come from Moses: their history, law and worship. Where did he get it from? Was he not taught it by God? How then can they say *The LORD does not see*? (v. 7). He *knows* their very *thoughts*, and that where their *thoughts* do not come from God's teaching *they are futile*, referring of course to their assumption that God is either ignorant of their actions or powerless to stop them.

Verses 12-15: Reassuring the faithful

True as all this is, it does not seem to be working at the time, for it is those who remain faithful who seem to be suffering under God's judgment. God knows about *the wicked*, but does he know about *his people*? The psalmist reminds them that there is more than one way of teaching – there is *discipline* (v. 12). One lesson is learned from *the law*, another from days of trouble (v. 13). When these occur, *his people* have two comforts: God will *grant (them) relief*, he does not try them without giving them grace to bear it; also he sets a trap: *a pit is dug for the wicked*. The word *till* shows this may take time, but it is certain to come because God must restore the moral balance, as described in verses 14-15.

Verses 16-19: Appealing for support

The psalmist has come to a clear understanding of God's place in the current situation. Although God *seems* inactive at the present, he is still the Judge and Avenger of the wicked and the guardian of his people. It is only a matter of time before he acts. This does not mean he will do it alone; his normal method is to use human instruments. So the writer calls on all who are still faithful to God and to him to join in resisting the enemy, *standing* with him *against evildoers* (v. 16).

To encourage them he adds his personal testimony (vv. 17-19). Time and again during his life he had stood on the threshold of death, but was rescued by divine intervention (v. 17). Even when he was not in this extreme danger, his faith would have given way if God in his love had not *supported* him, v. 18. *When* beset with *anxiety*, so that he could not even come to a decision, God gave him *consolation* and restored his *joy* (v. 19). The God who had never failed him would not let him down now. All who supported him would have that assurance too. Let this stir them to come and join in resisting this opposition!

Verses 20-23: Expressing full assurance

He is not saying that a resistance movement alone would overcome this attack. Ultimately it was down to 'the Judge of all the earth'. It was inconceivable that this God should be *allied* with a *corrupt throne* occupied by an enemy. His rule would be the opposite of God's, whose *decrees* bring blessing, whereas a corrupt ruler only brings *misery* (v. 20). Look what they are doing now, he says in verse 21. Are such going to govern God's people in his name? His answer is shown in his final conclusions: God will give strength to those who *take refuge* in him (v. 22). Then he will show himself Judge and Avenger in unmistakable ways; the language is very strong: *repay ... destroy* (v. 23).

Questions:
(1) In what way may we today pray for God to shown himself as Judge and avenger? (Rev. 6:10.)

(2) How can we reason from God's nature and works to convince and convict unbelievers? (See Acts 17:22-31.)

(3) Do you see the overthrow of evil and the Evil One as a co-operation between God and his people – through whom he is often said to defeat the powers of evil? (James 4:7; 1 Pet. 1:5-9; Rom. 16:20.)

Psalm 95

A Call to Praise

The Septuagint attributes this psalm to David, but the statement of Hebrews 4:7 is ambiguous, for 'in David' (a literal translation of the Greek) can simply mean 'in the Psalms of David' (the Psalter) rather than 'through David' himself. It is clearly written for public use in the temple, possibly on a particular occasion or festival. The occasion included either the reading or preaching of the word of God (v. 7) and may have referred to the recital of the Law at the Feast of Tabernacles. The Letter to the Hebrews uses it as a warning to Christians who were wavering from their faith in the gospel: they should remember what happened to the Israelites when they disbelieved and disobeyed what God had said to them in the desert. Worship is prompted by a right view of God, which in turn prompts a response to his Word. Both thoughts are present throughout the psalm.

A. The view of God expressed
Verse 1 describes him as *the Rock of our salvation*. God is a God who saves. The whole nation is a saved people (*OUR salvation*, emphasis mine): saved from bondage in Egypt, saved from the desert tribes and even from the desert itself (see the references to this period in vv. 8-10). Although the failure of their faith meant many died out there, God kept his promise and brought their children into the land. In spite of

subsequent disobedience, they are still his, and now have his chosen one as their king. This proves his *salvation* is sure – *he is the Rock*.

Verse 3 calls him *the great God ... the great King*. This is to distinguish him from *all* (other) *gods*: those worshipped in the land before Israel occupied it and those still worshipped by the surrounding nations (of which David had had a taste in Philistia, 1 Sam. 26:19). Apart from the fact that they were man-made, these were all localised gods (vv. 4-5): some gods of the underworld (*the depths of the earth*), some of the *mountain peaks*, and some of *the sea*. Israel's God is the universal God; all these places are *in his hand*.

Verses 6-7 speak of him as the **Shepherd** of his people. *Maker* refers, not to their original creation, but to his making of a special nation from one man, Abraham. These can call him *our God*, who is to them what a shepherd is to *the flock under his care*, that is, he is everything (cf. Ps. 23). He *cares* for them: leads, feeds and protects.

B. The response that such a God calls for
Verses 1-2: the **first** response is **exuberant praise**: *sing ... shout aloud ... extol*, using all the available resources, not only words, but *music and song*. There is no formality here, all comes from a full heart.

Verses 6-7a: the **second** response is to *bow down ... kneel*. True worship is not merely making a lot of noise, which can be a cover for an empty heart (1 Cor. 13:1). God is to be 'feared', treated with awe and love.

Verses 7b-11: the **third** response is to *hear his voice*. Do not drown his voice with your noise. He wants you to listen to him as well as shout and sing to him. Hear what he is saying: perhaps he wants to tell you to do something; perhaps he wants to make you a promise. Learn from your past history, your time in the desert from which God saved you. There the people grumbled and failed to be thankful because their *hearts* *were hardened* against him, due to the privations of *the desert* after the abundance of Egypt. At Rephidim they had 'disputed' with God (*Meribah*) because there was no water. Since God had supplied water until then and had only just sent them miraculous manna, this was testing and trying him (*Massah*). They were saying, 'Because he does not do what we want, therefore he is not "among us"' (Exod. 17:1-7). This provoked his anger and when it was repeated at Kadesh (Num. 20:1-3) that generation was debarred from entering the land.

Hebrews 3–4 applies this passage to the gospel, for God is speaking *Today* – in Gospel times – more clearly and fully even than he did in the desert. If our hearts are hardened in unbelief, as theirs were, we shall miss, not an earthly land but a heavenly home.

Questions:
(1) Is modern worship suffering from low views of God? Take a look at your church hymn book, or whatever you use.

(2) What is the right balance between exuberance and reverence in worship? (See 1 Cor. 13:1.) Have **you** got it right?

(3) Is worship complete or even true without the ministry of the Word?(See Acts 6:4.) Does failure to **respond** in faith and obedience nullify worship? (See Isa. 1:10-20; Rom. 12:1-2.)

Psalm 96

The Lord Reigns

First Chronicles 16 records the successful restoration of the ark to the tabernacle, after the first abortive attempt. It also specifies what psalms were sung on that occasion: parts of 105 and 106, and this one slightly abbreviated. The ark had spent some time in the hands of the Philistines, so the psalmist sees its recovery as signifying God's sovereign rule over all the nations.

Verses 1-3: Proclaim God's salvation to the nations!
A new song – words used in six other psalms – shows there is something special about this occasion: it celebrates one of the *marvellous deeds* which reveal God's *glory*, for it is not any miracle, but a work of *salvation*. Their deliverance from the Philistine confederacy was proof that God had a greater work of *salvation* to perform in the world. This is what they are to *proclaim among the nations*. The term used for *proclaim* means 'tell the good news', from the New Testament equivalent of which we get the word 'evangelise'. This was therefore an advance preaching of the gospel to the world.

Verses 4-6: Let the nations abandon their idols!
Since it is the Lord alone who saves, all who hear it should forsake *the gods of the nations*, which have been demonstrated to be but *idols*, literally ELILIM, a parody of ELOHIM, the most

common Hebrew term for God. ELILIM means 'worthless', for *idols* are made by man, whereas *the* LORD is not made but is the Maker *of the heavens*. This is the one who is now entering Jerusalem to set up his *sanctuary* there and shine with all his *splendour and majesty ... glory and strength*.

Verses 7-9: Let the nations turn to the Lord!
Merely to abandon their idols is not enough – they must acknowledge him. The expression *families of nations* means either that the nations themselves are *families* or that they are made up of *families*. Those who had been enemies of his people are invited to come with *an offering into his courts*. Of course, the idea that Philistines, Ammonites, Moabites and so on would process up to Jerusalem with gifts for the Lord is far-fetched. What is meant is that this is the logical response from those who hear what God has done. It stresses that it was not so much David who was occupying the citadel of a former enemy but the Lord himself. It therefore strikes a prophetic note, anticipating the time when a Greater than David would overthrow the prince of this world from his domination of the nations (Rev. 20:1-3), set up his kingdom and invite people of all nations to abandon their Satanic religions and worship him and his Father.

Verses 10-13: Let all nature join the song!
These verses enlarge on this future Messianic kingdom, on the time when the words *the* LORD *reigns* will have become a visible reality. Because he is a righteous king who administers justice (*equity*), there will be greater stability on the earth (v. 10). This will bring joy not only to people but to nature itself (vv. 11-12). For where God is known the natural creation is treated with the respect it deserves as God's handiwork and gift. The thought of a restored creation looks on to the final act of Christ's kingdom, when, on this second coming, he raises the dead and renews the universe (Rom. 8:18-25, cf. Ps. 98:7-9).

Thus three stages of the Lord's reign are brought out here: (1) when he occupied the citadel of Israel's former enemy, thus crowning the recent military victory; (2) when he came in Christ to overthrown Satan and offer salvation to people of all nations; (3) when he will come again at the end of the age to usher in his final perfect kingdom (1 Cor. 15:24-28).

Questions:

(1) How can we always be fresh in our personal and public devotions, even after many years? (See vv. 1-3 and Lam. 3:22-24.)

(2) How does this psalm (especially vv. 4-9) answer the view that so long as people are happy and sincere in their beliefs they should be left alone? (See Acts 17:29-31; Rom. 1:18-25.)

(3) Do verses 10-12 give us the basis for a Christian view of 'environmentalism'?

Psalm 97

The LORD Alone is King

God's universal sovereignty is again the theme, but in this psalm the message is more severe. God appears in awesome splendour and terrifying power. The psalm has similarities to 18. Those idolatrous nations who were called to worship him in 96 are warned what will happen if they do not. Even his own people must beware of contamination from evil and idolatry, but are assured of his favour if they heed the warning and faithfully worship him.

Verse 1: The Universal King
God proved himself King of the nations by subduing those countries that had warred against Israel (see Ps. 18). But *if the LORD reigns* over them, he *reigns* over *the earth*. In this case the most *distant shores* should *rejoice* in him, that is, worship him willingly, finding him a better God than their national ones. This is the theme of 18:43-50.

Verses 2-6: The Demonstration of His Kingship
Two themes intermingle here in this 'theophany' or appearance of God.

(1) The dazzling splendour of his being when it comes into view. There are allusions to the Red Sea and Sinai, and all is parallel with 18:7-15. He comes not just to be seen

but to act with irresistible power: *the mountains melt like wax* – not literally but meaning that no opposition can hold out before him.

(2) The righteous character of his reign (vv. 2b, 6). When he appears it is not in order just to strike terror into people, but to right wrongs and administer justice. This is a strong theme in 18, especially verses 20-29. Those who want to do right have nothing to fear from him, but the corrupt and the unjust should *tremble*.

Verse 7: The Fall of the Idols

Which of the *gods* of the nations can rival him in majesty, holiness and justice? His appearance and reign show up these so-called deities for what they really are: mere *images ... idols*. When the true God appears what can people do but *worship him*? Even the *gods* themselves, if they were real, would do so. This is another theme of 18, especially verse 41.

Verses 8-9: The Joy of his own People

The judgments which have spelt disaster on Israel's enemies have brought rejoicing to Zion, to those who gather at God's shrine there. For them it is good news when God shows himself to be the Most High over all the earth, for it takes their enemies off their backs. When he exposes the futility of their gods, it only serves to confirm that their God is the only true God. For the parallel in Psalm 18 see v. 46.

Verse 10: The Call to Holiness

Their exuberance, however, should be tempered with self-examination. To be under a holy and righteous God demands a similar life-style. This is basically clear and simple: *hate evil*, but it is not easy. He himself is there however to enable them by guarding *the lives of his faithful ones* from *the hand of the wicked*. Personal holiness is prominent in 18. See verses 20-29.

Verses 11-12: Joy and Rejoicing

These should be the prominent marks of people who have this awesome and just God on their side. They live bathed in constant *light* which is *shed* on them along with the spirit of joy. If they are *righteous* and revere *his holy name* they are entitled and expected to *rejoice*. What else can they do?

Questions:

(1) If God truly appeared in Christ, so that 'we have seen his glory' (John 1:14), why was he so unlike his description in verses 2-5?

(2) Why are those to whom God has never appeared in glory still without excuse for not worshipping him? (See v. 6 and Rom. 1:18-21.)

(3) If 'joy', 'rejoicing' and 'praising' were so prominent in the old covenant church, why are they so lacking in the church of Christ? (See John 16:20-22; Acts 2:46-47; Gal. 5:22.)

Psalm 98

Uninhibited Rejoicing

This psalm is similar in tone and even language to 96, so perhaps it is also connected with the return of the ark to the tabernacle. The joy of the writer knows no bounds (v. 11), so it must have been something very special.

Verses 1-3: Let all Israel praise the Lord!
A new victory calls for a new song (cf. 33:3; 144:9). To speak of it as *marvellous*, meaning miraculous, is no exaggeration, for God achieved it virtually alone, *by his right hand and his holy arm*. Because of this, not only has Israel enjoyed *salvation*, but God has received glory, for it was a display of *his righteousness* to *the nations* who had felt the power of *his right hand and his holy arm*. Verse 3 explains this: he had promised to look after his people, *the house of Israel*, in his *love and his faithfulness*. That he had done so would be evident to all who heard of it. No doubt the news would not have travelled far by today's standards, which makes *the ends of the earth* sound wildly optimistic. We must however view this as prophetic of another *salvation* yet to come, about which we shall see more in verse 9.

Verses 4-6: Let all nations praise the Lord!
Israel's victory came at the expense of other nations' defeat, so what was there for them to *shout for joy* about? This is where the prophetic note comes in again: *shout for joy* is the phrase used

by Zechariah in his prophecy of Christ's triumphal entry into Jerusalem to bring salvation (Zech. 9:9; Matt. 21:1-11). When the nations of the world came to hear of a Saviour from God coming into the world, they would be freed from their enmity against God and his people, would come to acknowledge his righteousness and become his worshippers.

Meanwhile Israel must do it for them, employing all the available instruments and using the whole team of musicians David was in process of setting up (1 Chron. 25:1-8). The blast of the ram's horn was particularly significant, for it was this that proclaimed the jubilee year and announced the accession of a new king (Lev. 25:8-12; 1 Kings 1:39). With the whole nation united under their rightful king, who had taken possession of its capital, Jerusalem, and with their enemies subdued, Israel was entering a new era. To seal it all, the ark of the covenant, the manifest presence of God himself, was on its way to the city: something to sing and shout about indeed!

Verses 7-9: Let all creation praise the Lord!
Calling on the natural creation to join in the praise is characteristic of the exuberance which marks a special occasion. We find it in other celebratory psalms such as 148. But it is more than that. It fits the prophetic tone that underlies this psalm. When the people of God are at peace and their enemies subdued, the material world functions best. War ceases to ravage the countryside, fields are used for growing crops, not fighting battles, and resources are used to harness the goodness of the earth.

This is why we find prophecies of Christ's coming lay a strong emphasis on order, harmony and prosperity in the natural world (e.g. Isa. 11:1-9). History proves that the earth is a better place for the coming of Christ and the spread of his gospel. Compare nations where the gospel has taken root with those where it has not, even today. This situation is still far from perfect and will be until the Lord returns to usher in the final restoration of the universe, which will renew creation as well as perfect the saints and destroy evil (Rom. 8:18-25). Verse 9 clearly puts the coming of *the Lord to judge* (rule) *the earth* as what should motivate this song of the earth.

Questions:

(1) How is God's single-handed victory over the nations (v. 1) fulfilled in Christ? (See Isa. 59:12-20; 63:1-6; Matt. 26:56; Heb. 10:14.)

(2) What do verses 4-6 tell us about the ultimate aim of the church's mission? (Cf. Matt. 5:16.)

(3) In what ways has the material world been improved by the conversion of nations to Christ? Is this still happening? Where?

Psalm 99

The LORD Sits Enthroned

The reference to God *enthroned between the cherubim* (v. 1) may indicate a feast day or celebration of a victory which has displayed his universal sovereignty. Such a God speaks through his prophets and is approached through his priests (vv. 6-7).

Verses 1-3: A Call to the Nations
As with 65 the people are gathered on Zion for a special celebration. Although it could not be seen, it was known that the holy of holies housed the ark of the covenant and that on top of it were the images of two cherubs, with their outstretched wings touching so that they formed a kind of throne. Here *the LORD reigns,* for *he sits enthroned between the cherubim* (v. 1; 2 Sam. 6:2). A cherub is not the winged naked baby of popular art and folklore but a mighty being wielding a weapon. Cherubs with swords guarded the gate of Eden after man's expulsion (Gen. 3:24). Ezekiel's extraordinary vision in chapter 1 is of these beings controlling the whole world, while they themselves are under the control of the Spirit of God.

This is why the psalm calls on *the nations (to) tremble (and) the earth (to) shake,* because *the LORD* who is *great ... in Zion ... is exalted over all the nations* (v. 2). The tabernacle or temple was there, not merely for the worship of one nation, but as a testimony to the whole world that *the LORD* who was Israel's

God reigns over all, and calls all to *praise (his) great and awesome name* (v. 3). This is really looking on to the time when Christ would take his throne and his gospel would spread from Jerusalem to the whole earth and bring the nations to God (cf. Isa. 2:2-3).

Verses 4-9: A Call to Israel
The universal theme does not dispense with the national one. During this age the Lord was Israel's *King* ruling over the offspring of Jacob (v. 4). The chief feature of his rule was his *justice*. This is not harsh but comes from his love. It is because he *loves justice* and loves his people that he has done *what is just and right*. So Israel is called on to *exalt the LORD our God*, not from a distance like the nations, but *at his footstool* (v. 5), that is, before the throne over the ark, where the 'Shekinah' light shone forth (80:1). While they are favoured above the nations they must still remember that God is *holy* – not merely morally perfect but an altogether higher being: eternal, pure and unchanging.

The holiness of God was revealed, not only in his awesome presence on Zion, but in the law he had given on Sinai, when he *spoke ... from the pillar of cloud (and) gave statutes and ... decrees*, so that they might be *kept* by his people (v. 7). But how touchingly this manifestation of holiness in justice and law is tempered by grace! For they were a flawed people, whose blemishes appeared all too obviously and frequently. This was why God gave them priests – not only of the sacerdotal kind like *Aaron*, but men like *Moses and Samuel*, who were not technically priests but *called on the LORD* when the people offended him (Exod. 32:11-14; 1 Sam. 8:6; 12:18-23).

Moreover, having given these intercessors to his people, he *answered them* (vv. 6, 8), by *forgiving* their offences. For though he *punished their misdeeds* this was not as much as they deserved. After the golden calf incident God said he would destroy them, but Moses prayed and God relented. In Samuel's time God viewed the people's clamour for a king as a rejection of himself, but Samuel's intercession saved the day. So if God deserved praise for the justice of his laws he equally deserved it for his mercy towards those who infringed them. So verse 9 repeats the refrain of verses 3 and 5, but with a difference. Verse 5 referred to the footstool to which Israel but not the nations could come. Verse 9 speaks of *his holy MOUNTAIN* (emphasis mine), perhaps with a slight ambiguity. Sinai, where the law thundered forth, was *holy* because *the LORD* spoke from there. But Zion was a *holy mountain* also, where God revealed the glory of his grace.

Questions:
(1) Do you feel a sense of the glorious presence of God when your church meets? (See Rev. 1:10-20.)

(2) In what way do the laws God spoke on Sinai reveal his perfect justice? (Take as an example Exod. 23:1-9.)

(3) Does your view of God and your relationship with him reflect the balance of his justice and mercy? (See Ps. 85:10; Rom. 3:21-26.)

Psalm 100

Joy in His Presence

This 'psalm of thanksgiving' (title) appears to be an invitation to gather at the tabernacle or temple to offer joyful praises to God. Its exuberance – even shouting is encouraged (v. 1)! – well befits the uninhibited singing that marked the Jewish Feasts. However, there is a problem. At first sight it seems to share the universalism of 67, with its call to *all the earth* (v. 1). Most commentators take this as the correct translation and interpret accordingly. The well-known paraphrases we sing today are based on this version: William Kethe's 'All people that on earth do dwell' and Isaac Watts' 'Before Jehovah's aweful throne'. However, only Israel was *his people, the sheep of his pasture* (v. 3), that is, in covenant with him, and only they could *enter his gates ... and his courts*. So how can *all the earth* be invited?

H. C. Leupold points out that the Hebrew word 'ARETS means 'land' as well as *earth*, and therefore the call may be to 'the inhabitants of the *land* of Israel'. The psalm does not refer again to other nations. On the other hand, the stress may be on *Know* (v. 3). The nations are to recognise that YAHWEH, Israel's God, is the true God who made Israel *his people, the sheep of his pasture* as a witness to the world and therefore a challenge to the nations to abandon their idols and worship the Lord. In this case the call to *enter his gates ... his courts* is used in a spiritual sense, as has already been expressed in 'come before him' (v. 2).

It can even be viewed Messianically, that is, as anticipating universal Christian worship and the proclamation of the gospel to the world. We want all people to worship our God joyfully, to come to him through Christ's death, that they too may become *his people, the sheep of his pasture*. Above all we want them all to know what we know: the everlasting goodness, love and faithfulness (v. 5) of God revealed in Christ our Saviour and Lord, who 'always lives to intercede for us' (Heb. 7:25).

But the challenge to us is: if we want *the earth* to express this fervent praise, we must be doing it ourselves. How *joyful* is our singing? How real is the sense that we *come before him,* that we are in the very presence of him who *made us* and entered into covenant relationship with us through 'the Good Shepherd' who 'laid down his life for the sheep'? How real to us is the sense of his eternal goodness, love and faithfulness? When we recapture this spirit perhaps *the earth,* or at least that part of it near where we live and worship, may take us seriously and think of joining us. People today have no time for unreal, insincere formalism.

Question:
Examine yourself and your church by considering the questions in the last paragraph.

Psalm 101

David's Godly Resolutions

Here is David making resolutions about how he will live and what company he will keep. In all probability they are connected with his accession to the throne, for someone who says they are going to silence all the wicked in the land (v. 8) must have the power to do it.

Verse 1: David's guiding principles
There is no *your* in the original: David *sings* of the *love and justice* by which he intended to reign, as well as the *love and justice* which are in the character of God and in the way God had dealt with him in recent times. *Love* is the HESED word – the covenant loyalty which bound God and his people together. God had been faithful to that in preserving David and bringing him out of the dire state he was in at Ziklag (1 Sam. 30) and into the kingship. This also fulfilled his promise to give the people a 'better king than Saul' (1 Sam. 15:28), one 'after his (God's) own heart' (Acts 13:22).

It had been about fourteen long years since God had first called David, most of them spent on the run from Saul. God had been showing great patience with Saul and at the same time testing the faith of David. Now at last his *justice* had taken effect: Saul, still unrepentant, was defeated and slain, leaving the way open for David to take the throne. Now he would make *love and justice* the basis of his reign over the people God had given him to govern. 'Do to others what you would have them do to you' holds for kings and commoners alike.

These principles he is to apply in three areas: his personal life, his appointments to the court, and his methods of governing.

Verses 2-4: What David required of himself

(1) *His personal integrity* (v. 2a). If he is going to reflect the character of God in ruling the people, he must first rule himself. This is why he uses the word *careful* – such a life requires conscious effort. He feels inadequate in himself and calls on the Lord: *when will you come to me?*

(2) *His domestic life* (v. 2b). A leader of God's people must be in control, not only of his own life, but of his family (1 Tim. 3:4-5). This was where David was to fail most, and with disastrous results for everybody. But at least he realized the need for it and made it a plank in his platform.

(3) *His aims and values* (v. 3a). As king he would set his sights primarily on avoiding evil. This had been the ruin of Saul's regime, which had been governed by *vile* things like ambition and jealousy. David would try to avoid all that, and to a considerable extent succeeded.

(4) *His role models* (vv. 3b-4). What examples would he follow? He is clear about this; his words are almost lurid – they spit at us. He is still feeling very hurt by the way Saul and his henchman have treated him. They were *faithless ... perverse ... evil*. One thing he is certain of: he will not go down that road. Neither did he, even when his comrades such as Joab wanted to. If anything, David leaned too much the other way.

Verses 5-7: What he required in his servants

David cannot govern alone – he must delegate (Exod. 18) and take advice (Prov. 19:20; 20:18). A ruler is influenced by his advisors (see, e.g. 1 Kings 12:14). Some otherwise good men have ruled badly through ill-chosen colleagues. David is clearest on the negatives; he will **not** have

- Censorious people who smear their rivals (v. 5a);
- Personally ambitious people, who are likely to bend the rules to suit themselves (v. 5b);
- Devious people, who say one thing and mean, and even do, another (v. 7, Prov. 12:5b).

He is clear too on the positives: his companions in office must be like-minded (v. 6). He has committed himself to being *faithful (and) blameless* (cf. vv. 1-2) and he can only work with such. Learning, skill and expertise are important, but valueless without integrity. To David, godliness comes before personality.

Verse 8: The method he would follow

This must be consistent with his personal and political aims. He who resolved to cut evil out of his own life and out of his government, must do likewise in his kingdom. Moreover, he is resolved to do it methodically and diligently: he would be down at the city gates where cases were heard and adjudicated *every morning* – if not in person then by a representative. All complaints and charges would be dealt with promptly. When Absalom later undermined this procedure he had to get up very early (see 2 Sam. 15:1-4)!

Questions:

(1) From what you know of David's subsequent life, how far did he keep his own principles?

(2) How does this psalm help us choose our political leaders and assess their performance? (Cf. Rom. 13:1-4.)

(3) Should Christians make resolutions? If so, what is there to guide us in our personal, domestic and social lives?

Psalm 102

The LORD Will Rebuild Zion

This *afflicted man's ... lament*, which was making him *faint* and pour out his heart before the Lord, is connected with the condition of *Zion* (vv. 13-16). It appears to have been reduced to stones and rubble, and little was being done to rebuild it. It may therefore be the *prayer* of one who grieved either over the destruction of the temple, which no one could repair because they were in exile, or over the slow progress of the rebuilding being made on their return until Haggai and Zechariah persuaded them to resume building.

Verses 1-2: Calling on God to hear
Before he comes to his specific prayer, this 'afflicted man' simply asks that *the* LORD will *hear* it (v. 1). This is because he interprets the present situation as a sign that God has turned away from them (cf. v. 10). His prayer *do not hide your face from me* (v. 2), shows that he feels this is just what God is doing; and his words *turn your ear to me* show that God does not appear to be listening. This is a great lesson in how to pray in a time of affliction: not only for the specific matter in hand, but for what God might be saying or doing through it. These or similar words feature in many psalms, showing how steeped this man was in the devotional literature of Israel.

Verses 3-11: Pleading the state of the people
He still has not come to his request and continues to seek
a favourable hearing from God. So he describes in detail the
physical effects the problem is having on him, hoping God
will be moved to take pity on him and grant his request when
it comes.

He is wasting away like a body thrown on the fire (v. 3).
He is so sick at heart he cannot eat (v. 4). This, combined with
the energy put forth in *loud groans,* has *reduced (him) to skin
and bones* (v. 5). Nor does he have anyone to share his grief
with; he is like a *desert owl* or one living *among the ruins* away
from human habitation (v. 6). He cannot sleep, he is like a *bird*
which sits *alone on a roof,* having lost its mate or its young (v. 7).
By day the only company he has is that of his *enemies* who
come merely to *taunt* and *rail against* him, possibly referring
to the Samaritans' mockery of their ruined building (v. 8)
(Neh. 4:1-3). The *name* of Jew no longer commanded respect
and wonder, as it had when they first returned (Ps. 126:2) but
was now a mere swear word.

His fast is only broken by eating *ashes* (and) drinking tears
(v. 9), which is an excessive act of humiliation, going beyond
the usual 'repenting in dust and ashes' (Job 42:6) to eating
them! There is good reason for this – that God's *wrath* seems
to be so *great* he has altogether cast them away, as a storm lifts
a tent from the ground and throws it aside (v. 10). His life is
as dark as an evening shadow and his strength *like grass* that
withers away for lack of water (v. 11).

Verses 12-17: Appealing to the everlasting God
Now another line of thinking comes into the matter. He has no
right to expect God to come into action merely out of pity for
a miserable man. But surely he will regard his own nature?
God does not change with our fluctuating fortunes and
feelings; he does not come and go like earthly kings, he *sits
enthroned for ever* and is great *through all generations* (v. 12).

Knowing this, he does not even have to ask, he can
confidently predict that God *will arise and have compassion on
Zion* (v. 13). The ground of this confidence is the promise of
God – not just that he has covenanted to *favour* Zion, but that

his *appointed time* to do so has arrived. The prophets predicted, not only the return from captivity, but the restoration of the land, the city and the temple (Hag. 2:9; Zech. 2:3-6). Jeremiah even specified the time (Jer. 29:10). The return proved that this time had arrived. Surely, having fulfilled that prophecy, God would go on to carry out the others?

There were signs that this was beginning to happen, for people were starting to take an interest in the site of the Temple, perhaps as a result of the prophesying of Haggai and Zechariah. For even the *stones (and) dust* which remained from the old Temple had become *dear* to them (v. 14) – more dear than when it had been a mighty edifice. They even felt a kind of *pity* for it, as though it were a person. He goes further: when it is re-erected and God again appears *in glory* among them (v. 16), and the whole land is restored, their enemies will change their tune and fear the name of the Lord, so that even *kings ... will revere your glory* (v. 15).

Then it will no longer be a case of weeping, pleading and self-affliction, for God *will respond to the prayer of the destitute* (v. 17). He is not interested only in the great ones of the earth, but has special regard for the afflicted (9:12).

Verses 18-22: Foreseeing great times ahead
The lower the state into which his people fall, the more glory there is in their restoration. As the Exodus proved to the nations in earlier days who was the true God, so will their full restoration from captivity do again. It will be spoken of in *generations* to come, so that *people* who are not even yet born will *praise the Lord* (v. 18). They will hear and speak of how they had cried out to him in their bonds and he from *his sanctuary on high* had *looked down*, heard their groans and released those *condemned to death* (v. 20).

Peoples in days to come will *assemble (in) Jerusalem (to) worship the Lord*, hear his *name ... declared* and join in his praise (vv. 21-22). This was not to be fulfilled in the way some might imagine, but in the age of the gospel. It would begin when many nations were present in Jerusalem at Pentecost and some acknowledged Christ as Redeemer. Then it would continue as the gospel was preached through the nations, causing many to accept Jesus as *the* Lord who had led Israel in Old Testament times. They would come to the 'Jerusalem which is above' (Gal. 4:26 cf. Isa. 2:2-3).

Verses 23-28: Reminding himself of his frailty
The return of his confidence has not made him complacent; he cannot forget what he and the people were like in their desolation (v. 23), and how he had cried to God at the beginning (v. 24a). But the God he prayed to is eternal and unchanging (v. 24b): he **was** the beginning – *earth (and) the heavens are the work of (his) hands* (v. 25).

It is not only such as he and the people who *will perish*, but the whole universe, which to God will be like changing his clothes (v. 26)! Just as when a person changes his clothes he himself remains, so it will be with God, and moreover his years will never end (v. 27). This is no depressing thought but our only hope, for those who are his *children* and his *servants live in (his) presence and are established before him* (v. 28).

Questions:
(1) Are there any points of comparison between the condition of the temple at this time and the church at present?

(2) How deeply do you feel it when the church is in a low state?

(3) Do you share the confidence of the psalmist that, if we humble ourselves, he will revive his church? (See vv. 13-16, cf. 2 Chron. 7:14; Matt. 5:3-5.)

Psalm 103

So Great is His Love

David had much to thank God for concerning himself, especially healing and forgiveness, which is why he begins by stirring up his own soul to praise God. But he soon moves on to speak on behalf of the people generally. It may have been composed to celebrate a deliverance from war or plague, or simply for an annual feast at which past history was recollected as a stimulus for praise. It chiefly exults in God's faithfulness to his covenant, which is as everlasting as he himself is. It forms a pair with 104, for both open and close in a similar way.

Verses 1-5: God's mercy to one man
How encouraging is verse 1! Even David was not always able to pour out his heart in praise to God spontaneously, but had to 'shake off dull sloth' and stir up his spirit. He also points the way to do this: recollecting *all his benefits*, those gifts and acts which show God is 'good to his people' (13:6, for 'good' is the same word as *benefit*). Nor is he vaguely generalising, but specifies: firstly, total forgiveness of *all your sins* (v. 3, your being addressed to himself); secondly, healing *all your diseases*, for sin is sometimes the cause of sickness, as David knew (Ps. 32:3-5); and thirdly, salvation from death and the darkness which lay beyond (v. 4).

How total these *benefits* are is seen in what follows: you are sure of his forgiveness because he *crowns your life with love and compassion*, you glory in this fresh experience of his love; your healing is total, for your appetite is restored and he *satisfies* it, so that you rise up with greater strength than ever, like an *eagle*, an emblem of tireless vigour (cf. Isa. 40:30-31). Now that he has warmed up his engine he can pick up his passengers!

Verses 6-14: God's mercy to Israel as his people

God's mercy to Israel is seen in the way he always takes their part when they are *oppressed* and sees they receive *justice* (v. 6). This goes back to *Moses* through whom he *made known his ways to the people of Israel* when he delivered them from Egypt (v. 7). But *his ways* were not just ways of *righteousness … for all the oppressed*, but also of mercy on the sinful. This recalls the time particularly in view at Tabernacles when, after hearing his will and entering into covenant with him at Sinai, they failed in their faith and obedience. Yet he showed he was not only righteous but *compassionate and gracious* (v. 8). He showed he was not *always* looking for faults for which to *accuse* them so that he could give vent to his *anger* (v. 9). In fact he did the opposite – he withheld it when it was deserved (v. 10).

How and why? Because *his love* is *so great*. David emphasises this with powerful illustrations. He looks up to *the heavens* as far as the eye can see (v. 11) – that is the height of God's love. He lowers his eyes and looks away to the horizon (v. 12) – that is the length of his love. He invokes the father-child relationship (v. 13) and says how often he refrains from punishment – that is the depth of his love. As a father does not expect too much from a young child, so God *remembers how we are formed … that we are dust* (v. 14). This leads to the next stage, for the scope of the psalm gradually broadens, from the individual to the national and next the human.

Verses 15-18: God's mercy to Israel as human beings

Though a special people they were still human and shared the weaknesses of *man* (v. 15). To us life may seem long, but in the light of eternity it is *like grass* – soon *gone*. The illustration of *grass* would carry more weight in the Middle East where the dryness gives it a very short life, since any there is soon eaten by animals or mowed by the farmer. But we in these more northern climes know what *wind* does to our *flowers* (v. 16: 'rough winds do shake the darling buds of May' Shakespeare), for 'frail as summer's flower we flourish; blows the wind and it is gone' (H. F. Lyte)

What is the answer? *The LORD's love* which is *from everlasting to everlasting* (v. 17). He who made nature is more merciful than she! His *love* pities our weaknesses and forgives our sins, and his *righteousness* protects us from all who would harm us. We have but to *fear* him, to live with a sense of his greatness and look up to him, *remembering to obey his precepts* (v. 18). 'Trust and obey' is 'the way to be happy in Jesus'!

Verses 19-22: God the universal King
The final stage is the cosmic: he is the God, not only of David, of Israel, and of man and nature, but of the celestial and supernatural realms. There he *has established his throne*, from which he *rules over all* (v. 19). His *mighty angels ... obey his word* (v. 20), all creatures visible and invisible *do his will*. The whole cosmos, all his works, unite to praise the Lord (vv. 21-22). If **they** do, why should not I? So he ends where he began: *praise the LORD, O my soul*.

Questions:
(1) How do you go about rousing your soul from sleep at the beginning of the day and warming your heart to praise and pray with fervour? (See Ps. 63.)

(2) Does Ephesians 3:17-19 throw light on verses 11-12 of the psalm, and do verses 13-14 help you see more of what Jesus meant when he invited us to pray to 'our Father in heaven' (Matt. 6:9, 7:9-11)?

(3) Do your prayers and praises reflect the scope of David's or are they lacking in perspective – too preoccupied with yourself and your immediate circumstances? (See Job 38:1-7, and read on if you have time).

Psalm 104

The Days of Creation

Some versions have ascribed this anonymous psalm to David, and it is certainly similar to 103 both in the opening and closing words and its general atmosphere of rejoicing in God's transcendent being and mighty works. It beautifully complements 103, which is somewhat subjective, praising God for his personal care and forgiveness, whereas 104 is more objective, looking at his created works as revealing how great and glorious he is.

The psalm closely follows the Genesis account of creation, keeping roughly to the order of the days. But it is more poetic than factual, designed to move us to praise God. While it follows the order of the days in Genesis 1 it goes beyond that chapter. He uses his own observations and reflections to bring out how God is still at work in the world, providing and caring for what he made long ago.

It has been compared to other 'nature songs' from the ancient near east, especially Akhenaten's 'Hymn to the Sun'. This was the Pharaoh who abandoned the galaxy of Egyptian gods and all their priests in order to worship only the sun in the form of a red disc (the 'Aten'). As a monotheist he comes nearest to the Hebrew religion, which may have influenced him, but he is still a long way from it since the sun is not God, only his creature. So, just as Genesis 1 is superior to the

Mesopotamian creation myths, so is Psalm 104 superior to Akhenaten's 'Hymn to the Sun'.

A psalm such as this would be very meaningful to a people who lived close to the soil and the animals, who depended on natural water supplies and derived energy from the sun. But it is a healthy exercise for us moderns to take on board that, behind all our mechanised forms of producing food and energy, there is still the natural world from which they are derived, and above all the God who created and sustains them.

Verses 1-4: God's personal splendour
He stirs his *soul* up to *praise the* LORD by picturing him as a glorious king apparelled with the *splendour and majesty* of *light* (v. 1), and making *the heavens (his) tent* (v. 2). This is beautifully rendered by Robert Grant in his great hymn where he says, 'whose robe is the light, whose canopy space'. This is the God of Day 1 (Gen. 1:1-5).

Then follows in verse 3 a poetic description of Day 2 (Gen. 1:6-8) in which the 'firmament' or 'expanse' is seen as the base of his dwelling place, which has now graduated from a tent to a building with a floor (*the beams*) and a ceiling (*upper chambers*). However, he is not confined there, he is not a king who stays in his palace, he moves abroad. Wherever there are *clouds* he is there; wherever *the wind* blows, there he is. Nor is he alone, but like a king he is accompanied by *his servants*, 'his angels' (NIV mg), who like him are everywhere, as *the winds* are, or as lightning (*flames of fire*) is (v. 4). Thus do verses 3b-4 go beyond Genesis 1.

Verses 5-9: Land and sea
Although based on Day 3 (Gen. 1:9-10) this goes further back than Genesis 1:2 to envisage an immovable *earth* (v. 5), subsequently covered with the deep, so that even the *mountains* were submerged (v. 6). Verses 7-9 poetically describe the separation of *the waters* from the land. They are spoken of as if they were an enemy who has to be rebuked and put to flight (v. 7). They are seen draining from *the mountains* to be confined to *the valleys* (v. 8) where they are perpetually held in (v. 9). Here is where his observation and imagination enlarges on Genesis 1.

Verses 10-18: Food for the creatures

He continues to describe the third day (Gen. 1:11-13), again appealing to his observation as well as God's revelation. Although God drained the water from the mountains down to the oceans, he did not leave them waterless, but caused *springs* to *pour water into the ravines* (v. 10). Thus creatures who live high up can *quench their thirst* (v. 11), *trees* can grow and *birds* can *nest in their branches (and) sing* happily (v. 13).

Thus watered, *the earth*, high and low, can bear *fruit* (v. 13), *grow grass for the cattle and plants for man* (v. 14). From this he can produce *wine ... oil ... and bread* (v. 15). *Trees* grow in profusion, even on mountains like *Lebanon* (v. 16). They become the homes of *birds* of many kinds (v. 17), also *wild goats* and *conies* (v. 18). All this the psalmist could see with his eyes, and know from Scripture that it was the provision of the God of creation, enabling him to do what he was seeking to do – to stir up his soul to praise God (v. 1).

Verses 19-23: Sun and moon

Here he moves on to Day 4 (Gen. 1:14-19) where the sun and moon divide day from night (v. 19). His own observation teaches him how both these daily periods are used by God's creatures. There are nocturnal ones: *the beasts of the forests,* who *prowl (and) roar* by night as they *seek their food* (vv. 20-21), then *steal away* to their *dens* when *the sun rises* (v. 22) and *man goes out to his work until evening* (v. 23). Then the process begins again. The order here of night and day reflects 'the evening and the morning' of Genesis 1.

Although this stanza has similarities to Akhenaten's 'Hymn to the Sun', it distinguishes the sun from God, its Creator and Ruler. Also, it puts to shame the Egyptian fear of sunset and darkness, showing that God and his creatures have a use for the night hours.

Verses 24-26: The sea and its creatures

Moving on to Day 5 (Gen. 1:20-23), he begins by referring back to his original desire to 'praise the Lord' (v. 1), which he fulfills as he observes the multiplicity of God's creatures and the *wisdom* displayed in their order (v. 24). For not only does he populate day and night with them, but the sea as well as the land. Perhaps he is composing his psalm on the top of *Lebanon* (v. 16) as he cries *there is the sea!* (v. 25). Its end is out of sight, it is so *vast and spacious*, but however extensive it may be, it is *teeming with creatures beyond number*.

There too is evidence of man's superior skill, for although made for the land, he has learned how to build *ships* and take to the sea (v. 26), something not envisaged in Genesis 1. He alludes, perhaps a trifle scornfully, to the sea monsters, real or mythical, such as *Leviathan*, feared by the ignorant, but to God just like a pet playing in a puddle!

With the mention of creatures and man, he has encroached on Day 6 (Gen. 1:24-31) which he now takes up.

Verses 27-30: Food for all

Day 6 describes not only the creation of beasts and people but also God's provision for them (Gen. 1:29-30). This is what he glories in here as he observes how they depend on God for their sustenance as they did for their creation (vv. 27-28). For he knows from experience that there are times when God *hides his face*, that is, withdraws his providing hand and gives us up to famine and drought. Then his creatures are *terrified*, knowing they will die, which they do (v. 29), unless or until he *sends (his) Spirit (to) … renew the face of the earth* (v. 30).

The allusion to *the Spirit* is interesting. In Genesis 1 he only appears at the very beginning (Gen. 1:2). But by the time of writing, revelation has moved on and *the Spirit* is seen as present in every part of creation, including man (Job 33:4) and here in the work of providence.

Verses 31-35: Glory to God

So he has achieved his aim – to move his soul to 'praise the LORD' (v. 1). Now he is full of praise (v. 31a), but recognises this is not his doing, but is simply sharing in *the LORD's* own joy *in his works*. Because *the LORD* rejoices, so does he (v. 34); and he wants to keep it like this *as long as I live* (v. 33), as he continues his *meditation* on his works.

There may be an allusion here to Day 7 (Gen. 2:1-3), when the whole work was complete and God saw it was 'very good'

(Gen. 1:31). All he has written, based on God's revelation and his own observation, is about what is 'good'. But of course this was composed long after that seventh day, and changes have come in through the entrance of evil and sin into the cosmos. Yet this does not shake his faith, for he sees how God continues to exercise his sovereignty by coming in judgment (v. 32). In this the psalmist fully concurs, indeed prays it may succeed in making *sinners vanish from the earth,* so that *the wicked (will) be no more* (v. 35). So, even in a world infected with evil and liable to God's judgment, he can still *praise the* LORD.

Questions:
(1) Compare the psalm with Genesis 1 from the standpoint of the priority of God. How many times does his name appear in Genesis 1, and how many in Psalm 104 (including 'he' and 'his')? What does this teach us about how to view Genesis 1?

(2) In our mechanised age and urbanised society how can we make Genesis 1 and a psalm like this meaningful?

(3) In a world with so much evil and suffering how possible is it for us to believe God 'rejoices in his works' (v. 31) and to share in his joy (v. 34)?

Psalm 105

What God Has Done

First Chronicles 16 tells us that the first fifteen verses of this psalm were sung when the ark had been recovered from the Philistines and was brought into the tabernacle. Parts of 106 and 96 were also sung on this occasion This does not mean these psalms were composed at that time. Possibly this writer used the material of 1 Chronicles 16 and expanded it for a later occasion. Recitals of Israel's history tend to mark later times, when the whole cycle of feasts was in operation, or even later times still, when the second temple was in use. Psalm 105 certainly forms a pair with 106: 105 links their recent deliverance with those interventions of God which had marked their earlier history; 106 dwells on the perversity of the people for which they had been sent into captivity. Thus 105 stresses God's faithfulness and 106 the people's unfaithfulness.

Verses 1-4: Full-hearted praise
The psalm begins on a high note; it bubbles over with enthusiasm for the praise of God. We today can still feel the exuberant joy of the Jews as they came together on what was clearly a special occasion. They could readily respond to the priest's or Levite's call to *give thanks to the LORD*.

So full of happy feelings is the author that he brings all aspects of worship together in these verses: *call on his name*

... glory in his holy name, that is, acknowledge who he is, how he has revealed himself; *make known among the nations what he has done*, for his people have nothing to hide but everything to boast of before the world; *sing praise to him*, for such an occasion demands more than words, it needs the emotions aroused by music to do it justice; *tell of all his wonderful acts*, for this recent event is only the latest in a whole history of marvels, which they are about to recount; *seek the Lord*, do not be content with thinking only of what he has done, but get a vision of who he is; *rejoice* in him and the sight of *his face*; especially *look to ... his strength*, take to heart the great power he has put forth in all these *wonderful acts*, so that he will receive all the credit and they may have the assurance that he, the Lord, is the one true God.

Verses 5-11: The acts of God
Before coming to particulars he brings before us the two great principles lying behind all the incidents he is about to recount.

Firstly, verses 5-7 show that they are all works that *HE (God) has done*. The narratives as they stand in the histories may attribute events to human actions; but the psalm brings out that behind them all lay God's initiative: they were *HIS miracles ... the judgments HE pronounced ... HIS judgments*. They were performed to show that *the descendants of Abraham ... and the sons of Jacob* are *HIS chosen ones* and *HE is the Lord our God*, (emphasis mine throughout) as he declared at Sinai (Exod. 20:1).

Secondly (vv. 8-11), they were performed to fulfill his *covenant* promises. The particular promise in view here is the gift of *the land of Canaan*, originally *made to Abraham*. This was passed on to *Isaac*, then *confirmed to Jacob*. The present generation are *descendants of Abraham* (v. 6), which is why he has restored them to the land, for that covenant is still in operation at the time of the composition of the psalm. However, that *old covenant* which contained the promise to give the land of Canaan to Israel would only last until Christ came and inaugurated the *new covenant*. God promised him a world-wide kingdom, which would make the need for a special land for one nation of no further relevance. The words *for ever ... for a thousand generations* therefore do not mean *endlessly* but are limited to the period of the old covenant.

Verses 12-15: The Patriarchs
The covenant people began *few in number*: Abraham and Sarah, then Isaac, then Isaac's family. They had no territory in Canaan but were *strangers in it* and *wandered from nation to nation* and *from one kingdom to another*. Yet, though they were foreigners, objects at the very least of suspicion, *he allowed no one to oppress them*, and even *rebuked kings* if they tried to. The king of Egypt was prevented from harming Abraham and Sarah (Gen. 12:17-20). Abimelech, King of Gerar, was rebuked by God for taking Abraham's wife from him (Gen. 20) and something similar happened later to Isaac and Rebekah (Gen. 26). Thus events which seem to arise out of human weakness are attributed to God fulfilling his promise.

Verses 16-22: Joseph in Egypt
As the history of the outworking of God's covenant continues, we see that the *famine* which drove Jacob and his family into Egypt was *called down* by God. Similarly, the treachery of Joseph's brothers was the means by which *God (had) sent a man before them – Joseph, sold as a slave*, as he himself later acknowledged (Gen. 50:20). Even the awful incident of Potiphar's wife and his subsequent imprisonment is seen as the way by which *the word of the LORD proved him true* (v. 19). This probably refers to Joseph's original dreams of pre-eminence (Gen. 37:5-11), since the statement is immediately followed by the reference to Joseph's promotion as Pharaoh's chief minister. It was thus that the way was prepared for Jacob's family to migrate to Egypt, where they were kept safe until the appointed time for them to possess the promised land.

Verses 23-36: Israel in Egypt
The psalm traces the way God fulfilled his promise of a land for his people. The one family was insufficient to possess it all. Had they remained there and increased they may well have been absorbed into the existing population. So *he called*

down famine (v. 16), and, preceded by Joseph, *Israel entered Egypt*, remaining there four centuries until their numbers had increased sufficiently for them to occupy the whole land of Canaan. After 400 years, however, they were so settled that it seemed unlikely they would go unless driven out.

But *the LORD made his people very fruitful ... too numerous for their foes* (the Egyptians), *whose hearts he* (the Lord) *turned to hate his people*. This began the train of events which eventually secured their freedom. They were enslaved and began to hate their lives in Egypt. Moses, after a long period of preparation in Pharaoh's court and the land of Midian, became their leader. He sought permission for a brief holiday for them so that they could worship the Lord. This being refused, a great battle ensued between the Lord and Pharaoh, in which the Lord sent a series of plagues culminating in the slaughter of Egypt's firstborn sons (v. 36).

The plagues are not recounted here in the same order as in Exodus. The ninth plague is put first (v. 28) since it was this one that broke the spirit of the Egyptians and made them willing for Israel to leave. Perpetual darkness was what the Egyptians feared most of all, for it meant their chief god, Ra, the sun, was dead. Pharaoh, however, remained adamant, for was he not the representative on earth of Ra? Most of the other plagues are then mentioned before the final crucial one, which struck at the heir to the throne who was destined to be Ra's representative. Finally, Pharaoh himself was overthrown and God's victory over the gods of Egypt was total. The thing to observe is that God is the subject of almost every verse of this passage, which is about what *HE* did, in line with the principle of verses 5-11 that the great events of Israel's history were his direct actions.

Verses 37-45: On into Canaan
Although the contest with Pharaoh had ostensibly been only about securing a short period away, in the event it led to their total and final departure: *he brought out Israel*. The Egyptians no longer wanted them to stay, but were *glad when they left* (v. 38). So God saw to it that they had ample provisions; they went out laden with silver and gold, and at full strength: *from*

among their tribes no-one faltered. Moreover he took care of them on the long, difficult journey across the desert, miraculously providing food and water (vv. 40-41). All because the time had come when *he remembered his holy promise* (v. 42).

As they left Egypt *with rejoicing*, so, to cut a long story short, they took possession of *the lands of the nations* (v. 44), the plural no doubt indicating that Canaan was occupied by several independent kingdoms. The land they entered was not virgin territory but was furnished with farms and homes, so that they *fell heir to what others had toiled for*, which would not have been so had they remained there all those centuries while they were increasing.

Last, but not least, is the purpose for which God did all this: *that they might keep his precepts and observe his laws* (v. 45). God had given them a great code of law governing their personal and social lives and prescribing the way he wanted to be worshipped. They could not observe this fully while under others' jurisdiction, so he set them free and made them independent in order that, as he had kept his side of the covenant, they might keep theirs. Thus this closing verse forms the link between this psalm and the next.

Question:
(1) How can you use verses 1-4 to boost the fervency of your devotion to him who is the true Temple? (See John 2:20-22.)

(2) When you read the Old Testament story do you observe the hand of God even where events are attributed to a human agency? Do you do this with your personal life and the affairs of the world? Jesus told us that, whoever may cause a sparrow to fall, his will is behind it (see Matt. 10:29-30.)

(3) Can you see from the climax of this psalm in v. 45 that you were saved and the church was created with a view to holiness? (See Eph. 1:4; Titus 2:11-14.)

Psalm 106

What the People Have Undone

This psalm is the counterpart to 105 (see the introduction to that psalm). God's covenant with Israel had two sides: what GOD promised and undertook, which was mainly to make Abraham's descendants through Jacob his own people and give them a land; and what THE PEOPLE agreed to do, which was to 'keep his precepts and observe his laws' (Ps. 105:45). Psalm 105 is a thanksgiving to God for the way he has faithfully discharged his promises down their history.

But history shows the people had not matched his faithfulness but disobeyed him at almost every turn. Their sins down the years are catalogued here and confessed with shame. But this is not all. The grace of God has triumphed over their sin, for in spite of it God is still 'good' to them and 'his love endures' (v. 1).

VERSES 1-5: THANKSGIVING AND PRAYER

In view of what is to follow, the call to *praise* and *give thanks to the* LORD (v. 1) is even more meaningful than in 105. For *the* LORD has shown just how *good* he is and how *enduring* is *his love,* not only in relation to the mighty acts he has performed, but in relation to those he has done them for – an ungrateful, perverse and rebellious people. So the question of verse 2 is a good one: what words indeed could be found to *proclaim the mighty acts of the LORD or fully declare his praise*, since there was little in the response of the people to encourage him? His forbearance, grace and mercy were as great as the acts themselves!

But this does not mean it makes no difference whether his people obey him or not. We have to distinguish between the whole nation and the individuals who composed it, just as we do between the church and its members. God kept faith with Israel for the sake of his name, to maintain his reputation as one who honours his promises. But this does not mean he blessed individuals in the nation equally. It is those who do his will: who *maintain justice (and) constantly do what is right* who are *blessed* by him (v. 3). So often we read of this distinction, especially in the prophets. Isaiah, for example, pronounces severe judgments on the wicked in Israel, but promises blessings to the faithful remnant (Isa. 3:10-11).

So the prayer goes up (vv. 4-5), for each individual: *remember ME, O LORD* (emphasis mine). The Lord may *show favour to (his) people* collectively, but this did not mean he would *show favour* to each individual equally. Each must seek him for himself; each must be true to his laws irrespective of what others did, in order to *enjoy the prosperity of your chosen ones, ... share in the joy of your nation* and so be able wholeheartedly to *join your inheritance in giving praise*.

VERSES 6-39: CONFESSION OF FAILURE
Verse 6 sets the tone for the passage

Although it is chiefly about what *our fathers did* and the recurring pronoun is *they*, it begins with *we*. The present generation was no better but *have sinned, even as our fathers did*. They may not have *sinned* in the same ways, but this did not make them any better basically. There was no guarantee that the spirit that had been in their *fathers* had not been passed on to them. So, as Daniel and Nehemiah both confessed on behalf of their own generation (Dan. 9:1-20; Neh. 9:5-37), *we have sinned*. The confession that follows not only divides into historical periods, but goes through a whole range of sins.

Verses 7-12: Unbelief at the Red Sea
This passage is an inspired reflection on the behaviour of Israel at the Red Sea, where, having escaped from Egypt, they found themselves hemmed in by sea, mountains and the Egyptian army. Even if it was not the Red Sea proper but only 'the sea of reeds' (NIV mg), it was still uncrossable on foot, and there was no time to build boats.

Their unbelief consisted in their failure to *remember your many kindnesses* (v. 7), and all that God had done to get them out of Egypt and set them up for their journey to Canaan. To say *they rebelled* may seem to be going too far, but it is justified when we recall the awful things they said at the time, recorded in Exodus 14:10-12. There was a deliberate, wilful element in it.

Nevertheless, God did not abandon them, but *saved them*, not for their sakes but *for his name's sake* (v. 8). His reputation for truth and power was being called in question. He had displayed *his mighty power* in the miracles of the plagues. But perhaps this situation – taking his people safely over the Red Sea with their enemies at their backs – was too much for him; in which case what he had done in Egypt would soon be forgotten. But, in order to *make his mighty power known, he rebuked the Red Sea and it dried up, led them through the depths (and) saved them from the hand of the foe* whom *the waters covered* so that *not one of them survived* (vv. 9-11). Whatever the effect of this on other nations, it revived the faith of Israel who *believed his promises and sang his praise* (v. 12), as Exodus 15 records.

Verses 13-15: Discontent in the desert
These verses probably refer to the incident in Numbers 11, although discontent over food had emerged before, particularly in Exodus 16, when, as a result of their complaints, God sent manna. Now they had tired of the manna and longed for the fish and vegetables they had enjoyed in Egypt. This was seen by God, not as mere natural *craving*, but as *putting (him) to the test*. So he punished it 'with a severe plague' (Num. 11:23). It is interesting to compare this with the way the same incident is treated in 105:40 (although this may refer more specifically to Exod. 16). In 105 it is reported as one of God's wonders for his people, whereas in 106 it is an example of the people's

sinfulness. As at the Red Sea they had forgotten the great plagues, so in the desert they forgot the Red Sea.

Verses 16-18: Envy in the camp

Numbers 16 describes in full the events lying behind these verses. Although Korah appears to have been the ringleader of this attempted coup, his name is not mentioned here, perhaps because his sin was so grievous that his name deserved to perish from the lips of the people. Ambition and jealousy are not uncommon among leaders, even in the church of Christ, but the terrible punishment inflicted on these men and their followers shows how great is God's hatred of it.

Verses 19-23: Idolatry at Mount Sinai

This goes back in time to their stay at Sinai when Moses had disappeared into the divine cloud on the mount and remained there so long that they thought he had gone for ever (Exod. 32). In order to keep the unity of the people, Aaron proposed making a god out of gold in the form of a calf, an idea they may have brought from Egypt. However good his intentions may have been, even though they may have seen it not as another god but a representation of their God, Moses clearly regarded it as idolatry: exchanging *their Glory for the image of a bull* (v. 20). Like unbelief and discontent, it was another way of forgetting *the God who saved them (and the) great things (he) had done in Egypt ... and ... by the Red Sea*.

But their sin was worse than unbelief and discontentment and this time the whole nation was threatened with destruction. It took the intercession of Moses with God, in which he even offered himself in their place, 'the righteous for the unrighteous'. Foreshadowing as it did the way of redeeming the human race which he had purposed through a greater than Moses, God relented. But the sin stood on record as a warning, which often went unheeded by later generations. Paul quotes verse 20 in Romans 1:23 when he is establishing the cause of God's wrath on the whole human race, leading up to the action of the One who *stood in the breach* and took that wrath on himself, enduring what God had refused to Moses.

Verses 24-27: Disobedience at Kadesh

Moving on in the story, they arrive at the border of the land of Canaan. The story behind this passage is recorded in Numbers 13–14. The case they made out for not entering the land was fear of the existing inhabitants, whom they thought too strong to be overcome. It seemed a reasonable argument, but fear has no place in the hearts of a people who had the Lord for their God. Again they had put out of their minds the great things God had already done and the powerful enemies from whom he had delivered them by his mighty acts. So he accused them of unbelief (v. 24), and disobedience (v. 25). The purpose of sending the spies ahead was not to enable them to make a decision as to whether or not to go in, but to help them prepare, and to sample some of the fruit of the land to encourage them.

This is why verse 24 says they *despised the pleasant land*. They were so fearful and foolish that they preferred to go on living in the desert to fighting their way into Canaan, when God had assured them they could overcome its people (Num. 13:30). So, as a punishment, he gave them their wish, except that it would last 40 years, until that generation of adults had died out.

Verses 28-31: Apostasy in Moab

Forty years later they had reached Moab. They had overcome several enemies and taken possession of their lands and now stood on the brink of entering Canaan. But right on the point of victory they commit the worst sin of all – apostasy. Numbers 25 records how, where Balaam had failed to persuade God to curse them, the Moabite women succeeded in luring them into immorality and idolatry. Here it was not a god of their own making, a representation of the Lord, whom they worshipped, but *the Baal of Peor*, a heathen idol, whose worship involved *sacrifices*, possibly even human ones, and certainly fornication with cult prostitutes. This *provoked the* LORD *to anger* on an unprecedented scale. 24,000 had already died of the plague when *Phinehas stood up and intervened and the plague was checked* (v. 30). For this Phinehas was assured of the blessing of Abraham, indeed of the gospel itself: it *was credited to him as righteousness* (cf. Gen. 15:6; Rom. 4:5).

Verses 32-33: Provocation at Meribah

The two occurences of water from the rock seem to be blended here. The first, before Sinai, is recorded in Exodus 17, when the people's complaint was seen by Moses as 'testing the Lord' and led to the naming of the place Massah and *Meribah*. The other, recorded in Numbers 20, is at the end of the 40-year period when they were back in Kadesh. This time Moses himself was in trouble, because God had told him only to speak to the rock not to strike it. But he not only struck it but did so in anger and with *rash words*. So the whole nation and its leader were guilty of rebelling *against the Spirit of God* (v. 33). God speaks by his Spirit, and if we disobey him we are resisting his Spirit, a sin which Stephen accused the Jews of committing many times (Acts 7:51).

Verses 34-39: Failure in Canaan

The final scene in the drama takes us on to their life in the land and the period of the Judges. When all should have been light and love, there was total failure. All the sins of past years seem to meet together here as they fail to *destroy the peoples* whose land they had taken over. Instead, they *mingled with the natons and adopted their customs*. This applied particularly to *the idols* they *worshipped* and the rituals they had to perform in doing so, even to the extent of offering human sacrifices, particularly of their children (v. 37). So instead of making the land holy, fit for the presence of God, they *desecrated* it (v. 38), and *defiled themselves* (v. 39).

This completes the horrendous catalogue of the sins of the forebears of the generation now assembled before the God who had put up with this behaviour through the centuries. Would they be warned and refrain from going down the same road? Surely what follows should decide them!

VERSES 40-46: THE JUDGMENT OF GOD

If the preceding passages have brought together all the sins of the people, this one sums up God's reaction to their sins. On each occasion recounted in this psalm God brought a judgment upon them for their sins. When, in spite of all this, he did give them that 'pleasant land' and yet they proceeded to desecrate it, his judgments were the more severe. He did as he had threatened (Deut. 28:64-68) and *handed them over to the nations* (v. 41). They were *ruled over* by those whose gods they had turned to and became *subjected ... to their power* (v. 42). *Many times* they relented, he forgave and *delivered them*, but *rebellion* was endemic in their hearts and they returned to their sin, so that it happened over and over again.

Bringing the matter right up to date, he speaks of their latest deliverance (vv. 44-46), which he allowed because he still pitied *their distress when he heard their cry* (v. 44). But he did it mainly because of his *covenant* and his *great love*. Their captors (possibly the Persians) *pitied* them and released them, although they still kept them in their empire.

VERSES 47-48: PRAYER AND PRAISE

The psalm began with praise and prayer and ends with prayer and praise: prayer that God will continue the work of restoration and *gather* more of his people *from the nations* into which they had been scattered, for so far few had returned. The motive for asking this shows there was real repentance, for their desire is to *give thanks to your holy name*. So the psalm closes with *praise* to the Lord *from everlasting to everlasting*, not interrupted by lapses into sin as it had been in the past. This alone is worthy of an everlasting God whose covenant and love 'endure for ever'.

Questions:
(1) (On vv. 1-5): are you personally enjoying the blessing he bestows on his church or is it passing you by? (See Matt. 20:30.)

(2) (On vv. 7-12): is your faith such that you can look back at what God has done, not only in the Bible but the history of the church and even your own life, and believe he will do it again and to even greater effect? (See Ps. 44:1-8.)

(3) (On vv. 6-39): to what extent are the sins of Israel, recounted here, common to the church through its history and at the present time? (See 1 Cor. 10:6.)

Psalm 107

The LORD's Unfailing Love

This psalm celebrates God's frequent deliverances of his people. Verses 2-3 suggest that the occasion was their return from exile, but the particular instances which follow could apply to many other periods of Israel's history. Nor are they all national ones; some may cover small groups or individuals. Moreover, the covenant background is quite pronounced. There is frequent reference to God's 'unfailing love' (vv. 8, 15, 21, 31, 43), but also to their sins against the covenant and the threatened punishments, set out in Leviticus 26 and Deuteronomy 28.

Thus it follows 105 and 106 appropriately. Like 106 it brings out the distressed state the people found themselves in because of their sins, and like 105 it shows how God delivered them when they turned and cried to him again. Its dominant theme is therefore thanksgiving. It begins on this note (v. 1), and every example of God's deliverance contains the same exhortation (vv. 8, 15, 21, 31).

Verses 1-3: Give thanks for the return from exile
The psalm begins, as do 105 and 106, with a call to *give thanks to the LORD* and for the same reasons: *he is good* and *his love endures for ever* (v. 1). The psalm is going to show how God's faithful *love* comes to the aid of those who find themselves in situations which are beyond the power of man. It begins with

the most recent experience and the one which has affected everyone: their deliverance from Babylon. What they could not do for themselves and no one else could do for them he has done: *redeemed* them *from the hand of the foe* (v. 2). The choice of the word *redeemed* goes well with the *goodness* and *love* of God, for in Old Testament thought redemption was the responsibility of the closest relative to pay for someone to be purchased from debt or slavery, conditions from which none could free himself (cf. Ruth 4:1-10).

In 106:47 the cry had gone up from a people suffering under God's wrath for their sins, that he would 'gather us from the nations'. Here they are rejoicing that he has already begun to do that (v. 3). But it was just a beginning, for the Jews were not only exiled to Babylon but scattered through its empire, from which they are now beginning to be *gathered*, as Isaiah prophesied (Isa. 43:5-7). The psalm is teaching them how to express their *thanks to the LORD*: by saying this (v. 2), that is, by joining in the words which follow, which acknowledge God's many other deliverances. These are examples for us all to take to heart (v. 43).

Verses 4-9: Give thanks for food and drink

The experience of being *hungry and thirsty* was a common one in the ancient Near East, particularly when travelling. You could not get far in that area without having to cross desert wastelands (v. 4). Their recent return journey from Babylon would have taken them across such terrain and would have made the 40-year journey of their fathers across the desert of Sinai more real to them. Where there is *no way to a city where they could settle* (v. 4), there is no access to food and water, so *their lives ebbed away* (v. 5).

What do God's people whom he loves do in such circumstances? *They cry out to the LORD in their trouble* (v. 6). What happened when they did this? In the journey from Egypt we know he fed them miraculously with water from the rock and food from heaven. But in this case *he led them ... to a city where they could settle* (v. 7). Verse 4 suggests the problem was that they were lost and *wandered in the desert; a city* was not far away but they could not find the *way* to it. So he *led* them there.

Verse 7 applies particularly to people who are not just away from home but have no home. For such God provides so that they can cease wandering and *settle* down. Then they can produce their own food and water. But since God has done it they should *give thanks* to him (v. 8), and recognise him as the One who *satisfies the thirsty and feeds the hungry* (v. 9). Notice the hint of the Redeemer of all here, for Mary's song takes up these words in Luke 1:53, as does Christ himself in Matthew 5:6.

Verses 10-16: Give thanks for release from prison
This experience would still be in the minds of the returned exiles. They had been kept chained in a prison (v. 10) and only let out to do *bitter labour* (v. 12). If through weakness due to malnutrition and overwork *they stumbled* on the road, *there was no-one to help them* to their feet. This was worsened by the fact that it was their own fault they were there, because *they had rebelled against the words of God* (v. 11), which had provoked his wrath against them.

Yet there was one thing they could still do. As the Lord's people and because 'he is good' and 'his love endures for ever', they could cry to him *in their trouble*. They had certainly done this in captivity as 137 shows. God's covenant promise was that if they did this with a penitent heart he would hear them, as he had their fathers in Egypt (Lev. 26:40-45). Solomon had prayed for this very thing when he dedicated the first temple (1 Kings 8:46-51) and here they were now in the second temple as a testimony to the fact that he has been faithful to his promise, and has *brought them out of darkness* and *broken away their chains* (v. 14). Who had more reason than they to *give thanks* to him as the one who *breaks down gates of bronze and cuts through bars of iron* (v. 16)?

Verses 17-22: Give thanks for recovery from sickness
Imprisonment and exile were not the only curses in the covenant for *rebellious ways*; there was also sickness (Lev. 26:14-15; Deut. 28:22, 59-61). Clearly the particular *affliction* here in view is sickness, as it caused loss of appetite and threatened life itself (v. 18). Sickness is not necessarily the result of sin (John 9:1-3), but it can be (e.g. Luke 5:20; James 5:15). This may well have

been part of their suffering in exile, but it was not confined to that time. Plagues characterised their original journey from Egypt and occurred during their lives in the promised land. Apart from these general visitations there were instances of individuals being struck down, as was David (Pss. 32, 38) and Hezekiah (2 Kings 20). Even the wisest could become fools, that is, behave like people who have no God (Ps. 14:1).

But the remedy is at hand and is the same as before: humbling and prayer (v. 19). This moved God, who *sent forth his word*, that is, gave his command for the sickness to be removed, so that they were *healed* and saved from death (v. 20). Again, he has done this, as all his other *wonderful deeds for men*, to prove *his unfailing love*, to which the expected response is again to *give thanks* to him (v. 21). But such was the seriousness of this situation that it called for more than words. Yes, let them *tell of his works with songs of joy* but also *sacrifice thank-offerings* and show they truly meant their gratitude. Perhaps this was Passover time and everyone contributed in some way by bringing an offering.

Verses 23-32: Give thanks for rescue from the sea
This is unlikely to have any connection with their recent exile, although Deuteronomy 28:68 does refer to being 'sent back in ships to Egypt'. In any case there is no reference here to sin and God's punishment, so it is more likely to refer to troubles at sea during ordinary voyages. Israel did trade by sea (1 Kings 9:26-28; 10:22, to which this passage seems to be referring) – see verse 23b with its reference to *merchants*.

However, the thought here is not so much of sinfulness as littleness. The Mediterranean, where their merchant ships would sail, could become very rough, and sudden storms were frequent even on their own lake of Galilee. Such a storm is described here and the vivid words of verses 25-27 show how small and weak are the strongest men in the face of the elements.

But the One behind this is God himself, who *spoke and stirred up a tempest* (v. 25). A storm is one of *the works of the LORD*, one of his *wonderful deeds* (v. 24). He who sends it can end it, so the answer again is to call to him, not here confessing particular sins, simply human frailty before the mighty power of God in nature (v. 28). How often has he by way of answer *stilled the storm* and *hushed the waves* (v. 29), thus making the mariners *glad* again, and able to continue their journey safely (v. 30).

Since he has done this, it is appropriate to give thanks to him, for he has done it out of *his unfailing love*. As the stirring up of the storm was one of *his wonderful deeds* (v. 24), so too was its stilling (v. 31). And what place more suitable to do so than *in the assembly of the people* (v. 32)? Perhaps there were those present who had actually been in this situation, for trading by sea may have been resumed since the return; if so they would be the first to respond.

Verses 33-42: Give thanks for the return of prosperity

In this final passage the format is altered: instead of describing a situation from the standpoint of the sufferers, it is all about what he (God) did. Also the usual refrain is omitted. This may be because, whereas the other experiences only applied to 'some' and 'others', this affected all, so the format is changed to draw attention to this. For it has to do with the fluctuating condition of the land itself. God could turn this land of *rivers* and streams *into a desert* and make it a *salt waste* (vv. 33-34). This too had been threatened on the people if they broke the covenant (Lev. 26:32; Deut. 28:16-18). This had certainly happened in recent years while they had been away and there had been few left to cultivate the land, so that it 'enjoyed its sabbaths' (Lev. 26:43), perhaps suggesting they had not been observing these. Psalm 126 speaks of how when they returned they 'sowed in tears'.

But equally God can reverse the process and return it to prosperity. Then *the desert* becomes *pools of water* enabling them to sow their *fields* and gather *a fruitful harvest,* so that *their numbers increased* (vv. 35-38). But the process could happen all over again; indeed it had since their return (v. 39-40). Because they had neglected God's house and put their resources into their own houses, the land had again come under his curse and not yielded its increase (v. 39-40; Hag. 1:6). But once they had put this right and finished the temple, the blessing returned and they again enjoyed an increase (vv. 41-42).

Verse 43: Learn the lessons

Here is the indication that the psalm had been composed, not only for that occasion and even just for that people, but for *whoever is wise*, whoever wants to know how to walk with the Lord. There are lessons to *heed* here: about human frailty, physical, moral and spiritual; but chiefly about *the great love of the LORD* who forgives, redeems and restores.

Questions:

(1) How does the Old Testament use of the word 'redeemed' (v. 2) throw light on what it involved for Christ to redeem us from the power of sin, death and Satan? (See Heb. 2:10-18.)

(2) We who know 'the great love of the Lord' in Christ can apply these experiences to our salvation. How do you see these five scenes as pictures of the various states of sin from which Christ saves us?

(3) How often and with how much fervour do you 'give thanks to the LORD' for these aspects of his redemption you have just been considering? (See Eph. 1:3; 1 Pet. 1:3.)

Psalm 108

Victory Celebrations

This psalm appears to have come from the heat of battle.
The victory was not yet won but it was sure. Such an event
called for special praise – 'a new song'. Led by the Spirit what
David does is to make one new song out of two old ones. He
takes Psalm 60, composed in similar circumstances when the
war still hung in the balance, and cuts off the cry of despair
(Ps. 60:1-4). But how should this be replaced to make the psalm
approximately the same length and probably fit the tune
'Lily of the Covenant' ? Why not take the words of a psalm
composed under similar circumstances? David looks back
over his previous experience. There had been a time when
his fortunes had been at rock bottom: Saul had finally caught
up with him. He was in the mouth of the cave while David
was in the back. It seemed all was over. Yet God turned the
tables and put Saul at David's mercy. When David spared him
it shamed Saul into confessing he had been in the wrong and
into acknowledging David would become King. In Psalm 57
David expressed both his great fear when at the back of the
cave (vv. 1-4), and his praise when God in his providence
delivered him (vv. 5-11).

What more suitable passage than the latter with which to
begin his new song? It was the intervention of providence again
– this time on behalf of the nation in general and his throne in
particular. It was also a demonstration to *the nations* that God

reigns (v. 3) and that his reign is one of *love and faithfulness* (v. 4). Thus what was old is taken to express something new. David could now say, with greater sincerity even than when spared in the cave, the words of verse 5.

Questions:
(1) Should this encourage us to put passages of Scripture together to show how God's dealings with his people are progressive? See Paul's use of verse 5 (57:9) in Romans 15:9.

(2) How does this psalm teach us the way to use repetition effectively,not tediously? (See 2 Pet. 1:12-15.)

(3) How does this psalm teach us to use Scripture to interpret our personal experiences and those of the church?

Psalm 109

A Curse On All Traitors

Here is David complaining of a fierce attack that is being made on his character. This had been done by Saul in David's early years, and was done towards the end of his life by his son Absalom. But it may have happened at other times too, for David was not universally popular. His reply is fiercer than their words as he launches into one of his great imprecations. See the Introduction (Vol. I, p. 18), for an explanation of imprecatory passages.

Verses 1-5: David prays to God about this blow
Although the psalm is a bitter complaint and includes a fierce imprecation, David still approaches God in an attitude of worship: *O God whom I praise,* and waits for what God has to say: *do not remain silent.* He then outlines the situation which calls for God to break his silence and speak. The conspiracy was not a mere whispering campaign but an open attack. David feels besieged by their *lying tongues* and *words of hatred* (vv. 2-3). Nor was this being done by an isolated individual; a number were involved. David had seen these men as his friends, and now they were his accusers (v. 4). They were men who knew him well, so that their lies would seem credible. Bitter as this was to him, David restrains himself, remembers *I am a man of prayer* and gives himself to *prayer* (v. 5).

Verses 6-15: David pronounces God's curse on them

God has not remained 'silent' and is answering David's prayer, for the Spirit of prophecy again comes upon him. Prophets have authority to declare God's judgment on sinners. This is what David is doing here, except that, being *a psalm* addressed to God, the prophecies take the form of a prayer, using words like *let* and *may*. This does not bring a note of uncertainty into the matter; nor does it mean David is voicing his own vindictiveness, which would be inconsistent with what he had just said about his 'friendship' towards them and his prayer for them. But now the Holy Spirit takes him up to pray *against* them. The change to the singular in verse 6 is because he is now concentrating on the leader of the campaign, the one who had been closest to David and therefore chiefly responsible.

This is not one 'curse' but a whole string of them:

(1) **Verses 6-7**: he will be brought to trial for his libellous words. He who accused his king will himself be accused – not by a true witness interested only in justice, but by *an evil man* who will stop at nothing. The NIV margin suggests 'the evil one', which is in line with the word *accuser*, which is 'Satan'. Nor will God answer for him if he appeals to him: *may his prayers condemn him* (v. 7).

(2) **Verse 8**: He will suffer an early death, either because he has been found *guilty* (v. 7) and condemned, or because nemesis will overtake him by illness, accident or murder. Thus he will lose *his place of leadership*. This is the verse quoted by Peter with reference to Judas in Acts 1:20, whose act was the last word in treachery, whose *days were few* and who was deprived of his apostolic office and replaced by another. It was Jesus himself who had pronounced this curse on Judas: John 13:18.

(3) **Verses 9-15**: his family too will suffer because of this. No-one will take care of the offspring of such a man, for they would be regarded as sharing his curse. His absence will leave his estate to the mercy of *creditors* and *strangers* (v. 11) from whom orphaned children would be unable to rescue it. Much of this passage is based on Exodus 20:5, God's judgment on the descendants of those who apostatize from him. This is further

evidence that David is not speaking from personal pique but pronouncing the judgment of God's word.

Verses 16-18: David justifies his imprecatory prayer
The word of God is clear, both in Old and New Testaments, that there is no mercy for the unmerciful (Matt. 18:21-35; James 2:13). So David is in line with Scripture in verse 16. On this basis he can justify the prayer he has just prayed. For these men had shown no mercy to David and his few followers, but *hounded (them) to death*, leaving them *poor ... needy (and) ... broken hearted*. In verses 17-18 he goes further to declare that the curse has already fallen on them. Follow the margin in verse 17 ('and it has') rather than *may it*; they were already given up to judgment.

Verses 19-20: David intensifies the curse
With this justification David's words become even stronger. He prays for God's judgment to tighten round them so that they cannot escape it (v. 19). In this way God would 'pay them back', as we say, for their *evil* words and actions.

Verses 21-25: David pleads for God's deliverance
The God who deals justly with oppressors deals mercifully with their victims. Such is David just now: from his position of power and wealth he has been reduced to utter feebleness, physically as well as mentally and emotionally (v. 22). He has become such an emaciated figure (v. 23a) that he is *an object of scorn* (v. 25), like an insect alighting on a person, which he just shakes off (v. 23b).

Verses 26-29: David prays God will turn the tables on his accusers
Now he makes God's character rather than his own condition the ground of his prayer (v. 26). If God turns the tables he will get the glory (v. 27), for it will be clear that David has not done this – he is too weak. Thus he believes blessing can come out of this and he will ultimately rejoice (v. 28) because God has demonstrated his faithfulness to those who trust him, by letting his justice fall on those who shame him (v. 29).

Verses 30-31: David praises God in anticipation of his deliverance

So in the midst of his plight, which was unchanged at the time of writing, he foresees himself back *in the great throng* that gathers in the house of God to *praise him*. In verse 31 he uses an expression he had used when these troubles first began, (in Ps. 16:8): that God *stands at (his) right hand*. He has lost his 'right hand man', who is but a man, whereas his true advisor and protector is the Almighty God.

Questions:

(1) Is there still a case for praying *against* those who deal treacherously with Christ and his gospel? (Cf. Matt. 5:44 with Jude 9-11.)

(2) How do we guard against a spirit of vindictiveness when unjustly attacked? (See 1 Pet. 2:19-25; 3:13-18; 4:12-19.)

(3) Is it true historically (and currently) that the cause of Christ has suffered more from its alleged friends than from its sworn enemies?

Psalm 110

King and Priest

David, whose psalm this is, utters an oracle, verse 1a, either given him directly from God or through a prophet, for the Lord says to *my Lord* is literally 'the oracle of Yahweh to my Lord'. While originally my Lord may have meant the King, perhaps David himself, Jesus made it clear it referred to him (Matt. 22:41-44). David is in prophetic mode, as in 109, but what a different message! Here he is not predicting a curse on a traitor but a blessing on a faithful one whom he calls My Lord. How far David understood what he was saying we do not know. But it is clear to us in view of Jesus' own use of the psalm. There are two parts to the oracle.

Verses 1-3: His enthronement as King
Sit at my right hand means 'receive authority to rule in my name'. The implications are brought out in what follows. Although his *enemies* are still active, the decisive act which has led to his exaltation guarantees their ultimate defeat. The fact that the Hebrews saw the Egyptians drowned in the Red Sea does not mean they would have no more trouble with the ungodly, but that that victory guaranteed future victories; God would deal with other enemies in like manner. So we find in the Old Testament that when Israel was faced with enemies they were frequently reminded of that occasion, and not just at Passover.

For example, when confronted by the Babylonians, Habakkuk appealed to this event (Hab. 3:8-10).

Verse 2 confirms this: his enemies will not be able to prevent the expansion of his kingdom. David first established himself on *Zion*, then extended his territory in all directions. This is now becoming fulfilled in the growth of Christ's kingdom through the *sceptre* of the gospel, which first went forth *from Zion*, when he was proclaimed 'Lord and Christ' at Pentecost (Acts 2:33-36). Then the apostles, their colleagues and successors took the word to the nations.

Verse 3 develops this latter thought. Christ does not work alone to establish and extend his kingdom. He has a vast volunteer army, as had Joshua and his successors when they sought to take possession of Canaan (cf. Judg. 5:2). It is not clear whether verse 3b refers to the king himself or his *troops*. The niv margin appears to opt for the latter. It could be translated 'your young men come to you like dew from the womb of the morning'. Dawn gives birth to dew which is fresh every morning. So those who fight for and under Christ in his holy war are 'new every morning' and 'renewed day by day'.

Verses 4-7: The King as Priest

This is stated even more strongly than the first message, for it is made with an oath: *the Lord has sworn* – the oath of one who *will not change his mind*. Kingship and priesthood were never vested in the same person during the term of the old covenant, so it needs to be said that *the Lord* is making no mistake here. Also, he appeals to the precedent for this in the case of Melchizedek (Gen. 14:18-20) and Hebrews 5:5-10 and 6:19–7:28 bring out how well this ancient Priest-King prefigured the ministry of Christ as Priest and King. When the old covenant was made, although the offices were split, Israel still had kings and priests to provide adequately for a people redeemed from a great enemy but facing others as they served their king and their God.

The closing verses, (5-7), depict the final victory of the Priest-King. His enemies will not resist him for ever. The day of his wrath, often called 'the day of the Lord' in both testaments, is coming, when he will crush and judge them. The victory will be total: over the proudest and mightiest *kings* (v. 5), over the remotest *nations* (v. 6a); and even over supernatural powers, *rulers* (v. 6b, cf. Eph. 2:2; 6:12). Thus the Red Sea experience is to be repeated, but totally and finally. Nothing will delay him (v. 7). The quick *drink* at the *brook* recalls Gideon's three hundred totally dedicated warriors marching boldly and decisively against the Midianites (Judg. 7).

Then will come the final triumph: *he will lift up his head.* Like a Roman general he is chaired from the battlefield and cheered into the city. This no doubt often happened in the history of Israel – all due to the original great redemption commemorated at Passover, previewing the redemption of Christ, which itself guarantees the final defeat of the enemies of the Lord and the triumph of his people.

Questions:
(1) Look up the quotations of and allusions to verse 1 in the New Testament and work out how they build up a picture of Christ's person. Look them up in this order: Matthew 22:44 and Hebrews 1:13; Acts 2:33-36; Acts 5:30-31 and Romans 8:34; 1 Corinthians 15:25 and Hebrews 10:13.

(2) Consider verse 4 in the light of Genesis 14:18-20 and Hebrews 5:5-10. What should Christ's Melchizedek priesthood mean to us?

Psalm 111

The Goodness of God

This and the next psalm form a pair: both begin 'Halleluyah' or *Praise the Lord*; both are 'acrostic', that is, they work their way through the 22-letter Hebrew alphabet, beginning each line with a different letter. Each verse has two lines except for verses 9-10 which have three. They are also paired as regards theme: 111 is on the goodness of God shown in 'the works of his hands', such as his provision of food, which links the desert journey with the harvest, celebrated particularly in the Feast of Tabernacles. 112 follows, bringing out how the man of God seeks to emulate him in generosity.

Verse 1: Purpose stated

The writer vows to express his wholehearted thanks to the Lord (*extol*), which immediately indicates he is going to concentrate on God's 'works', since it is primarily for these that we give thanks. Several synonyms are used for his works in the verses that follow. If this is not David or another king it is clearly someone high up, possibly the high priest, since he has an important place both in what we might call the cabinet (*the council of the upright*) and the whole congregation (*assembly*).

Verses 2-9: Purpose fulfilled

He now proceeds to carry out his vow, beginning in a general way with a word for *works* which refers to what he has *made* rather than simply what he has *done*, that is, his created *works* (v. 2). That these are *great* is evident from the interest and pleasure they arouse: *pondered by all who delight in them*. This remembrance of creation formed part of the Feast of Tabernacles.

Turning to his *deeds* (v. 3), that is, his works in providence, he is full of wonder at them; they are *glorious and majestic*, not only in themselves but in what they reveal about God – his everlasting *righteousness*. He has not brought things into existence only to abandon them to their own whims, but sustained them, so that the light of the sun, the fruit of the earth and the skills of man display his glory and majesty.

As well as the normal continuing providential works, there are special ones which he calls *wonders* (v. 4): intervention on behalf of his people, which show that as well as being righteous he is *gracious and compassionate*. So that his people might never forget this about him, he has *caused his wonders to be remembered* by appointing special feasts, such as Tabernacles. This feast is probably in view in verse 5 – his provision of *food for those who fear him*, such as he made by supplying manna on the long journey across the desert (long in time rather than distance!). This he did in spite of all their unbelief and rebelliousness, simply because he had promised to do so in his *covenant* with them.

Their arrival in the *land* of promise and conquest of it from *other nations* was likewise not due to their enthusiasm and skill, but *the power of his works* (v. 6). This began with the overthrow of Jericho, the fortress town which guarded the entrance to Canaan, encouraging them to believe Moses' words that 'the LORD your God will be with you wherever you go' (Josh. 1:9), until the whole land was in their possession.

This leads him to reiterate what *the works of the* LORD prove about him: he is *faithful and just* (v. 7). What he has undertaken to do for all men he has performed; what he has promised to his people he has delivered. Occasions like the feasts are a great encouragement to reaffirming confidence that *all his precepts are trustworthy* – whatever he says he does. Having surveyed the past they can look to the future and see it as equally secure, for the Lord does not change: *his precepts ... are steadfast for ever and ever* (v. 8). He never lies or speaks evasively, but always *in faithfulness and uprightness*.

The greatest proof of this lies in his work of *redemption*, which matches or even exceeds his work of creation and providence (v. 9). For this *covenant* of grace is more glorious than his covenant of nature (made after the Flood) or his covenant of law (made at Sinai). This one is *for ever*. So his epithets for God mount to a height: *holy and awesome is his name*. How much more do we feel this, who know his full *redemption*, of which Israel's was only a preview!

Verse 10: Response required

The appropriate response to one who is *holy and awesome* is *fear*, not in the sense of terror (unless we disobey him!), but of high regard leading to the heartfelt praise with which he began. It has been pointed out that the psalm blends a variety of literary traditions: historical (vv. 4-6), legal (vv. 7-8) and now *wisdom*. This gives the thought a lovely balance, showing that those who by remembering his deeds confirm their faith and go on to *follow his precepts*, grow in *wisdom (and) understanding*. Such people are not moaners or grumblers but those who give God the *eternal praise* which rightly *belongs* to him.

Questions:
(1) F. D. Kidner points out that the words of verse 2 adorn the entrance to the Cavendish Laboratory in Cambridge, the scene of many scientific discoveries. How would you relate these words to scientific research and vice versa? Do Daniel 1:4 and Acts 7:22 help?

(2) What have you personally experienced or observed in others or the world generally that moves you to admire God's providential acts?

(3) If this high view of God is 'the **beginning** of wisdom', how does it continue and grow? (See Col. 1:9; James 1:2-5; 3:17-18 (James is the New Testament's 'Book of Wisdom').

Psalm 112

The Blessedness of the Righteous

This psalm is companion to 111 with its similar acrostic structure (see the introduction to 111). It takes over where 111 leaves off, expounding what 'the fear of the Lᴏʀᴅ' (111:10) is. As 111 is about God's goodness, so 112 is about how someone who *fears* God emulates him and thus is *blessed*.

Verse 1: Blessedness pronounced

Like 111, it begins with 'Halleluyah' or *Praise the Lᴏʀᴅ*, since it is from him 'all blessings flow'. Chiefly his blessing falls on *the man who fears* him. This fear is expressed in a similar way to 111:10, that is, by knowing and obeying his word: 'commands' in 111:10 and *precepts* here. That fear is not the same as terror is clear from the words *delight in his commands*. Those who have high views of God and appreciate the goodness which 111 dwells on *enjoy* knowing and obeying his word. If they did not and it made them miserable, how could they be called *blessed*?

Verses 2-9: Blessedness described

In what ways is the God-fearer blessed?

(1) *In his home and family* (vv. 2-3). After God himself the godly person's chief concern is for *his children*; like Job (in ch.1) he is concerned that they should follow his footsteps by being *an*

upright generation and an influence for good *in the land. Mighty* is similar to the 'greatness' God promised to Abraham and his descendants (Gen. 12:2). This promise therefore is God keeping his covenant undertakings. God enables them to do this by providing *wealth and riches*, which are clearly not for living in luxury and self-indulgence, but for doing good (as will be seen later). In this way the *righteousness* of the godly man *endures for ever*. **He** does not continue, but what he was and stands for does.

(2) *In adversity* (v. 4). The *darkness* may refer to trouble in his own life or to moral decline in society. Whichever it is he continues to live as a *righteous man, gracious and compassionate* – God's own qualities (111:4)! In this way he is *a light for the upright*, that is, an encouragement to other godly people who may be wavering in such times.

3) *In normal life* (v. 5). His main principle in the conduct (of) *his affairs,* his business life or other occupation, is *justice*: he will be honest and fair, but if necessary go beyond 'the rate for the job' and be *generous and* lend *freely*. He will be blessed in this too, for *good will come* to him.

4) *In trials* (vv. 6-8). Righteousness, justice and generosity do not always mean popularity. Such a person can have *foes* – jealous people who hate him for his position, wealth or even godliness because it exposes their sinfulness. He may hear *bad news* of how they have harmed his business or his family, as Job did, and may threaten his own person. But *he will never be shaken* by this, he *will have no fear* (stated twice) because *his heart is steadfast ... secure*. He is *trusting in the* LORD, he has a good conscience and knows God is on his side. So like Job he knows God will eventually vindicate him and *he will look in triumph on his foes*. He will not end in obscurity but *will be remembered for ever*.

5) *In prosperity* (v. 9). Perhaps this verse indicates he is now enjoying that 'triumph' and expressing his gratitude by resuming his former practice (v. 5). Or perhaps he is carrying on doing good in spite of his 'foes'. He maintains his principles of fairness and generosity come what may, *his righteousness endures for ever*. This makes him even more respected by society: *his horn*, his reputation, is *lifted high in honour*. What

greater blessing can one have than that of being honoured by God and man for integrity and kindness?

Verse 10: Wickedness cursed

Here are the *foes* over whom he has *triumphed*. They have been exposed as *wicked*. There are no blessings for them, but only the opposite: they are *vexed*, not encouraged, by the sight of godliness blessed; they get very angry and *gnash (their) teeth*; they are frustrated in their attempt to get their hands on the godly man's wealth and satisfy their *longings*. Their frustration ruins their health and they *waste away*. What a contrast to the blessings of a God-fearing life!

Questions:
(1) Is your study of God's word and care to obey it a 'delight' to you, or only a duty which would make you feel guilty if you did not do it? (See Pss. 1:2; 37:4.)

(2) How concerned are you that the principles you hold will be followed by the rising generation? (See Eph. 6:4.)

(3) How do you maintain your godliness in times of unpopularity and criticism? (See John 15:20-21.) How do you continue being generous in spite of adverse circumstances? (See 2 Cor. 9:6-11.)

Psalm 113

Who is like the LORD?

This psalm is the first of six (113–118) which were put together and called 'the Egyptian Hallel', to be used at the great feasts: Passover, Pentecost and Tabernacles, after the Jews' return from exile. Their deliverance from Babylon was seen as a repeat of the exodus from Egypt. This psalm might have been written for the celebration of one of these feasts some time after the work had been resumed on the temple.

Verses 1-3: The call to praise

This psalm begins with a call from the priest or Levite leading the service to *praise the LORD* (v. 1). It was addressed to the whole people (v. 2), who came to be called *servants of the LORD* after their return from exile (Ezra 5:11; Neh. 1:10), although the term had been used of them as early as Leviticus 25:55. Isaiah brought it more into prominence with his 'servant songs': 42:1-4; 44:1-5; 49:1-7; 50; 52:13–53:12, in which Israel's high calling and great sufferings merge into those of the Messiah.

It is for his *name* they were to *praise* him, that is, for what he has revealed of himself as 'God' and '*the LORD*', the mighty and faithful one who has shown himself to be true to his *name* in their restoration from captivity and the re-erection of the temple where they can meet with him. Such a God deserves *praise* which is both **perpetual**: *now and for evermore*, and

universal: *from the rising of the sun to the place where it sets,* that is, from east to west. This concept is found in Psalm 50, Isaiah 45:6 and 59:19 and Malachi 1:11 where it anticipates the coming of the Gentiles to worship the one true God.

Verses 4-9: The God who is praised
There can be few more all-embracing descriptions of God in such a small space even in the rest of Scripture. His **transcendence** is spoken of in verses 4-5 in superlatives. He is supreme in the earth: *exalted over all the nations,* including the foreign powers at present governing Judah, which is the motivation for the universal worship of verse 3. Moreover, he is Lord of *the heavens* too, the supernatural sphere and all who inhabit it; whatever *glory* these beings have, he outshines it. For he is sovereign over the universe, *the One who sits enthroned on high.* He is beyond compare: *who is like the LORD our God?* a favourite theme with the prophets, especially Isaiah, who expatiates on it from 40:12 to 41:4, and Micah, whose name means 'who is like the Lord?' and who makes this the climax of his message (Micah 7:18-20).

In this psalm his uniqueness does not lie merely in his absolute sovereignty, his transcendence, but in his **immanence,** that he *stoops down to look on the heavens and the earth* (v. 6). So high is he that he has to *stoop* to see *the heavens* let alone the earth! But he does so, and it is in this that his uniqueness lies, for while some gods or views of God stress his transcendence and others his immanence, only the Bible combines the two.

The proof lies, as in 146:7-9, in his record of helping the lowliest whom others neglect. The inspiration for verses 7-9 is the Song of Hannah (1 Sam. 2, especially v. 8). In ancient Israel a woman was regarded by people as a second-class citizen, and a childless woman little better than a harlot, cursed by God for some sin. When Hannah gave birth in answer to prayer she saw it as being *raised ... from the dust and ... the ash heap* (v. 7), and put alongside *princes,* for not only was she favoured with a man-child, but one who was wholly given to serve the Lord and destined for great things.

Likewise verse 9 recalls 1 Samuel 2:5. She had prayed with such anguish that Eli the priest thought her drunk. But when she became *the happy mother* of a son she needed no stimulants to inspire her to 'rejoice in the LORD' (1 Sam. 2:1). This generation of Jews had also been humbled to *the dust*, made lower than the low, slaves again to a foreign power. It had been a *barren* time with little reason for bringing forth *children*. But their God who *sits enthroned on high* had not forgotten them and now they were at least *settled ... in (their) home*, even if they were not yet *seated with princes*. That was a hope to come, as Mary's Song shows (Luke 1:46-55). But for now this was enough to inspire them to *praise the LORD*.

Questions:
(1) How is verse 3 still being fulfilled? Think about the lines from the evening hymn: 'The sun that bids us rest is waking our brethren 'neath the western sky, And hour by hour fresh lips are making thy wondrous doings heard on high'.

(2) Why is a God both transcendent and immanent essential for salvation? How are these qualities seen in the incarnation? (See John.1:1-5, 14, 18.)

(3) How does what Christ has done for us go beyond verses 7-8? (See Eph. 2:1-7.)

Psalm 114

Trembling at the Presence of the LORD

This psalm celebrates the sovereignty of God over his natural creation through which he established Israel as his people and provided for them. It might have been composed for the Feast of Pentecost, especially as it sounds the note of universality characteristic of Pentecost.

Verses 1-2 bring out the contrast between the people's past experience in Egypt and their present settlement in the land of promise. They had been a minority, subject to *a people of foreign tongue*, with whom they could scarcely communicate, yet who enslaved them. The use of the name *Jacob* draws attention to the weakness of their position then, and contrasts with the name God gave *Jacob* after he had 'struggled with God and men and overcome' (Gen. 32:28). Now through God they had *overcome* the most powerful nation of that time!

But there is more: they now have a King more powerful than any Pharaoh, for they are *Israel his dominion*. The God who overthrew Egypt is their King, so who can touch them now? But there is still more: although divine and supernatural he dwells among them, for *Judah* has become *his sanctuary*. No doubt this (Zion) was where they were gathered for the feast, to celebrate those past events because of which they are enjoying their present peace and prosperity.

Verses 3-4 show the poet dramatically reconstructing these events, but looking at them from God's point of view, rather than that of those who experienced them. Although God's name is not mentioned, it was he at whom *the sea looked* (the Red Sea) and from whom it *fled*. It was God's appearance from which *the Jordan turned back*. As God had opened the gates of Egypt to let them out, so he opened the gates of Canaan to let them into the land he was giving them – both these by turning back the waters of rivers.

In fact wherever God appeared nature reacted. Verse 4 refers to Sinai, which God personally visited. Exodus 19:18 speaks of smoke and fire on Sinai rather than dancing, so this verse probably refers to the nearby *mountains and hills*. They are depicted as skipping *like rams ... (and) lambs*, rejoicing to see their maker and keeper. For though at the time Israel was afraid of God when he descended on Sinai, looking back they see the glory of it, for it was there they were brought into that covenant relationship which made them what they were on that day. So now they could join in the dance of the *mountains and hills*.

Verses 5-6 seem to marvel at the strangeness of this behaviour on the part of nature, even its humour, as if asking 'Are we supposed to take this seriously? How can it be? What is the point of it?'

Verses 7-8 reply with some sternness. The God whose appearance provoked that behaviour is still present. All should take it seriously and behave appropriately – with awe: *tremble*. This applies first to Israel itself (for the word rendered *earth* means 'land' as well as *earth*), then to all nations of *the earth*, for the whole *earth* is the Lord's and if he comes and visits it, all should acknowledge him. Here is that universal note again, so characteristic of the Feast of Pentecost, anticipating the ultimate Pentecost when the gospel would extend his kingdom far and wide.

This is confirmed in verse 8. He is the God who takes particular care of his people and when necessary can overcome the most unpromising of circumstances. At Horeb he *turned the rock into a pool* (Exod. 17:6) and at Kadesh *the hard rock into springs of water* (Num. 20:11). This was a token of the fertility he would bestow on his land, which was now being celebrated at Pentecost. Without the water, the rain, the springs and the rivers, where would the harvest be?

The ultimate fulfilment of this was in Christ who came to open up 'a spring of living water welling up into eternal life' (John 4:13-14) and this for all who would receive it (Rev. 22:17).

Question:
Consider the range of emotions the appearance of God evokes, from awe to joy, from trembling to dancing. Does this reflect your reaction to him in your personal devotions and church gatherings?

Psalm 115

Soli Deo Gloria!

The psalm celebrates a deliverance from calamity (v. 2) and a victory of God over idols (vv. 3-8), leading to a rededication of the nation to God (vv. 9-13) and an ascription of praise to him (vv. 14-18).

Verses 1-3 set the tone by giving God alone the glory of this victory. God's power and love for his people, in fact his very existence, had been called in question (v. 2), and God acts quickly to restore his honour and prove his power to do whatever pleases him (v. 3).

Verses 4-8 show how the people's eyes had been opened to the futility of man-made gods, whether Egyptian, Philistine, Assyrian or Babylonian, who now appeared ridiculous to them in their total uselessness.

Verses 9-11 call on them to forsake any hankering after these gods and commit themselves wholly to the Lord.

Verses 12-13 follow this train of thought. If they learned the lesson of God's victory (vv. 1-8), heeded the call of verses 9-11, they could be assured of God's help in the future. This confidence grows as the psalm develops.

Verses 14-15 reveal a renewed spirit of prayer for each other. Prayer is addressed to the LORD ... *of heaven and earth*, as also in

Verse 16. Jesus taught us to remember 'When you pray say, "Father in heaven"'. This God is concerned not only about his own abode but ours – *the earth* which *he has given to man*.

Verses 17-18 show why God has done this for them and spared them from death: so that they could live to *praise* him in the future. During Old Testament times little was revealed as to what lay beyond death. It was seen as a place of darkness and silence called 'Sheol'. Christ conquered death by his resurrection and ascended to prepare a place for believers with him. Through him Christians have the glorious hope of being transported to a sphere in which they are no longer 'dead' and 'silent' but live for ever praising God (Rev. 4:8; 7:15).

Questions:
(1) Can you recall any times of unfaithfulness to God which led you into trouble, but from which God has delivered you?
(2) Are you using your deliverance to continue in his praises?
(3) What in present-day life corresponds to 'dumb idols' (vv. 4-8)?

Psalm 116

At Death's Door

The God of Israel was a God who healed diseases (Ps. 103:3). No doubt what is described here was a not uncommon experience for the people, who are thus provided with a psalm to express their gratitude. We are told of how King Hezekiah was struck with a fatal illness, of which he was providentially cured, so that he went up to the temple of the Lord to give thanks. Perhaps this was the psalm he used (2 Kings 20:1-11).

Verses 1-6: Recollection

The intense emotion with which the psalm begins is shown in the Hebrew which reads literally 'I love because the Lord hears my voice, my supplication' (v. 1). The lack of an object for the verb *love* is matched by a similar lack in verse 2 for *call* and in verse 10 for *believed*. This reflects spontaneity, but is somewhat clouded in translation. If this was Hezekiah he is so filled with wonder at the extra fifteen years added to his life in answer to prayer that he resolves to spend it calling *on him* (v. 2).

The emotion continues as he recalls his recent near-death experience in verses 3-4. *Death* had held him in its grip and there seemed no way he could escape it (v. 3). He felt *the anguish of Sheol* even before he was in it, so close was he to death. There is a play on words here: *the anguish of Sheol FINDS me and I FIND trouble and sorrow*. The tenses are present as he re-lives his experience. The same applies to verse 4: *I called on the name of the LORD: O LORD save me*, compare 'Remember, O LORD, how I have walked before you faithfully and with wholehearted devotion and have done what is good in your sight' (2 Kings 20:3), a prayer accompanied by bitter tears, but a prayer heard.

Verses 5-6 state the reason why his prayer availed. It was not the prayer itself, nor the obedient life he had pleaded, but God: his **nature** as *gracious ... righteous (and) full of compassion* (v. 5); and his **office** as the one who *protects the simple-hearted*, that is, those who come to him with a childlike dependence and trust, as children to a father. The Lord has proved all this to him in that *when I was in great need, he saved me*.

Verses 7-11: Deliverance

That re-lived experience is over and he can *be at rest*, not only from the physical pain that obviously racked him, but from the *anguish ... trouble and sorrow* (v. 3) that accompanied it as he stared death in the face. Before the coming of Christ and his resurrection the godly normally lacked the hope with which Christian believers face death. So to say *the LORD has been good to me* is to say, not that he is taking me to be with him in glory, but that he has left me to live here for a little while longer.

This is confirmed in what follows. He faced *death* with *tears* and doubts which is probably what he means by his *feet ... stumbling* (v. 8; cf. 73:2). Now he is restored to *the land of the living*, reflecting his dread of moving into the company of the dead. Now, instead of *stumbling* he can *walk before the LORD* (v. 9). It shows that the best of men under the old covenant lacked any real hope in death and clung to life. Death was entering the unknown world of shadows away from God.

Now he feels somewhat ashamed of his weakness, especially the weakness of his faith, which had only just been maintained. He had just enough faith to voice his affliction in the ear of God (v. 10), and had certainly lost faith in his fellow-men (v. 11). Perhaps they had come to him like Job's friends offering false hopes which made him conclude *all men are liars*. So it was God alone rather than his faith in God or humanity that brought him through. This opens the way for the thanksgiving that follows.

Verses 12-19: Thanksgiving

The question of verse 12 shows that his feeling of gratitude to God for his recovery is at least as intense as his feeling of anguish had been in his sickness (v. 3). This matches the welling up of love in his heart which he had expressed brokenly in verse 1.

He answers his own question in three ways.

(1) He simply accepts the deliverance God has given him (v. 13). It is possible he is making a 'drink offering' to God to symbolise his gratitude, but, as F. D. Kidner points out, the main thought is what God is giving **him** rather than the reverse; and *lift up* is misleading since the expression simply means 'take in my hands', that is, receive what God is giving me. This is confirmed by the fact that the words for both *goodness* and *salvation* are plurals – God had done a multiplicity of things for him. He had spared him the pain and sickness he was enduring, saved him from death and its aftermath, shown him compassion (v. 5), appeared as his protector (v. 6) and given him a new lease of life, a not inconsiderable one too – fifteen years. This is why he is finding it difficult to know how to *repay the Lord* who has so lavishly showered him with blessings. All he can do is accept them, hoping that this is the thanks God likes.

(2) He *calls on the name of the Lord*, the third time this expression has appeared in this psalm. He 'called on his name' when he was at death's door (v. 4) – 'called on his name' to save him. When he knew God had heard him, he resolved to go on 'calling on the name of the Lord' as long as he lived (v. 2). He would make prayer his first line of action in every situation. Now he is beginning this new way of life by 'calling on him' in praise and thanksgiving.

(3) He fulfills *his vows* in public *in the presence of all his people* (v. 14). Whether he had made formal vows when in his extremity we are not told, though this was common practice. But it may just mean the vows he had repeatedly made as a godly man and especially as king. There is a hint of this in verse 9, which indicates a desire to live his life in the Lord's company and in a way pleasing to him. If he had died he

would have lost the ability to do this; now he has recovered he reaffirms his commitment to it.

Unquestionably the most powerful expression of his thanks is the question of verse 12: the feeling that God had done so much for him that there is just no way anything he says or does can be an adequate return. This is what delights God most. Verse 15 seems to bear this out, if we take precious to mean 'costly'. A human life is the most valuable thing in all creation (Mark 8:36-37), so that to yield it up in death is the costliest act we can ever perform. But God regards it the same way! Notwithstanding the billions who have come and gone, each one is *precious* or costly to him too. The note of astonishment with which he says this is perhaps the highest form of thanksgiving.

The remaining verses repeat and underline what he has just been saying. In verse 16 he reaffirms his commitment to the Lord. He had been held in chains by death, and now that God had released him all he desired was to be bound to him with the *chains* of a *servant*. The three-fold use of that word shows how utterly devoted he wanted to be to the Lord's service.

Verses 17-19 repeat the sentiment of verses 13-14 in different words. This time he is making some kind of *offering, a sacrifice*, either a drink *offering* or a burnt *offering* (v. 17). In verses 18-19 he repeats what he said in verse 14, for this is no mere formality or passing whim; he is utterly sincere and determined. Let all *his people* who gather *in the courts of (his) house*, let all *Jerusalem* hear his words that they may bear witness to them and see how well he keeps them in the remaining days of his life. He is not ashamed!

Questions:
(1) Compare the attitude to life and death expressed in this psalm with Paul's in Philippians 1:20-26.

(2) What fresh meaning does Paul give to verse 10 in his quotation of it in 2 Corinthians 4:13?

(3) If an Old Testament person cannot adequately express his thanks for what God has done for him, how can we, in view of the gift of Christ? (See John 3:16; 2 Cor. 9:15.)

Psalm 117

Short but Broad

This shortest of all the psalms is a fitting doxology to the previous pair, beginning and ending as it does with 'Halleluyah' or *Praise the* LORD. The call here, however, is not to Israel but *all you nations ... all you people* (v. 1). The blessedness he promises to those who know him and his goodness are offered to all who will acknowledge him as *the* LORD, the one God sovereign over all. This involves turning from their idols and their sins, and is thus a call to faith with the promise of salvation.

It is doubtful if this message was actually broadcast to *all the nations*, unless it refers to those from foreign parts attending a feast. It is therefore best to see it as the psalmist's aspiration, or even as a prophecy of the day when the gospel would go forth in all the world. This is how Paul used it in Romans 15:11 when he spoke of Christ's Gentile mission.

In Romans 15:8 he said this mission was to 'confirm the promises made to the patriarchs', which is what lies behind verse 2. At the time of Abraham God promised to bless all nations through Abraham's descendants (Gen. 12:1-3). The psalmist is praising God for his *faithfulness* to that promise, which he must keep because he who made it *endures for ever*. Moreover, ultimately it stems from his *love towards us*, which is *great*, literally 'prevails'. It has continued notwithstanding the wickedness of man and the treachery of his people. The time would come when it would 'prevail' over sin, death and Satan, when Christ came, died, and rose again.

Question:
Do you share the psalmist's enthusiasm for the nations to be brought into Christ's kingdom? Is it evident in your support for evangelism and missions? (Rom. 1:14.)

Psalm 118

Victory Celebrations

This psalm is celebrating a victory (v. 15) snatched from the jaws of defeat (vv. 10-12) A great service is taking place in the temple towards which the people are processing (vv. 19-20). But it is looking on to a still greater victory and cause for thanksgiving: the words of verses 22-23 are quoted by Christ in Matthew 21:42 and by Peter in Acts 4:11.

Verses 1-4: United thanksgiving
Verse 1 was to become a standard temple doxology: see 105:1; 106:1; 107:1; 136:1. It acknowledges that the nation's victories and prosperity stem, not from its own skill, power or virtue, but from God's faithful covenant love. This is the most extended form of the doxology (but cf. 115:9-11) as it embraces the whole nation: Israel (v. 2); the priesthood (*house of Aaron*) (v. 3); and all however lowly who revere their God (*those who fear the* LORD) (v. 4). The praise of God and his covenant unites the people of God.

Verses 5-9: Heartfelt testimony
For what was this exuberant thanksgiving being offered? For a great rescue act: the nation, personified here by the priest, had been trapped and *cried in anguish* to the Lord, who set them free (v. 5). There is a beautiful balance in the Hebrew here:

'from a narrow place I called to the Lord; the Lord answered me with a broad place'. So they had learned once again that *the* LORD *is with me*. How often had God taught them that! There are lessons to learn from this (vv. 8-9), about trusting the Lord rather than man, for however high and mighty man becomes, he cannot guarantee safety. God had proved that he was not on the side of the big battalions but of those who trust him.

Verses 10-14: Dire straits
How often verses 8-9 had been proved right! Their whole history was one of divine deliverances. The wording of the second line of verses 10-12 reminds us of the encounter with Goliath: 'I come to you *in the name of the* LORD *Almighty*' (1 Sam. 17:45). Then it takes us on through the long struggle that ensued. All these they had faced *in the name of the* LORD and in the faith that they were God's servants. This had always secured victory, however far they were *pushed back* (v. 13).

This goes right back to Moses, for the words of verse 14 were those with which Moses and the people celebrated their release from Egypt and the crossing of the Red Sea (Exod. 15:2). The Exodus is the model of all rescues, right up to our redemption in Christ, which means that every Christian can say these words.

Verses 15-18: Uninhibited joy
The greater the danger the greater the salvation, and the greater the salvation the greater the rejoicing – not just in songs but *shouts of joy and victory* (v. 15). They were still camped in their *tents* when news of victory came.This recalls the time when they had lived in *tents* to cross the Sinai desert. This explains the further allusion here to the Exodus: the expression *the* LORD's *right hand* was first used in Exodus 15:6, 12. The repetition of these words shows the exuberance of this rejoicing. There is nothing like joy for strengthening assurance, so in verse 17 we hear the writer expressing great confidence about the future. But he is by no means fantasizing. He is well aware of his and his nation's weaknesses and even sins (it is for these God *chastens*). If all that is over now it is not down to them but to *the* LORD. They were utterly in his hands – he could have, but he did not, *given (them) over to death* (v. 18).

Verses 19-24: Triumphal entry

So far the songs and shouts had gone up from outside the city. Now the procession has arrived at the gates and the leader calls for admission (v. 19). This is all symbolic. The army had already returned, but they were re-enacting its victory as an act of thanksgiving to God, to whom all this is attributed. So he calls them *gates of righteousness*, the way into the place where the *righteous* God dwells with his *righteous* people (v. 15). It is *the gate of the Lord*, through which only those in covenant with him *may enter* (v. 20). Normal life went on in the city like any other city, but for today they are interested in one thing: *giving thanks to the Lord* (vv. 19b-21) for *becoming my salvation*.

The greatness of this salvation is beautifully illustrated by a metaphor from building in verse 22. As the leader surveys the gates he sees how they are surmounted by a *capstone*. He imagines how this had been lying around in a quarry and passed over by *the builders*. Yet under God's direction it is now head of all the others. This had been the experience of the nation throughout its history. So this is a special day, *the day the Lord has made*, a day for rejoicing in him.

Verses 25-26: Fervent prayer

Past deliverances do not dispense with the need for prayer for the present and future. What has happened once can happen again. There are still enemies around, and his own people are not perfect. So the cry goes up: *O Lord, save us!* – go on saving us! The word is that from which HOSANNA comes, used by the people of Jerusalem on a later triumphal entry – that of the Messiah himself (Matt. 21:9), likewise rejected by the builders, but made by God the 'chief cornerstone' (Matt. 21:42).

Perhaps verse 26 is the response of the High Priest receiving the procession, since they came out of *the house of the Lord*. His words echo those of verses 10-12. He had conquered *in the name of the Lord*, returned in the name of the Lord and now was welcomed *(blessed) in the name of the Lord*.

Verses 27-29: Willing offerings

All is now ready for the climax: the sacrifices of thanksgiving on *the altar*. So the priests continue their prayer: *the Lord is God*, which is the basis of all.

This same Lord and God has revealed himself to his favoured people: *he has made his light shine* (recalling the original priestly blessing of Num. 6:25). It seems best to go with the NIV margin 'Bind the festal sacrifice with cords and take it to the horns of the altar.'

That done, all that remains is to *give thanks* yet again, not so much for this safe and triumphant return but for what it proves: *you are my God* (v. 28). So we end where we began: with the faithful enduring love of God.

Questions:
(1) How does this psalm help us foster the spirit of thanksgiving in ourselves and our churches? (See 1 Thess. 5:16-18.)

(2) Would more emphasis on the praise of God produce greater unity in our churches? (See vv. 1-4 and Rom. 15:5-6.)

(3) Consider the use of verses 6-7 in Hebrews 13:5-6. How does the apostle apply the words to encourage Christians in a very different situation?

(4) 'The joy of the Lord is your strength' (Neh. 8:10). Does your experience confirm this (vv. 15-17)? Conversely, do you find lowness of spirit goes with loss of assurance? (See 1 Pet. 1:3-9.)

Psalm 119

The Word of God

This psalm is notorious for being by far the longest in the whole collection, but since it is divided into 22 stanzas, it does not make tedious reading. In fact it can be approached as 22 separate psalms, since each stanza is 8 verses long, similar to many of the shorter psalms.

(1) Why is it such a long psalm?
The reason for its length lies in the manner of its composition. The author chose to make it an 'acrostic', that is, to base it on the 22-letter Hebrew alphabet. There was nothing new in this; it is used in Psalms 9–10, 25, 34, 37, 111, 112 and 145. But whereas the other acrostic psalms have only one verse per letter (or two in the case of 37), 119 has no less than eight. This is why you will find that your Bibles head each stanza with a Hebrew letter. That is the letter with which each verse of that stanza begins.

(2) Why did the author employ this method?
Possibly because he chose to use eight different terms to refer to what we would call 'the Word of God' or 'Scripture'. It is true he did not use each of the eight in every stanza – the composition is not as artificial as that. But he used one of them in every verse apart from verses 84, 121 and 122. F. D. Kidner describes it thus: 'like a ring of eight bells, eight synonyms for Scripture dominate the psalm, and the twenty-two stanzas

will ring the changes on them ... freely, not with a bell-ringer's elaborate formulae.' He also calls it 'an alphabet of prayers and reflections on the word of God.'

This does not mean he was trying to be clever and show off his skill with words. There is a message in his method. He is emphasising one of the two chief foundations of old covenant religion: the word of God revealed in Scripture. The other was the Temple worship, with its daily, weekly, monthly and yearly ceremonies.

(3) When was the psalm written and by whom?

No one knows. The psalm is anonymous and there are no clues to link it to an historical event, as we find in other anonymous psalms. **Some** assign it to the period after the exile in Babylon before temple worship was restored. Great stress was placed on the law of God at that time, as we see from Ezra's ministry. The Book of Deuteronomy seems to have come into prominence at this time and the psalm has some allusions to it.

The first century historian **Josephus** ascribes it to David and his assistants late in his reign, following the rebellion of Sheba. David is looking back over his experiences and bringing out the centrality of God's word in his life. This explains the themes of knowledge, understanding, wisdom, comfort, prayer and commitment that recur throughout it.All these were ways by which he knew and communed with God and God with him. It is the full flowering of that delight in the law of the Lord described in 1 and witnessed to in 19.

(4) What is the chief THEME of the psalm?

This is the Law of God, the TORAH, a term which occurs some twenty-six times, more than any other. This does not mean he is exalting over all else the code of laws dictated to Moses on Sinai and repeated on the bank of the Jordan. 'Law' (TORAH) and 'laws' are different. The 'laws' are part of the Law. TORAH means 'teaching' and refers to the whole written revelation. It includes narrative (history), poetry and prophecy. The stories, poems and sermons are as much God's word and teaching as are the laws.

In the Hebrew Bible 'the Law' covered not only the books of Moses but most of the histories too. In fact, sometimes the whole Old Testament was called 'the Law'. For example, in Matthew 5:17 the full title 'the Law, the prophets and the writings' is shortened to 'the Law and the prophets', and in verse 18 is shortened even more to 'the Law'. Jesus 'accomplished' not just the legal requirements but the prophecies too and even the history!

This explains why the Law meant so much to the writer of 119. How much of Scripture existed in his time depends on when it was written. If it comes from David's reign it would cover the books of Moses – Joshua, Judges and possibly some of the material contained in 1 and 2 Samuel, plus Job and many psalms. These books contain all types of material found in the Old Testament and would enable the author to glory in God's great works of creation, providence, salvation and judgment, as well as his commands, warnings, promises and blessings. But the later it is dated the more of his word was available.

(5) What are the VARIATIONS on the theme?
The other seven terms are virtually synonymous, but can be seen to bring out different shades of meaning. All come into the first eleven verses.

'EDOT: 'statutes' (v. 2, KJV 'testimonies'). These are practical principles governing behaviour. 'Testimony' is a good translation showing how God's word 'testifies' to his righteousness and against our sinfulness.

PIQQUDIM: 'precepts' (v. 4) – the 'fine print' of the Law, showing how closely it examines and defines our conduct.

HUQQIM: 'decrees' (vv. 5, 8, KJV 'statutes'). The word means 'engraved' and brings out the binding force and permanence of God's Law.

MIZWOT: 'commands' (vv. 6, 10, KJV 'commandments'). This draws attention to the authority with which the Law came, stressing God's right to determine the basis of our relationship with him.

MISPATIM: 'righteous laws' (v. 7, KJV 'righteous judgments'). These are the rules which govern the relationship between man and man, of which there are plenty in the Law code and many examples in the stories. They were particularly a guide to judges in deciding guilt in cases brought before them.

DABAR: 'word' (v. 9). This is the most general term of all, akin to TORAH itself, covering the whole of God's revealed truth.

IMRA: 'word' (v. 11). It is a pity the translators do not distinguish it from DABAR by the use of a term such as 'promise', to which it particularly refers.

All this brings out the richness not only of the TORAH but the whole of Scripture as we know it, including the New Testament, which has all these aspects of the word of God. It explains why the psalmist was able to expatiate on this one theme in twenty-two eight-line poems. It challenges us to value the revealed word more. As Leupold says, 'we can never think or say too much about the word of God.'

(6) What is the VALUE of the psalm to Christians?

1. *It teaches us that the primary purpose of the Bible is to know God.* For all his preoccupation with the 'word' and 'the Law', the Scriptures are to the writer only a means to an end – the knowledge of God himself. He only valued the Scriptures because they came from God. Do not overlook the word that comes into almost every verse: 'your' (or 'his'). Evangelicals today are in danger of over-emphasising the Bible **as a book**. This is done in good faith because of the fierce attacks launched against it in the past two centuries. But we must not over-react into bibliolatry. Be careful to read the psalm as an encouragement to seek, find and know God for himself through his word. This is the nature of the knowledge, wisdom and understanding which the writer finds in God's word (e.g. vv. 98-100, 104, 169). It is not mere knowledge of the facts and ideas, but of God himself that matters: it is through knowing **him** that we understand the world and ourselves, and perceive clearly the way we should live: 'in your light we see light' (36:9).

2. *It shows us the richness of God's word.* You cannot describe it in one term, you need as many as you can lay your hands on. You cannot say all there is to say about it in a few lines.

Even the alphabet is not long enough, you must go through it eight times! All this without repeating a sentence! And it is woven together in the most elaborate form known to any poetry ever composed. C. S. Lewis says it is 'like embroidery, stitch by stitch through long quiet hours for love of the subject and delight in leisurely disciplined craftsmanship'. This does not glorify elaboration for its own sake, but reflects the intricate pattern of the Scriptures themselves. These thoughts should take us back to the Bible to observe the way this book stretching over many centuries is woven by its divine author into an observable pattern. But, like a huge mosaic, it requires long contemplation to discern it. We should not stop there, however. As just said, it is a means to knowing God. So supremely it reveals the richness of God's character and actions.

3. *It displays the blessings to be derived from God's word.* The first word of the first psalm is 'blessed', meaning truly happy in the sense of having a peaceful mind and a joyful spirit, the kind of happiness Jesus described in the Beatitudes. There is a sense in which the whole psalm collection is about how to obtain and enjoy the blessing of God. The particular contribution of this psalm (which also begins with the word 'blessed') is that we enjoy his blessings through knowledge of his word. Through his word we may experience:

- **liberty**: from sin (v. 133) and from narrow-mindedness (vv. 45, 96). Instead of being preoccupied with self-gratification we are released to know and understand what lies outside our little world and enter into the mind of God himself;
- **light**: which is partly theoretical knowledge coming from study and learning (vv. 34, 73, 125, 130, 144, 169) and partly the application of this knowledge to practical living, light to our 'feet' and our 'path' (v. 105);
- **life**: a frequently-occurring term , for it is the Word which through faith gives spiritual life (v. 144), which preserves it ('preserve my life' is one of the most frequent prayers: vv. 25, 50, 107) and which revives it when it flags;

- **stability**: for he writes as one who has known adversity and is surrounded by adversaries, but does not have the resources to remain stable under these batterings. Verses 23, 49-50 are examples of how he would use the word of God as a firm foundation at such times, with the result that he could speak of enjoying great peace (v. 165). Along with this goes

- **comfort in affliction**: for he is one who knew 'affliction' in general (vv. 67, 71) and persecution in particular (vv. 23, 51, 61, 69, 78, 85-6, 95, 110, 121, 150). As a normal human being this depressed him, not only because it caused pain and inconvenience, but because it reflected godlessness in society (vv. 53, 126, 158). He was being afflicted unjustly because he was a righteous man who testified against the sins of his contemporaries. That they should hate godliness and love evil so much was discouraging. But the word of God brought him comfort (vv. 50, 54-5, 165). Because of this he lived to be thankful for his affliction (vv. 67, 71). This is the great advantage believers have over others: they resort to the medical or psychological doctor, but for us the word of God is our medicine and comfort. All these themes are developed in the New Testament through concepts such as 'eternal life' and 'perseverance'.

4. *It evokes feelings of love for God.* Just as Bible readers are in danger of bibliolatry, so are we in peril of intellectualism, of deriving from God's word only doctrines and rules of conduct. While this is right, it is not all there is. If we also use the Bible as a means of communion with God, it will move us to love him more. This is what we find here: frequent outbursts of love (vv. 97, 113, 127, 159). This love is expressed in two main ways:

  - **longing** (vv. 20, 40, 81-82, 123, 174). This must mean more than 'I've lost my Bible' or 'I've forgotten to put it in my luggage'. It means he was looking for more than just the print on the page; he was looking to find God there, to see him in all his perfection, and he was not content until he had felt something;

• This came when his longing was satisfied and he had found what, or rather whom, he was seeking (vv. 47-48, 103). The two are put together in verse 174. Satisfaction with our earthly and fleshly longings can be disappointing. In the things of God the opposite is the case: it exceeds our expectations (1 Cor. 2:9). We feel like the Queen of Sheba when she **saw** the glory of Solomon of which she had only heard (1 Kings 10:6-7). God in Christ is even better. The 'delight' is so great it only increases the longing for more. 'We taste thee, O thou living bread, and long to feast upon thee still' (Bernard of Clairvaux). The godly life is a cycle of longing and delighting. If the Old Testament poet found this in 'the Law', how much more will we find it in the Gospel!

We shall find more blessings as we work our way through the psalm. This is best done by private meditation, but it may be helpful to suggest the main themes of each stanza.

(7) The Course of the Psalm

The psalm follows no consistent train of thought, though there are often connections between the theme of one stanza and the next. The twenty-two stanzas are best used, one at a time, perhaps one a day, for private meditation and personal devotion. They can be used in conjunction with your regular reading and study of the books of the Bible, either before other reading or after, or both. The following outline is not exhaustive and simply highlights particular themes that emerge.

Verses 1-8: Aleph

The stress here falls on **keeping God's word**. The word *keep* comes in verse 2 and is explained by other terms such as *walk* (vv. 1, 3), *obey* (vv. 4, 5, 8) and *learn* (v. 7). The true servant of the Lord is not content with a cursory reading of the word, he wants it to govern his whole life. He wants his *ways* (v. 5) to be God's *ways* (v. 3). Then he will enjoy God's *blessing* (vv. 1-2) and will be kept from sin (v. 3) and its consequent *shame* (v. 6). This will fill his *heart* with *praise* (v. 7) and strengthen his commitment to obedience (v. 8).

Verses 9-16: Beth
If the question arises *how can (one) keep* God's law, especially
when he is *young* and lusty (v. 9), the answer is that the same
word which commands also enables. So the emphasis here
is on **the power of the word**. It has power to purify (v. 9), to
restrain from wandering (v. 10) and to keep from sin (v. 11).
This evokes a further outburst of *praise* (v. 12) and *rejoicing*
(v. 14), so that God's word comes to be supreme in speech
(v. 13), thought (v. 15) and feeling (v. 16).

Verses 17-24: Gimel
The concern here is for God to **reveal** more of **the meaning of
his word** (v. 18). The more we understand it, the more we will
want to *obey* it (v. 17). Realising that we are in an alien society
which cannot answer our longings (v. 19) makes us desire
this knowledge all the more (v. 20). This sense of alienation
is brought out more in verses 21-23, and the thought of those
who are *astray* from God makes his word even more a delight.
God's *statutes* give him the *counsel* he can find nowhere else
(v. 24).

Verses 25-32: Daleth
This tells us how he feels about the **alien society** he lives in.
It gives him grief and sorrow (vv. 25, 28), causes him heart-
searching (v. 26) and moves him to prayer (vv. 25b, 26b,
27a, 28b, 29, 31b). Whether he realises it or not, his prayer is
already being answered, for his resolution to be faithful is
strengthened (vv. 30-32).

Verses 33-40: He
Since every verse of this stanza is a prayer, we are shown
here **the interdependence of the word and prayer**. Prayer
is essential to *understanding* the word (v. 34), since it comes
from God and only he knows what he means by it. But the
writer also needs God to enable him to govern his behaviour
by the word (vv. 33, 35). Since what we do results from what
we feel and want, he prays that his *heart* and *eyes* be turned
from what is *selfish* and *worthless* and fixed on God's *statutes*
(vv. 36-37). He is not going beyond the bounds of God's will

in this, for it is his *promise* (v. 38). Nor is this presumption, for his *laws are good* (v. 39), given to keep us in God's *fear* and away from *disgrace*. His total dependence on God and his word is expressed in his *longing* for them (v. 40).

Verses 41-48: Waw
The note struck here is of **spoken witness to the word**. He needs the word's inward assurance of God's *love* and *salvation* (v. 41) in order to *answer* those who *taunt* him (v. 42, cf. 1 Pet. 3:15). He is utterly without self-confidence about this, fearing his answer will be *snatched* from his *mouth* and he will clam up (v. 43). He also realises that practice must go hand in hand with profession (vv. 44-45). Then he will without *shame* be able to *speak of (his) statutes* even *before kings* (v. 46). For he will be speaking from the heart out of a *delight in* and *love for (his) commands* (v. 47). All this fills him with praise: *I lift up my hands* (v. 48).

Verses 49-56: Zayin
One thing he can certainly 'bear witness to' is the *hope (and) comfort* he has derived from God's word (vv. 49-50). For, as already mentioned in verses 25-32, he lives in a society estranged from God in which the *arrogant mock* the godly. Whether he is referring to the idolatry which set in after David's time or to the sheer indifference and worldliness that characterised David's own time, we do not know. But it stirred his righteous soul to anger (v. 53), while at the same time intensifying his resolution to obey the word (v. 51) and increasing the strength and comfort he found in it (v. 52). So he not only thinks and speaks but also sings of God's *decrees*, wherever he is (v. 54), even in sleepless nights (v. 55). He is now firmly established in this practice (v. 56).

Verses 57-64: Heth
Coming on top of the thoughts, experiences, prayers and resolutions of the previous stanzas, this one expresses an **intense devotion to the word of God**. But he is no bibliolator – it is God himself he finds in his word: *you are my portion, O Lord* (v. 57), and therefore it is God whom he loves and

obeys. He keeps himself in God's presence (v. 58), to enjoy his promised grace and enable him to live in conscious obedience (v. 59). Nor is this a vague resolution to get his *ways* right at some unspecified time – he will do so now (v. 60), whatever the consequences (v. 61). This makes him so full of *thanks* he gets up in the middle of the night to express them (v. 62). He does not want to keep all this to himself, but to share it with *all who fear you* (v. 63); indeed if possible with all *the earth* (v. 64).

Verses 65-72: Teth
In contrast to some of the preceding thoughts, this stanza dwells on **the chastening effect of God's word**. Twice he refers to being *afflicted* (vv. 67,71). This seems to have come, not from illness, but from his treatment at the hands of the ungodly, to whom he has already referred. Here he calls them *arrogant (and) callous* (vv. 69-70) because of their attempts at character assassination. But he is resilient, for he knows God is good and what he does *is good* (v. 68). So his prayer corresponds to this: that God will *do good* to him (v. 65) and teach him *good judgment* (v. 66) – the ability to discern good and evil. With this approach he does not care about the wealth of the wicked, for he has a richer treasure (v. 72).

Verses 73 – 80: Yodh
Now that he is getting on top of his sufferings, he is able to turn them to positive advantage, so that through them he can **witness to the goodness of God's word**. As God's personal creation, this is his prime responsibility (v. 73). First, he can be an encouragement to other God-fearers because his afflictions have not depressed him but have increased his *hope in (God's) word* as coming from the faithful and righteous one (v. 74-75). This does not make him self-sufficient, for he is still relying on the *promise* of God's *unfailing love (and) compassion* (vv. 76-77). These thoughts lead him to a full prayer ministry: for his and God's adversaries (v. 78), for his fellow-believers (v. 79) and for himself, that he will not fail in his witness and so be *put to shame* (v. 80).

Verses 81-88: Kaph

The foregoing does not mean that he says good-bye to adversity. It means that as his adversities continued and even increased, so did he continue and increase in faith, which makes this stanza about **perseverance in the word**. Thus we find him here in deep affliction: his *soul faints* (v. 81), his *eyes fail* (v. 82), he is like a withered discarded *wineskin* (v. 83), suffering persecution from the *arrogant* (vv. 84-86), so that he is almost *wiped ... from the earth* (v. 87). But each time he mentions his afflictions he re-affirms his *hope in your word* (vv. 81b, 83b, 87b), ending with a prayer-cum-recommitment (v. 88). The latter verse perfectly states the so-called doctrine of 'the perseverance of the saints': God preserves their faith and they persevere in obedience.

Verses 89-96: Lamedh

That he attributes his perseverance to the Lord and not himself comes out very strongly here in this lovely panegyric on **God's faithfulness**. The God who *established the earth* so that, unlike human creations, it does not disintegrate (v. 90) is the God who has spoken in his word (v. 89) which is still with us *to this day.* (v. 91). The fact that he was still alive to say so proves it (vv. 92-93). Nor is he out of the wood yet (v. 95) and he must still depend on the word and prayer (v. 94). Through all this he has learned a valuable lesson: not to expect *perfection* in this world and life, which is not a pessimistic viewpoint, for he is certain of it in eternity (v. 96).

Verses 97-104: Mem

As if he could not speak more highly of it, here we have an expression of **glorying in the word**. He *loves* it so much he cannot even say *how* (v. 97)! He wants to think of nothing else (v. 98), in fact it has almost become his food (v. 103). Two aspects stand out: first of all, the wisdom, *insight (and) understanding* it has given him. The word teaches him more than the *teachers and elders* who rely on human knowledge (vv. 98-100). Second, it governs his behaviour, enabling him to avoid *every evil (and) wrong path* (vv. 101, 104). Thus the word is not just an intellectual feast (v. 103) but also a sure guide to living (v. 102).

Verses 105-112: Nun
In the midst of all the darkness of personal affliction and
public hostility, he needs *light* on his *path* (v. 105). In answer to
this he finds the word that gives comfort is also a **guide**. The
guidance he seeks and finds is not merely about how to come
to a decision on a problem, but much greater: how to be true
to his *oath* of obedience (v. 106). His sufferings have weakened
him (v. 107) and his life is still in danger (v. 109) because of the
plots of his enemies (v. 110). But he is still prayerful (v. 107b),
thankful (v. 108), resolute (v. 109b) and joyful (v. 111). So the
lamp is still shining on his *path*, lighting up even *the end* of the
road (v. 112)!

Verses 113-120: Samekh
Though he has light on his path he must still come to terms
with the darkness.This stanza therefore focusses on **the word
and the wicked**. They are *double-minded men* (v. 113) who,
as members of the holy nation, outwardly conform to its
traditions, but whose hearts are far from his *law*, so that they
cannot claim, as he can, to *love* it. They are *evil-doers* (v. 115),
who *stray from (God's) decrees*, but in their *deceitfulness* try *in vain*
to hide their disobedience (v. 118). To God they are *like dross*,
fit only to be discarded (v. 119). This estimate of his enemies
has the effect of making him more dependent on God (vv. 114,
116-117)). At all costs he must avoid becoming entangled with
them (v. 115), not because he feels superior but because they
would only hinder him from keeping *the commands of God*,
and thus being rejected (and) discarded like them. What God
thinks of the wicked only serves to make him more in awe of
the God who has given the laws (v. 120).

Verses 121-128: Ayin
These insights into God's way with the wicked, while they
make him tremble lest he also should go astray (v. 120), at
the same time increase his **assurance through the word**. On
this basis he is able to claim God's protection (vv. 121-122).
His unwavering desire for *salvation* from the dominion of
evil makes him bold to appeal to God's *love* (vv. 123-124). His
faithful service of God's *statutes* encourages him to ask for God

to act and vindicate his *broken law*, presumably by punishing the wicked (v. 126). Of one thing he is sure above all others – that he *hates* all this evil against which he is praying. Evildoers may amass their *gold*, but he has something better and purer: the *commands (and) precepts* of God (vv. 127-128).

Verses 129-136: Pe
The thought of the superiority of God's word to the ways of the wicked leads to this expression of the **satisfaction** to be found in it. He *obeys* it not because he has to but because it is *wonderful* (v. 129). In a confused world it is the source of *understanding* (v. 130) and he cannot get enough of it (v. 131). Not that this gives him any rights before God; it is all of *mercy* (v. 132). He is still vulnerable to the dominion both of his own sin (v. 133) and *the oppression of men*, from which only God can *redeem* him (v. 134). Moreover, the mere words of the law are not enough – he needs a sense of God's own glorious presence (v. 135). He is so close to God he shares his grief over the way his law is flouted (v. 136).

Verses 137-144: Tsadhe
His *zeal* for God's law reaches something of a climax here, with the thought that it is **thoroughly proven and guaranteed to last**. His *words* are as *righteous* as his person and as *trustworthy* as himself (vv. 137-138). While he himself is still in the fire because his *enemies* do not live as he does, the *promises* themselves have endured the fiery trial and proved pure (vv. 139-140). So in a way what is happening to him making him *lowly and despised* (v. 141), enduring *trouble and distress* (v. 143), does not matter since God's *law is true* (v. 142) and *right* (v. 144) and his *commands* are his *delight*. Best of all, they will go on being all this *for ever* (v. 144), because they are *everlasting* (v. 142).

Verses 145-152: Qoph
A previous stanza (33-40) brought out, as this one does, **the connection between the word and prayer**. There his prayer was to understand the word, whereas here it is to know **the power of the word** to enable him to remain faithful against

the background of his own weakness and the strength of the opposition. Verses 145-148 show him not just saying prayers but calling out *with all (his) heart*, getting up early and even praying all night. His plea is based on God's *love* (v. 149), something those who are *far from (his) law* can know nothing of, hence their *wicked* conspiracies (v. 150). But since he keeps near God's law, *the* LORD himself is *near* him. Whatever happens this will always be so, because, as affirmed in the previous stanza, his word is *established ... to last for ever* (v. 152).

Verses 153-160: Resh

He knows his prayer will avail because **the word guarantees deliverance**. His concern is lest *the wicked* get their way with him because of the intensity of the suffering they are laying on him (v. 153). But his constant remembrance of God's *law* and trust in his *promise* (v. 154) give him hope, because they are in a God of *great compassion* (v. 156). On the other hand, *the wicked* have no hope of *salvation* because they ignore his word (v. 155). His loyalty remains constant in spite of persecution (v. 157) and he has no love for *the faithless* (v. 158), since God's *precepts* are his *love* (v. 159). He has a sure ground on which to pray: that God's love for him is assured by his words which are *true ... righteous (and) eternal* (v. 160).

Verses 161-168: Sin and Shin

The central thought of this stanza and one of the highlights of the whole psalm is verse 165, which states the theme of **peace through the word**. His sufferings have reached a climax in that it is no longer just the people but *rulers persecute me* (v. 161). Verse 163 may suggest that *the rulers* had gone over to idolatry (*falsehood*) and were trying to force others to follow suit. But he remains firm in his adherence to God's word (vv. 161, 163). Nor does he do so in a legalistic way but retains his spirit of wonder as of one who has just unearthed huge treasure (v. 162). So he just cannot stop praising God for his word: *seven times* virtually means 'ceaselessly'. So he is not worried about what others do, even to him, for he has *great peace* and *nothing* is going to trip him up (v. 165). He can patiently *wait* for God's time to save him (v. 166a) and meanwhile continue his life of obedience (vv. 166b-168).

Verses 169-176: Taw

The closing stanza is virtually a summary of the main themes of the psalm and thus brings out **the all-sufficiency of the word of God**. In it he finds *understanding* (v. 169), deliverance (v. 170), a spirit of *praise* (vv. 171-172, 175) and the *help* of God to obey him (v. 173). But assurance is not the same as triumphalism and he ends (v. 176) with a confession of human sinfulness, for the *lost sheep* analogy is identical with the Bible's teaching on sin, found in Isaiah 53:6 and the mission of Christ in this world: to seek and save the lost (Luke 15:1-7; 19:10). This is the psalmist's chief interest: that God will *seek* him and vindicate his trust in his *commands*.

Psalm 120

The Consolations of Prayer

This is the first of fifteen Psalms under the Title *A Song of Ascents* or 'Marching Song', for travellers to sing as they made their way to Jerusalem to celebrate one of the annual feasts. This does not mean they were all composed for that purpose. Some may well have originated on other occasions, then later been collected together and issued for use in connection with Israel's feasts. This one may have come from David, for it fits well with his experience when he was forced into exile with the Philistines (see Appendix, p. 245). However, it is appropriate for those who, as a result of wars, were living in foreign lands where they were subject to persecution, on which they reflected as they travelled the road to Jerusalem.

Verses 1-2: Praying to God is worthwhile
Verse 1 suggests that the writer, and those on whose behalf he speaks, has learned to bring his *distress* to *the* LORD, and has found *he answers* his cry. His principal problem is false accusation (v. 2): he and his friends live among enemies who want to bring them down, and if true crimes cannot be found to do this, false ones will have to serve. This is what he is bringing to God in prayer.

Verses 3-4: Praying to God is awesome

The God he prays to is a God of truth who hates lies, especially if they are told against his own people. So, as is seen in David's psalms, his spirit of prayer becomes a spirit of prophecy, and he pronounces a severe punishment on their lives. The form in which he utters this prediction (v. 3) is that of the familiar oath or curse: 'May God do so to me and more also' (Ruth 1:17; 1 Sam. 3:17; 1 Kings 2:23, which the NIV translates *May God deal with me ever so severely*). This is similar to David's prophetic curses in Psalms 12, 35, 52, 59, 64, 140 and 141. He is warning them as well as reassuring himself that it will be worse for them than for him. In verse 4 he spells out the details: those who have sharpened their tongues like *sharp arrows* will be pierced with them; and those whose words have been as destructive as fire will themselves be consumed by flames. The *broom tree* had a particularly hard wood which burned fiercely and long. The psalmist may be speaking of a physical punishment or the counter-charges God will bring against them when he calls them to account.

Verses 5-7: Praying like this is justifiable

Meshech (and) Kedar were barbarous places: the first in the Black Sea area, very remote from Israel, of which they had only heard tell; the second was nearer home – the south Syrian desert, but inhabited by Bedouin with no settled home. Whether this was literally where the writer was living or not is unclear. The point is that these people were behaving like barbarians towards him. He is therefore justified in calling down God's curse on them . This is especially true since he never sought a quarrel with them. He has even attempted to make peace, only to have it all thrown back in his face.

Questions:

(1) What do verses 1-2 teach you about always bringing your trials to God in prayer? (See James 1:2-5.)

(2) What do verses 5-6 teach about the difference between the Israelite and the Christian in relation to the ungodly? (See John 17:15-19; 1 Cor. 5:9-10.)

(3) In verse 7 how does the psalmist anticipate Christ and the Christian? (See Matt. 5:9, 43-48; Eph. 2:14-18.)

Psalm 121

A Safe Journey

Some of these *songs of ascents* are appropriate for the start of a journey, some for its course and others for the arrival. This one is for use on the journey itself and therefore has a different preposition in the title: *A song FOR the ascents* (emphasis mine). It appears to be in the form of a dialogue: the person speaking in verses 1-2 is addressing someone else in verses 3-8. Some think this refers to the encouragement of his fellow-travellers; others that it is someone speaking to himself, as in Psalms 42 and 43.

Verses 1-2: The pilgrim calls for help
In verse 1 *the hills* of Jerusalem have come into view. He still has far to go and is faced with a climb at the end. Even before that point there are many hazards: rough, dangerous terrain, beasts, bandits and exposure to the elements by day and night. Who will *help* him reach his destination safely?

He reminds himself that *the hills* of Zion are the abode of his God. This God is no mere localised deity, like the pagan idols, but *the Maker of heaven and earth* (v. 2). If God has done such a great thing as that, he can do the lesser one of seeing his servant through his journey. Whatever he encounters on the way has been created by the God he is going to meet and is therefore under his control.

Verses 3-8: The pilgrim is promised help
The general promise of verse 2 is now spelt out in detail,
either by the pilgrim himself or another encouraging him.
Is he worried lest his *foot* slips on the rough ground, that he
might break an ankle or fall over a precipice? 'The Maker of
heaven and earth' will not let it happen (v. 3a). Is he anxious
that while he sleeps at night or stops for a doze during the day
he will be attacked by bandits or beasts? His God is Spirit and
needs no sleep. Has he not undertaken to *watch over Israel* by
day and night? Is he not his people's protector? If he protects
all *Israel*, he will *watch over* an individual Israelite (vv. 3b-4).

The same applies to other possible dangers such as the
rays of *the sun* with their fierce heat (v. 5). *The* LORD will
afford him *shade*, as if he stood by him holding a parasol over
him! Is there danger from *the moon by night*? Does this refer
to lunacy? More likely it simply means the extreme change
of temperature which characterises those parts and would
particularly affect those who had to spend the night in the
open. To those who trust *the* LORD no harm will come from the
cold of a clear moonlit night.

This same God has promised to *keep* his own from *all harm*,
to *watch over your life* as a whole (v. 7). That includes this
particular bit of it. He will not only see his pilgrims safely
through their journey *coming* to Jerusalem, but *going* back
from it as well. This is indeed a model for all the comings and
goings of life, *now and ... evermore*, this one and all the others,
indeed the final *going* from the earth.

Question:
How does this psalm apply to the Christian's 'walk' or
'pilgrimage' regarding such things as the hazards of the
journey, the strengthening presence of the Lord and our final
destination? (See 2 Cor. 5:7 [AV]; Heb. 12:1-3.)

Psalm 122

In Jerusalem

*D*avid, to whom the psalm is attributed, is seeking to express the feelings of those gathering with him for the feast. God has now brought his worshippers safely to his shrine, which they are on the point of entering as they sing this psalm. Fear of the hazards of the journey has given way to a sense of wonder at being in such a place as Jerusalem and they pray for God's blessing to remain on it. Other songs which express similar sentiments are 48, 84 and 132.

Verses 1-2: Going in
The words of verse 1 may be those of the high priest welcoming the worshippers into *the house of the Lord*, an expression which was used even before the temple was constructed (1 Sam. 17, 24), since it simply meant a place where God could be approached, not necessarily a solid building. The welcome brings great *rejoicing* to those who have arrived, whether from near or far. David catches the sense of wonder in verse 2, well expressed in the GNB: 'And now we are actually standing inside the gates of Jerusalem!'

Verses 3-5: Going on
These verses express admiration for the city of Jerusalem, with which visitors from afar would be particularly impressed.

David and his army had conquered the city from the Jebusites early in his reign. At the time it was probably a collection of tents and hovels. Now they had transformed it into *a city that is closely compacted together* or 'restored in beautiful order and harmony' (GNB). The term for *closely compacted* is the same as that describing the coupling together of the coverings of the tabernacle (Exod. 26:11).

This type of building symbolised the unity and harmony of the nation under its king and its God. For though there were many *tribes*, they were all *tribes of the Lord* going up to the one place to *praise the name of the* one *Lord, according to the statute given to Israel* (v. 4), which required them to assemble there three times a year (Exod. 23:14-17).

Not only was worship conducted there but justice was administered at David's throne of judgment (v. 5). There miscreants could be charged and sentenced and people have their disputes settled.

Verses 6-9: Praying for
No one must assume that everything was now perfect and there was no room for improvement; nor that there were no dangers to disturb what they already had achieved. Wars could arrive from without or strife arise from within. The rebellion of Absalom shows what could happen. So David issues a great call for prayer. No doubt he and his counsellors were doing all they could to protect the city and preserve the nation's unity. But ultimately these depended on God's blessing, which must be evoked by prayer.

Verse 6a calls for prayer and verses 6b-7 are the response (if only Christians today would respond as quickly to their pastors' calls!) which asks that they be kept *secure* from outside trouble and have *peace* among themselves. There is real love in the words of verse 8: his concern is not so much for himself as for his *brothers and friends*, those who would suffer most if the city came under attack or if rebellion arose from inside. Worst of all, God's own honour would be damaged if Jerusalem ceased to *prosper* (v. 9). For the people did not just bring themselves to the feasts but came laden with gifts: money and sacrifices. They would only be able to do so if the city was enjoying *prosperity*.

Questions:
(1) Have we lost a sense of wonder and joy at meeting together with the Lord and his people? (See Acts 2:42-47.)

(2) Is this concern to guard the unity present in our churches today, and is this concern expressed in prayer? (See Eph. 4:3.)

Psalm 123

A Cry for Mercy

The mood of the pilgrims here is very different from either of the previous psalms. Perhaps it was for use on those occasions when they had been passing through a time of defeat, persecution or even slavery, such as they endured in Babylon. If the latter is the case it would give greater meaning, not only to the reference to *slaves* in verse 2, but to the cry for *mercy*. For they had brought their troubles on themselves by their sins and could only come humbly back to God.

Verses 1-2: Humbling before God
In Jerusalem they would see 'the thrones of the house of David' (122:5). But he was only the representative of the One who occupied the throne of the universe. To God they were *slaves* who wait in the presence of their *master* or *mistress*, looking just for a motion of the *hand* and then going out to obey. For they had been disobedient servants and needed his *mercy*, for which they looked to him as steadfastly as a servant looking for a sign from his *master*.

Verses 3-4: Pleading for mercy
The *look* is now clothed in words – a plea for his *mercy*, repeated in order to impress him with their sincerity. The ground of their plea is not their innocence, which they could not protest, but their suffering, for they had *endured much contempt and ...*

much ridicule. Whether or not their bodies had been afflicted, their feelings certainly had. They need to be reassured that they are esteemed and loved, and that by their God himself.

Question:
Do you know what it is to have failed God and suffered for it? Does this psalm help you to return to him? (See Hosea 14.)

Psalm 124

A Remarkable Escape

This psalm was for use after some great military victory which had been snatched from the jaws of defeat. Calling it *A song of ascents* or 'Marching Song' shows that David composed it for the returning warriors to sing as they marched home and went up to the temple to acknowledge God's hand in their escape.

The words *let Israel say* in verse 1 suggest someone taught them the song and was leading it. The most notable feature of it is the absence of self-congratulation. The victory is ascribed entirely to the *help of the Lord* (v. 8), to the fact that he *had been on our side* (v. 1).

As for themselves, they had been on the point of extinction. At first he states this literally: *men attacked us* (v. 2), *their anger flared against us* (v. 3). Then he describes it in vivid pictures. First, the enemy is likened to a monster who would have *swallowed us alive*, that is, would have completely destroyed them with a blow. In verses 4-5 he changes the picture to a flood. The area in which the battle was fought contained many wadis, dried-up streams that in a storm can suddenly become a raging *torrent* which *sweeps away* everything in its path. This describes the suddenness with which the attack would have come, resulting in total destruction.

Lastly, in verses 6-7 he likens them to a bird caught in a *fowler's snare*. The more it struggles to get free the more it is *torn by (the) teeth* of the snare. The only way to escape is for the *snare* to be *broken* by another party. This is what *the* LORD had done for them: given them a victory against all the odds. Though the forces against them were formidable the one who was *on our side* is none other than *the Maker of heaven and earth.* Those against them on the other hand were only *men* (v. 2); the word used is ADAM, a reminder of 'the ground' from which human beings are made. What can the ground do against its Maker? How can clay challenge the potter?

Question:
Can we really talk of God taking sides? Does Romans 8:31-39 help us to an answer?

Psalm 125

Unshakable Faith

Again the people have been under threat from evil-doers. Whether these were from outside the nation or within is not clear, But what is clear is that God has not allowed them to retain control. This has greatly encouraged the people's faith in God's covenant, a worthy sentiment with which to come to his temple.

Verses 1-3: Their renewed confidence in God
As they see Mount Zion coming into view, surrounded by even higher mountains, they are reminded of two things. Firstly, (v. 1) *the foundation* on which their faith in God is based – a covenant promise which is as unchangeable and unshakable as Mount Zion itself. This is not because there is anything different about its geology or geography, but because God chose it for his dwelling (46:4). Second, God's protection of his people, reflected in the mountains surrounding the city (v. 2), which shelter it from storms and invaders (cf. Zech. 2:3-5).

God has just proved this once again (v. 3); he has not allowed *the sceptre of the wicked* to *remain over the land allotted to the righteous*, but has broken up the confederacy formed against them. Here is another covenant reference: the land was *allotted*, divided among the tribes by lot on God's own instructions (Josh. 13:6), and *the sceptre*, the right of rule, was given to the tribe of Judah (Gen. 49:10). For God knows their weakness, how easily they can be influenced away from him. If they followed the ways of the nations and even worshipped their gods when they were independent, how much more likely would they be to do these things when they were occupied! Then who would witness to the true God and walk in his ways?

Verses 4-5: Their prayer for God's continued goodness
The fact that their security and independence were guaranteed by God's covenant did not mean they could sit back and take it for granted. Then, as now, God carries out his purposes and promises through the prayers of his people. The two-part prayer is all-embracing. To *those who are upright in heart* (v. 4) – his covenant people whom he has again delivered – they pray that God will *do good*. This shows they are not relying on themselves as a special people, even on the fact that they are *good*, but on the goodness of God, a divine quality integral to the covenant (2 Sam. 7:28; Ps. 23:6).

Verse 5 can also be translated as a prayer: '*may the* LORD *... banish with the evildoers ... those who turn to crooked ways*'. Whether *the evildoers* are Judah's enemies or disloyal members of their own nation, or both, is not clear, but it shows that profession of trust in the Lord must be shown practically in right behaviour. 'Faith without works is dead' and those who merely say 'Lord, Lord' but do not 'do the will of my Father' are liable to be banished from the presence of God for ever, just as much as total unbelievers (Matt. 7:21-23; 25:31-46).

Questions:
(1) If Judah's security lay in the covenant of an unchangeable God, on what is the church's security based? (See Matt. 16:17-18.)

(2) Under the old covenant the godly were geographically separated from the ungodly. How is the position of Christians under the new covenant different? (See John 17:13-19; 1 Cor. 5:9-11; 2 Cor. 6:14-18.)

(3) What guidance do verses 4-5 give on praying for believers and unbelievers respectively?

Psalm 126

Facing Hardship

This psalm marks one of those occasions when they went up to Zion, perhaps on the anniversary of their return from captivity, hence the title *song of ascents*. By this time the return is a happy memory and they are facing the hardships of restoring their buildings and their farms, while being harassed by enemies (Ezra 4) and sometimes devastated by plague (Joel 1). This explains the contrast between the two halves of the psalm.

Verses 1-3: Recalling the past
There is a note of nostalgia here as they celebrate the time *when the LORD brought back the captives to Zion*. It had been a *dream* come true (v. 1). In Babylon they had 'wept by the waters' (137:1); now their *mouths were filled with laughter*. In Babylon they had refused to sing and hung up their harps (Ps. 137:2); now their *tongues were filled with songs of joy* (v. 2a), as Isaiah had promised (Isa. 49:8-13; 52:8-10).

Isaiah had also prophesied that other nations would hear of this and marvel, so that Israel would fulfill its role as God's 'witness' to the world (Isa. 43:10-13; 44:8). This had indeed happened: *the LORD has done great things for them*, they were saying (v. 2b). As they recall these days they recapture something of their *joy* and wonder (v. 3). If the uncircumcised were excited as mere spectators, how much more will they be who are beneficiaries of *the great things ... the LORD has done*?

Verses 4-6: Facing the present

The novelty of being back in the land had worn off as they tackled the task of restoring their land to its former glory. The word for *restore* (v. 4a) is the same as that translated *brought back* in verse 1. As the NIV margin shows, the word *captives* is also repeated. This may mean they are asking God for more of their people to return home. Only 50,000 had come back under Sheshbazzar and they were hard put to it to do all that needed doing: rebuilding the temple, resettling the villages and re-cultivating the land, while fending off their enemies. If so, this prayer was answered when Ezra led more exiles home in 458 (Ezra 7).

The simile in verse 4b may refer, however, to the need for better fertility of the soil. Haggai spoke of the poor harvests they were having in spite of the work they were doing (Hag. 1:6). He interpreted this as God's judgment on their neglect of the temple. So they were praying for God to remove his hand of judgment and stretch out his hand of blessing by fertilising the land and doing so quickly and abundantly. The reference to *the streams in the Negev* is explained by a passage in Lucretius ('On the Nature of the Universe', Book 6, lines 711-737). The Nile and its tributaries empty into the Mediterranean, but at the height of the hot dry season the northern monsoon holds it back, causing it to overflow and irrigate the surrounding land. This was seen as God 'turning' nature. The psalm is praying for such a 'turning' now – quick and abundant.

Verses 5-6 bear out that the state of the soil was their primary concern here. The words sound like those of a priest or prophet assuring them God has heard them, but may answer them in a different way from what they had asked. They would have to work the land in the normal manner by going out with *seed* and doing everything necessary to ensure it grew: ploughing, hoeing, watering. They must not expect quick miraculous results. It would be hard, they would *sow in tears*, probably because their stomachs were empty and their children crying. They would go out *weeping carrying seed to sow*, but they must bear this or nothing would happen. But they are promised that they *will reap* and sing *songs of joy* as they do so. They will *return carrying sheaves* and sing more *songs of joy*.

Although the primary reference is agricultural, it may be taken as a token of the restoration of their whole life as a nation: social, political, commercial and spiritual. All would be restored – but not overnight nor without much hard work and suffering on their part.

Questions:
(1) Do you still recall your release from captivity to sin through your conversion to Christ as a dream come true? (See 1 Cor. 15:9-10.)

(2) Do you believe that if he will God can bring about a sudden change in the spiritual life of church and nation comparable to the overflowing of the Nile? (See Acts 4:31.)

(3) Until such a time comes are you prepared to work hard for fruit in the normal way: by sowing the seed of the gospel and hoping to see a time of reaping? (See Gal. 6:7-10.)

Psalm 127

God the Builder

What was originally Solomon's reflections either on his coronation or his wedding appears to have been re-issued for use as a *song of ascents*, possibly on the occasion of the rebuilding of the house of God after the exile.

Verse 1a: Building the house of God
It had been David's dearest wish to build *the house* of God and it was his son Solomon who achieved it. Now it had to be done all over again because of its destruction by Nebuchadnezzar. As in the past, so now *the* LORD must be in it or *the builders* would *labour in vain*. Resources were in short supply and enemies were molesting them. They could not do it without God.

Verses 1b-2: Protecting the city of God
The walls of the city were also broken down and it was essential to rebuild them. Security must be kept up, *the watchmen* must *stand guard*. Again he realises the limitations of human effort and the need for *the* LORD to *watch over the city*, lest their own efforts should prove *in vain*.

Not only that, but if they relied on themselves they would wear themselves out with work and anxiety (v. 2). Looking to God and trusting in him would enable them to take rest and enjoy *sleep*. It is true that *toiling* was part of the punishment on fallen man (for the word used is that of Gen. 3:17), but for those he saves from punishment, this toil is tempered by peace of mind and rest of body.

Solomon seems to be setting himself up as an example to the people here, for he refers to *toiling for food*, which was not what he was setting out to do (v. 1). But for the people toiling for food was their daily employment and could be an anxious one. Let them see how Solomon went about his great tasks and follow his example in their smaller ones.

The precise translation of the last line of verse 2 is uncertain. If it is as the NIV text gives it: *he grants sleep to those he loves*, then he is saying: 'if you are so poor you feel you must work day and night, or if when you go to bed you cannot sleep for anxiety, then remember the Lord *loves* you, and will not see you die of hunger.' If the marginal reading is correct, he is saying, 'It is not all down to you; God does not sleep, and while you are unconscious he is working to supply your needs because *he loves* you'. In fact, it literally reads 'his beloved' (KJV), which was the name originally given to Solomon (2 Sam. 12:25). Solomon was seeking to live up to his name.

Verses 3-5: Raising a family

If God's promise to David was to materialise – that his dynasty would last throughout the days of the Kingdom of Israel (2 Sam. 7:13), then Solomon must have *sons*. He reminds himself that though he has a part in this process, they are ultimately God's gift: his *heritage* to his people and his *reward* to those who were faithful to him (v. 3). The *sons* of the king would make his dynasty secure, safeguarding it against rivals within and enemies without. They would be *like arrows in the hand of a warrior* (v. 4).

In this matter also he seeks to be an example to the people as he adds: *blessed is the man whose quiver is full of them* (v. 5). *Sons* strengthen any family, not just the royal household. In those days to be childless was a reproach for which a couple would be despised (1 Sam. 1). But when a man went down to *the gate* of the city, where people gathered for social and business purposes, and took a number of *sons* with him, he would be respected. If there were a dispute to be settled in the court (which also met at *the gate*), his sons would support him and he would not be *put to shame*. Later, they would be there to support him and his wife in their old age.

The sad thing about this psalm is that ultimately Solomon failed on all three counts referred to in this psalm. He failed to maintain the purity of the worship of God and introduced idols (1 Kings 11:1-8). His hold on the kingdom was insecure and it fell apart at the end of his reign (1 Kings 11:9-12). His many marriages did indeed produce *sons* but failed to gain him respect and power (1 Kings 11:14-26).

Questions:
(1) What corresponds to 'building the house of God' in these New Testament times? (See Matt. 16:18; 1 Cor. 3:9; Eph. 2:19-22.)

(2) Who are the 'watchmen' over God's 'city' now, and how do they keep watch? (See Isa. 62:6-7; Matt. 26:38.)

(3) What advice does verse 2 give us to ensure a good night's sleep? (See Ps. 37:7; Phil. 4:6-7).

Psalm 128

Domestic Bliss

Although not ascribed to Solomon this psalm may well be a response to the previous one. Solomon has voiced his aims on becoming king and now the priest or people express their concurrence and pray that these aspirations may be realised through the blessing of God. There is a progression of thought from the individual (vv. 1-2), to the family (vv. 3-4), to the nation (vv. 5-6).

Verses 1-2: Personal blessing
Verse 1 states a truth very much at the heart of Wisdom literature, which is in turn based on the covenant: that the blessing of God comes basically from the individual's attitude to God: *fear*, leading to obedience, which means to *walk in his ways*. This was how Moses expounded the covenant on the border of the promised land in Deuteronomy 28, the first five verses of which are particularly relevant to the psalm. Let Solomon observe these principles and his aims will be realised. He will be an example and encourage *all who fear the* L*ord* in their *walk* with God.

Such a relationship breeds a spirit of co-operation with him: *your labour* attracts his blessing, so that *you will eat the fruit* of it and *prosperity will be yours*. Solomon expressed this co-operation in different terms in 127:1-2 when he spoke of 'the builders' labour' needing 'the Lord' to 'build the house' and 'the watchmen standing guard' but having the Lord also 'watching over the city'.

Verses 3-4: Domestic blessing

Solomon had made raising a family one of his aims as king. These verses go further to promise happiness to this growing family. At the heart of it is *your wife* who is said to be *within your house*, using a term which probably refers to that part of it which was the particular domain of the woman. A home cannot be happy unless the woman is. She is likened to *a vine* not only for fruitfulness but beauty (Song 7:8-13) and joy (Judg. 9:13).

The *sons* which Solomon had called 'a heritage from the Lord' (127:3) are seen here in their familiar place *round (the) table*, as the woman was seen in her place. A king, or any working man, would spend much of his day outside the home and see his children chiefly at meals. Here they are presented as the hope of the future: *olive shoots*. The *olive* was basic to Israel's economy, used both in cooking and medicine. This again stresses the importance of the children, but with a different metaphor from 127:4-5. The picture of the *olive* shoot indicates their tender state and need for nourishment if they were to fulfill their promise in coming days. None must take this happiness and hope in children for granted – it depends on sustaining that personal godliness with which the psalm began (v. 1): *the man* who is *blessed* in his home is *the man ... who fears the Lord* (v. 4).

Verses 5-6: National blessing

From the individual and the family the psalm moves on to the whole congregation assembled on *Zion*, from there to the whole city, *Jerusalem*, and finally to all *Israel*. As the blessing moves outward so it also stretches onwards to *all the days of your life*, and further still to *your children's children*. Self, home, church and nation are interdependent. There can be no domestic joy without personal godliness, no national peace and prosperity without strong family life. The church too (*Zion*) has a vital part to play. It is also true in reverse: a stable nation enables the church to flourish unhindered, so that the families which comprise it can benefit, as ultimately does the individual. If only these ideals had guided Solomon all his days!

Questions:
(1) Compare verses 1-2 with what Paul says about co-operating with God in Christian service. (See 2 Cor. 6:1).

(2) What do verses 3-4 have to teach Christians today about family life? (See Eph. 5:22–6:4).

(3) Can the all-inclusive blessedness of this psalm be expected today?

Psalm 129

Celebrating Freedom

This psalm, like several of the *Songs of ascents*, particularly 126, may be connected with a thanksgiving for their deliverance from captivity in Babylon. In 126 they were addressing the problem of the barrenness of the land, which was hindering their recovery. But other troubles were beginning to loom up in the shape of unfriendly neighbouring peoples who were not pleased to see the Jews back in their land (Ezra 3:3). This was to become critical later; meanwhile they bring it to God and derive encouragement from their past deliverances.

Verses 1-4: What God has done for his people
These verses, being in the first person singular, are probably those of a precentor speaking or singing, not on his own behalf but that of the whole people, and urging them to join with him: *let Israel say* (v. 1). *Israel* is pictured as a mature adult whose history has been one of being *greatly oppressed from ... youth*, that is, from their early history in Egypt. Many nations had tried to destroy them, but had never *gained the victory* (v. 2).

Sometimes they had inflicted terrible sufferings on them, as severe as if they had run a plough over their backs, digging deep furrows (v. 3). But their God, *the* Lord, *is righteous* and always acts according to his character, never forgetting his call and promise to them. So once again, in releasing them from Babylon, he has *cut (them) free from the cords of the wicked* (v. 4). Having got the Babylonians off their backs, there was never any doubt he would deal similarly with any others who came against them.

Verses 5-8: What God will do for his people
It is not certain whether the verbs are to be taken as wishes and prayers, as NIV, in common with many others, does (*may ...*), or as assertions ('will'), as some, such as H. C. Leupold, do. Since the prayer is virtually an imprecation, it carries the same weight and certainty as a definite prophecy.

The verses describe a complete turning of the tables on their enemies. This had happened to Babylon, and any who followed their example would *be turned back in shame* (v. 5), as the Babylonians were before the Medes and Persians. The consequences are vividly pictured in the simile of *grass on the roof* (v. 6), that is, little tufts which grow out of the mud plaster but come to nothing. Such grass is useless for hay – *the reaper cannot* even *fill his hands* with it, let alone gather it in his arms. Similarly the blustering and harassment of these difficult neighbours will come to nothing.

It was customary for passers by to greet reapers with the blessing of verse 8 (cf. Ruth 2:4). Other nations certainly will not do this in the case of Israel's enemies, who have withered away like grass. The implication is that, far from enjoying the Lord's blessing, they are under his curse, whereas Israel, whom they tried to destroy, is being blessed by God.

Question:
(1) When people will not 'get off your back', do your thoughts go to the one in whom verse 3 was fulfilled? (See Isa. 50:6; Matt. 27:30.)

(2) What does the psalm teach us about the normal experience of the church and its members? (See Acts 14:22.)

Psalm 130

Forgiveness

This *Song of Ascents* may have been used as a preparation for one of the great annual events. With its stress on sin and forgiveness it best fits the great Day of Atonement. Nine days after the Feast of Trumpets, on the tenth day of the seventh month, Israel observed the Day of Atonement. This was probably the high point of the year and included some unusual features. The high priest had to wear special white linen garments; two goats were used, one of which was sacrificed as a sin offering and the other released into the desert; and the high priest made his annual entrance into the holy of holies. The details are in Leviticus 16 and 23:26-32.

The psalm does not touch on the ritual as such, but deals rather with the way a person prepared himself for this day. The title *A Song of Ascents* refers to the journey of the worshippers to the shrine and the psalm reflects the thoughts appropriate to the day. Leviticus 16:29, 31 refer to this preparation of heart in the words 'you must deny yourself' (NIV) or 'fast' (NIV mg). But the word is literally 'afflict yourselves' (ESV) or 'your souls' (KJV, NKJV). This is exactly what the psalmist is doing – probing *the depths* (v. 1) of his soul, facing the reality of his sinful state and finding forgiveness and redemption in God's promises.

Verses 1-2: Crying for mercy
There is real emotion here: *cry ... hear ... be attentive*. To say the same thing three times in different ways shows deep passion. The cry is for *mercy*, for he has plumbed *the depths* of his soul and found sin deeply rooted in it. The priest was going to confess the sins of the people over the 'scapegoat', but these would be of an external nature. It was for each worshipper to get to the root cause of these – a depraved nature. The Day of Atonement ritual might avail to lift the judgment on the nation, but could not restore the relationship between individuals and their God. Only personal forgiveness could do that, and this depended on one thing: not the meticulous observance of the ceremony or the extent of the fasting, but the *mercy of the* Lord.

This is why the psalmist begins by saying he is crying *out of the depths*: he wants God to look pitifully on him as on one in a filthy pit unable to get out on his own (cf. 40:1-2).

Verses 3-4: Finding forgiveness
Here begins what F. D. Kidner calls 'the steady climb towards assurance'. Although it is the psalmist who is speaking, he is clearly uttering thoughts God has given him. The first step of the climb is to realize the wonder of the fact that God does not deal with sinners as we might expect him to. In the case of believers he does not *keep a record of sins,* for he has wiped the slate clean (Heb. 10:17), he does not proceed like a policeman or prosecutor and amass the evidence against them with a view to sentencing and punishing.

If he did this, there would be no hope: *O* Lord *who could stand? But* he does not, *for with you there is forgiveness*. The God he has appealed to is a God of *mercy*, and to show *mercy* is to forgive. This does not make it a cheap option. We all know how costly forgiveness is. For God it is even costlier, for justice must still take its course, there must be payment, suffering and death. Under the old covenant this involved the slaughter of animals (bulls and goats were sacrificed on the Day of Atonement); under the new, the suffering and death were endured by God himself in Christ. But this achieved what the animals never could (Heb. 10:1-10). Indeed, it was only because of his purpose in Christ that forgiveness was possible through animal sacrifice.

That this assurance of forgiveness is only open to the contrite, to those who share the sentiments of verses 1-2, is clear from its effects on the psalmist: *you are feared*. True forgiveness does not breed complacency and carelessness; quite the opposite, it creates an even greater awe of God, as of one whose love is more humbling than his holiness!

Verses 5-6: Longing for God

If 'fear' sounds a nebulous term, then it is spelt out here in the description of its effect on the psalmist. It makes him long, not to escape God's punishment, but **for** God himself: *I wait for the* LORD. Nor is he basing his *hope* on feelings but on *his word*. The Day of Atonement was celebrated because God prescribed it, not out of whim but so that his people might have a solid basis for their forgiveness. It was a Day of *Atonement*, that is, for reconciliation with the God against whom they had sinned. The ritual was probably the most vivid of any ceremony: the goat over whom the sin had been confessed was let loose, never to be seen again, as if God was saying, 'You will hear no more about those sins you have confessed today'.

To crown it all, the high priest entered the holy of holies, that is (in Old Testament terms) into the very presence of God. This he did, not for himself, but as representative of all the people. The forgiven sinner could feel: 'I have been brought near to my God!'. This thought serves only to intensify his longing for God, as verse 6 expresses. Ask a soldier on night-guard what he is looking forward to and he will say, *for the morning*. The soul which has 'been to hell and back' cannot have enough of God.

Verses 7-8: Encouraging others

But assurance of forgiveness is not the only fruit: those who feel love for God express it in love for the brotherhood. The soul which has truly experienced forgiveness and reconciliation wants everyone to share it and does its utmost to encourage them. Observe the clarity of his thoughts on the matter: he is clear as to what God is like, a God of *unfailing love*; and on

God's chief work, *full redemption*, expounded in verse 8, which hints at the gospel which would bring that total forgiveness lacking under the old covenant and open the way into God's presence, not merely symbolically but really (Heb. 9:7-10).

Questions:
(1) Can you identify with the cry of verses 1-2? Does it matter? (See 1 John 1:8-10.)

(2) Does the thought of Christ suffering on the cross humble you more even than the realization that God is holy? See Watts' hymn: 'When I survey the wondrous cross'.

(3) Are our difficulties in testifying to the gospel due to a shallow experience of God's love and consequent indifference to others? (See 2 Cor. 5:11-15.)

Psalm 131

Be Still My Soul

David, to whom this psalm is ascribed, endured many perplexing experiences in his life, from the time he fled Saul's court right up to his last days, which were clouded by the rebellions of Absalom and Adonijah. Sometimes he complained bitterly about them, but he has found peace. This was the right frame of mind for pilgrims going up to the house of God, especially if times were troublesome. This explains the use of this Psalm, whatever its original circumstances, as *A Song of Ascents*.

Verse 1: Pride and ambition renounced
David had not sought the throne – nothing could have been further from his mind when he was watching sheep. But when it came he accepted it, and when the prospect seemed to have been removed by Saul's enmity he accepted that too; he could walk away from it – literally in fact, for *I do not concern myself with great matters* is 'I do not *march* after honours'. His retreat to Nob (1 Sam. 21) meant he was accepting this from the Lord. His *eyes* were not set on high office. Perhaps he was not yet ready for it – the reins of power were *things too wonderful* for the youngest son of a family from an obscure village who had grown up looking after sheep.

Verse 2: Peace and contentment embraced
I have stilled and quieted my soul indicates that this had been a struggle, as other psalms have shown. But it has been successful: he is *weaned* from the craving for fame and power, just as a *weaned child* is released from its frantic craving for the mother's milk. Like the *weaned child* with its mother, David is content just to be near God.

Verse 3 may have been added when the psalm came into **liturgical use**. It exhorts the people to learn from the earlier struggles of their king: not to expect too much in and from the world, but to put their *hopes in the LORD*.

Questions:
(1) Are you restless, unsatisfied, over-active? If so, is it due to pride and ambition? Do you feel you are not where you deserve to be, that your worth is going unrecognised or unrewarded – at work, home, the church or in life generally? These are questions for your heart to search rather than for your mind to enquire. (See Jer. 45:5.)

(2) How can pride and ambition be conquered? Take encouragement from the fact that even David had to struggle for it. Then look again at Matthew 5:3-10; 20:20-28.

Psalm 132

The LORD has Sworn

The allusions to David here do not come from him but from someone who is appealing to David's resolution to build a house for God, and to God's covenant promises in connection with David's resolution. This person was likely to have been David's successor, Solomon, who in his prayer dedicating the temple included verses 8-10 of this psalm (2 Chron. 6:41-42).

It is not certain whether the whole psalm was sung at that moment or whether it had been sung as the procession moved in, which would explain the title: *Song of Ascents*. Because of this title, some would date the psalm with the other 'pilgrim' or 'marching songs' (120–134). It could, however, have been adapted later for inclusion with these, but the most likely origin was Solomon's dedication of the temple. It is based on David's resolution to house the ark of God in Jerusalem (vv. 1-10) and the promise God gave him of a permanent dwelling for it and of a long-lasting dynasty for himself.

Verses 1-6: David's wish is now fulfilled
The temple Solomon was now dedicating was the one David his father had wished to build (2 Sam. 7:1-3). He wanted to replace the temporary structure in which he had housed the ark when he first brought it from Kirjath-Jearim to Jerusalem (2 Sam. 6:17). David was not permitted to build the Temple

(2 Sam. 7:5-7), but still deserved credit for bringing the ark from an obscure village to the city of God. This is what is being referred to here.

In Eli's time the ark had been captured by the Philistines (1 Sam. 4:10-11) but because it only brought them trouble they returned it to Israel, where it eventually found a home in Kirjath-Jearim (1 Sam. 6:21–7:2), in verse 6 called *Jaar* and in 2 Samuel 6:2 'Baalah'. There it remained throughout the judgeship of Samuel and the reign of Saul. It was not until David became king of all Israel that any attempt was made to bring it to the capital. Indeed, the wording of verse 6 suggests its whereabouts had become uncertain: there was a report that it was in *Ephrathah*, a term usually referring to the region around Bethlehem, though some say the environs of Kirjath-Jearim were known by that name, which may be what is meant by *the fields of Jaar*. Verse 6b seems to indicate that they *came upon it* almost accidentally!

When David heard this he was determined to bring it to his own city in order that the proper worship of God might be resumed. The wording of verse 5 suggests David saw the ark as the place where *the Lord* dwelt. The oath or *vow* he swore (vv. 2-5) are not recorded in the accounts in Samuel or Chronicles and must have been found in a document available to the writer but which has not come down to us. But we are told of the disastrous first attempt to bring up the ark (2 Sam. 6:1-11). This in no way lessened David's determination; rather it caused him great heart-searchings, which is probably the true meaning of the word translated *hardships* (v. 1). This is how it is used in Leviticus 23:26, 29, although it is translated 'deny yourselves' in the NIV.

It is this that Solomon is asking God to *remember* as the great temple that now housed the ark is dedicated. In humility Solomon is not pleading his own zeal or effort, but attributing the credit to David's original work in restoring the ark to Jerusalem. This thought forms the opening of Solomon's prayer of dedication (1 Kings 8:17-21).

Verses 7-12: The ark is housed in the Temple
Next the procession moves into the temple itself (v. 7) and there Solomon dedicates it to the Lord, as recorded in 1 Kings 8 and

2 Chronicles 6–7. His prayer ends (2 Chron. 6:41-42) with the words of verses 8-10. He has sought in his prayer to cover many eventualities: personal injury, defeat in war, drought, famine, plague and national sin. But the most important thing was that God should *come to (his) resting place* and dwell there (v. 8), that he would make the officiating ministers worthy of the privilege of leading his people in joyful worship (v. 9) and that he would *not reject* the prayers of *his anointed one* – Solomon himself as king (v. 10). Again he pleads the name of his father, David, for it was the thought of God actually coming to 'dwell on earth with men' (2 Chron. 6:18) that chiefly astonished him and of which he felt so unworthy. 'I do not expect you to do this for me,' he seems to be saying, 'but do it *for the sake of David your servant*', the one who originally initiated this whole enterprise.

But even David was unworthy of such privilege. Ultimately the plea must be based, not on David's *oath* to God but his to David (vv. 11-12). This was the promise God made when he refused David's request to build him a house (2 Sam. 7:11-13). The wording is different in the psalm, especially in referring to it as a *covenant*, which meant that as well as being a promise it also imposed conditions on those with whom it was made (v. 12).

Verses 13-18: God promises his blessing
That the Lord did *not reject* Solomon's prayer is clear from the answer he gave in 2 Chronicles 7:11-22. This is what is celebrated in the final part of the psalm. As miraculous fire had come down from heaven on David's sacrifice when he brought the ark to Jerusalem (1 Chron. 21:26), so it did again on the offerings with which Solomon accompanied his prayer of dedication of the Temple (2 Chron. 7:1). The glory of God appeared (2 Chron. 7:2) and later God spoke to Solomon to assure him he had prayed successfully (2 Chron. 7:11-22).

These verses are a summary of that answer. First comes the promise that God will dwell there, not because they had built him a house which he could not refuse, but because *he has chosen Zion (and) has desired it for his dwelling* (vv. 13-14). Because of this they need have no worries about the food supply (v. 15). The prayer of verse 9 will also be answered: worship will be led by worthy *priests* and offered by joyful *saints* (v. 16). The dynasty will continue and go from strength to strength (v. 17). *Enemies* will not prevail against them but their kings will remain, wear *the crown* and be *resplendent* (v. 18).

If we ask why things did not turn out like this, the answer is that the promises were always conditional, and kings, priests and people failed to keep the conditions (v. 12 and 2 Chron. 7:17-22).

Questions:
(1) Do we feel about God's presence in our church what David felt about the ark dwelling in Jerusalem? (See Eph. 2:21-22.)

(2) How do you understand verses 9 and 16 in the light of the New Testament's doctrine of 'the priesthood of all believers'? (See 1 Pet. 2:9-10.)

(3) How are the resolutions, prayers and hopes of the psalm only really fulfilled in Christ? (See John 1:14; 1 Cor. 15:25.)

Psalm 133

Together

It is possible that David (title) originally composed this psalm to mark the reuniting of the tribes on his accession to the throne of 'all Israel and Judah' (2 Sam. 5:5), then, after the tabernacle worship had been resumed in Jerusalem, he re-issued it as *A song of ascents*. It follows 122 well: the people have now entered the courts of the Lord for the festival service and are exulting in their unity in him, which becomes the theme of the psalm.

Verse 1: The sheer pleasure of unity in God
The NIV has omitted the opening word 'behold' or 'look!', which not only draws attention to their *unity* but marvels at it. From whatever tribe or family they have come, they are *brothers*, for God was the nation's Father (Isa. 63:16; Mal. 2:10). The land he gave them was their home where they could *live together*. In a way it is a pity the translators have added the words *in unity* since *together* is quite adequate. People can *live* with each without being *together*; *unity* is *together*ness. This became the basis of the *unity* and fellowship of the early church (Acts 2:44, 46). For a people to have this spirit is both *good* in the sight of the Lord, and *pleasant* and enjoyable to them.

Verse 2: The fragrance of this unity

Now follow two pictures of the beauty of this unity, to bring out what a 'good and pleasant' thing it is. It has the fragrance of *precious oil*, some rare exotic and expensive perfume, such as the elaborate concoction used for anointing *Aaron* (Exod. 30:22-33). This reminded them that they were not only a nation **with** a priesthood, but a nation **of** priests (Exod. 19:6), for the *oil* spilled out on to the high priest's robes on which the names of the twelve tribes were woven. This was a model for the church's great High Priest, on whom God *poured* his Spirit as *oil* was *poured* on *Aaron*, and who himself *poured* the Spirit on the members of his church. The Holy Spirit flows from Head to body. There is no greater joy for Christians than to smell the fragrance of Spirit-given fellowship. Gifts of the Spirit are good, but what binds them all together is love (Col. 3:14). So Paul followed up his passage on spiritual gifts with his great ode on love as 'the most excellent way' (1 Cor. 12–13).

Verse 3: The refreshment of this unity

In a hot and dry land, *the dew* could be collected in containers and used as water. *Hermon*, their highest mountain with the coolest nights, was famous for its *dew*. It refreshed and could be *even life*. But there was something better on *Mount Zion* – *there* they experienced *the blessing* of *the LORD* himself – his presence, more refreshing than *dew*. In fact *life* itself – not passing away as soon as the sun shone, but *for evermore*. The 'togetherness' of the church of Christ is the evidence of God's gift of eternal *life*.

Questions:

(1) How much enjoyment do you derive from being 'together' with God's people? (See Acts 2:46.)

(2) Is the fellowship of your church attractive to the outsider? (See Acts 2:46-47; 2 Cor. 2:14-16.)

(3) Does the fellowship in your church revive your spirits and restore your assurance when you are low? (See Col. 2:5.)

Psalm 134

By Night

In 121 the pilgrims were on their journey; in 122 they had arrived at their destination; 133 sees them at worship, and now in 134 the festival service has come to an end. What now?

Verse 1: The worship of God goes on
The servants of the LORD are the Levites who were on duty day and night (1 Chron. 9:33). God has so blessed the meeting together of his people for the feast (133:3) that they want it to go on; so they call on the Levites, whose duty it was to *minister by night in the house of the* LORD to take over while they go their ways. The Levites were divided into groups and assigned periods of duty (1 Chron. 23:6; Luke 1:8). But the whole spirit of these psalms was that whatever went on in the tabernacle or temple was done on behalf of all. The whole nation was continuously at worship through the priests and Levites, even during the hours of sleep.

Verse 2: Prayer and praise continue
This is a developed repetition of verse 1: 'let the duty Levites remain *in the sanctuary (and) lift up (their) hands* in prayer and *praise (of) the* LORD.' *The sanctuary* can mean either 'the holy place' where the light and incense burned, to which only the

priests and Levites had access; or 'in holiness', reminding them that God only accepts the prayers and praises of those who are clean (Pss. 15; 26:6; 66:18). Now that we are all priests to God, this duty and its qualification devolve on us all (1 Tim. 2:8).

Verse 3: God's blessing persists

This is probably the Levites' response to the appeal of verses 1-2. Far from taking offence or giving grudging agreement, they immediately invoke God's blessing on them as they leave. They do so in the boldest language – that he who is their LORD is *Maker of heaven and earth*, and no mere local deity. Yet he is present locally in order to *bless you from Zion*.

Questions:
(1) Now that all believers are priests, consider how the perpetual worship of God is carried out, how Malachi 1:11 is fulfilled in these gospel days, as expressed in the hymn ('The day thou gavest, Lord') which contains the lines 'the voice of prayer is never silent'.

(2) Apply verse 3 to our great high priest interceding to bring the blessing of God down on us (Heb. 7:25-28).

Psalm 135

So Much to Praise God For!

This psalm seems to have been put in juxtapostion to 134 because of the similarity of its opening. Perhaps 134 was an exhortation to the Levites to continue their worship through the night (134:1), whereas this is about daytime worship. So this includes, not just the Levites, but all the people (v. 19). It goes into much detail about what God is to be praised for.

Verses 1-4: Calling all ministers

Earlier in the dedication ceremony they had asked God to equip their ministers for their office (132:9) and God had assured them he would do so (132:6). In the light of this the people now call upon those *who minister in the house of the Lord* (v. 2) to do their duty and *praise the name of the Lord.*

They urge these *servants of the Lord to praise the Lord* (v. 1) first for himself, that he is good, then for his reputation: sing praise to his name (v. 3), that is, praise him for the way he made himself known in all he has done from creation onwards. This will be spelt out in verses 5-14. If the words *that is pleasant* (v. 3), refer to the act of praising him rather than to *his name*, a further motive for praising him is the sheer enjoyment of it. How could it be otherwise when we think of what we are to him: like Israel we are *his chosen ... his own ... his treasured possession* (Exod. 19:5; Deut. 7:6; Titus 2:14; 1 Pet. 2:9)!

Verses 5-12: Praise God for his sovereignty in creation

The writer speaks in his own name: *I know*, but on behalf of
king, priests and people into whose mouths these words are
put on this great occasion. He is enlarging on the 'name' of
the Lord (v. 3), how he has revealed himself. The first way
we encounter him is in his created works. Though we were
not there when he originated them, we experience him in the
way he still governs them as it *pleases him* (v. 6). If the *clouds
rise*, if *lightning* and *rain* follow, if *the wind* blows (v. 7), it is
because he wills it. This applies right across the board: *in the
heavens and on the earth, in the seas and all their depths* (v. 6).
Other nations believed these forces all acted independently
and some attributed deity to them. But his people *know* that
the LORD directs them and is therefore *greater than all gods* (v. 5,
cf. Exod. 18:11; Ps. 11:53; Jer. 10:12-13).

Verses 13-14: Praise God for his promise

So far so good. This was all working out. Here they are in their
own land with a new building dedicated to the worship of the
one true God. Here they are freely worshipping without the
pressure or even the company of idolators, and without an
idol in sight. But what of the future? Will it go on like this?
They were very vulnerable – a tiny nation surrounded by
hostile peoples who did not acknowledge their God.

They are reminded that their God *endures for ever* (v. 13). He
is not going to retire now that they are settled into their new
temple; he is not going to leave them on their own. What he
has been in the past he will be *through all generations*. So they
can count on him to *vindicate his people and have compassion on
his servants* (v. 14). So long as they remain in the same mind as
they are that day, all will be well.

Verses 15-18: Compare him with the other Gods

Having looked at their God and his works, their attention is
now directed to the gods of *the nations*. The words used echo
those of a former occasion when God saved them from the
Philistines and Samuel held a great service in Mizpah, in which
115 was central. The rest of this psalm is virtually identical to
that one. The point being made is that the gods themselves

are powerless and lifeless, but so are those who *make ... and ... trust in* them (v. 18). They are blind and deaf to the God who has demonstrated his power and glory in creation and redemption, and so *their mouths* have nothing worthwhile to *speak*, but only *lies*. This is similar to what Paul teaches in Romans 1:18-20. Those who worship lies will become liars (144:7-8).

Verses 19-21: Praise God everybody!
In view of what *the Lord* can do and the so-called gods cannot do, the praise of his people should be directed exclusively to him. So the call goes out to all ranks: to the nation as a whole – *Israel* (v. 19a), to the priests and Levites (vv. 19b-20a), to the 'God-fearers' – foreigners who remained or immigrated there (v. 20b). Let them gather to *Zion* in *Jerusalem*, for it is there *the Lord dwells* and receives his people's praises. So the psalm ends where it began: *Praise the Lord!* If only they had continued in the spirit they felt and showed on the great day of the dedication of the temple!

Questions:
(1) Is praising God 'pleasant' and delightful to you? Do you enjoy it, or do you have to find something else to do if you want to enjoy yourself? See Psalm 37:4 and Romans 14:17 and look in a concordance for the amount of times these terms (joy, delight, etc) are used in connection with the worship of God.

(2) Do you have the firm conviction of this psalm about God's place in the universe? Can you say 'I know' or does modern thought cast doubts on it? (See Heb. 11:1-3.)

(3) Consider how people become like what they worship, which today means money, sex, power, fame, stars, pop idols, etc. Are you becoming like the One you worship? (See Rom. 13:14.)

Psalm 136

God's Everlasting Love

The refrain that accompanies every verse of this psalm was originally used at the dedication of Solomon's temple (2 Chron. 5:13). There is no reason why it should not have been sung repeatedly in the regular worship. However, this practice would have suffered a setback in the devastating wars with Assyria and Babylon, and ceased altogether during the captivity. Jeremiah, who encouraged Judah to surrender to the Babylonians, predicted that a time would come when Jerusalem would be re-inhabited, people would live there happily and this refrain would again be sung (Jer. 33:10-11). So perhaps this psalm was specially composed for the first service after the return; verses 23-24 certainly hint at this.

Verses 1-3: God's everlasting love
This being a psalm of thanksgiving, the words *give thanks* begin each of the opening three verses. This section *gives thanks to the Lord*, not for anything he has done but for who he is. He is unique, for *he is good* (v. 1), whereas all else is tainted with evil; even 'the stars are not pure in his eyes' (Job 25:5). He is therefore supreme: over all supernatural beings (v. 2), and earthly potentates (v. 3). Whatever name they give themselves, whether *god* or *Lord*, he is that supremely.

But what they are chiefly celebrating on this occasion is his covenant *love* (HESED), enshrined in his name of YAHWEH (*the* LORD) and proved to be everlasting. There had been a seeming interruption in the expression of his covenant love during the long years of captivity, but now they can see that was not really so. Everything he has done from the beginning until now is the expression of his *love which endures for ever*.

Verses 4-9: His love in creation
This description combines the Genesis 1 account which brings out the *wonders* of creation (vv. 4, 6-9, cf. Gen. 11, 6, 16) with the Proverbs account which draws attention to his *wisdom* in creation, verse 5 (Prov. 3:19; 8:22-31). These verses, with their repeated refrain, come nearer than anywhere in Scripture to an answer to the question 'Why did God create the universe?' Answer: to express his *love*.

Verses 10-16: His love in redemption
From verse 9 to verse 10 is a big jump for it is a move from Genesis 1 to Exodus 12. Much happened in between which forms the background to verses 10-16: evil came in, man sinned, fell from God's grace and lost paradise, sin increased to such an extent that God washed all humanity away in the Flood. But man did not improve and eventually God chose one family as his own and gave them a land. They left this, however, and became enslaved in Egypt for centuries. If God's plan were to succeed, if his *love* were to prevail, his people must be set free. The way this happened is described in Exodus and summarised in these few verses. That this 'redemption' was not the final answer to the problem of evil was to be shown in the appearance of his Son who came to release, not one nation, but the whole human race, not from human hands but from the power of evil, sin and death. But the underlying cause was the same: God's everlasting love (John 3:16; Eph. 1:7; 2:4-5).

Verses 17-20: God's love in judgment
'Judgment' and 'love' may sound strange companions, but if God's people are to be released, then those holding them in their power must be overcome. The destruction of Pharaoh

(v. 15) was necessary if they were to be released from Egypt, and the overthrow of the Amorite kings was necessary if they were to occupy the promised land. So it was all part of God's everlasting love and, as with redemption, a rehearsal for what Christ was to do in order to set us free. He had to put our sin to death (Rom. 6:1-7; 8:3), defeat the powers of evil which led us into sin (Col. 2:15) and go on to destroy those teachings, practices and false gods who were deceiving most of the human race (2 Cor. 10:4-5; Rev. 20:1-3)

Verses 21-22: God's love in the gift of an inheritance

This is why God acted as he did in the two previous sections, why he brought Israel out of Egypt and overthrew the Amorites – to open the way for his people to live in the land he had given them. The word *inheritance* shows this was their right as his sons. Israel was God's chosen and adopted son (Hosea 11:1) and he would allow none to keep them from their inheritance or their inheritance from them.

In my judgment, this does not imply that the land belongs to the Jews in perpetuity, nor justify present day 'Israel' occupying the land at the expense of those who have lived in it for generations. For, as with redemption and judgment, this is a rehearsal for 'a better inheritance', that is, the kingdom of Christ which has replaced the kingdom of Israel and is given to all he has redeemed. Even this 'kingdom which cannot be moved' is only part of the full inheritance, which is, not that he dwells among us, but that we dwell with him in that place Christ has gone to prepare (John 14:2) which is called 'the new Jerusalem ... the new heavens and earth ... the paradise of God'.

Verses 23-26: God's love in restoration

So the psalm comes right up to date and *gives thanks* for this most recent restoration when he *freed us from our enemies*, the Babylonians (v. 24). Although they returned to their land in a very *low estate* (v. 23), he has *remembered* them. Though the fields were untilled, he *gives (them) food*, so that they have been able to work on restoring their cities and especially setting up their altar in order to resume his worship, as they were doing that day. So with what full hearts can they *give thanks to the God of heaven* for that *love* which has kept them down the years and still *endures* (v. 26)! Let us remember that the love which achieved our salvation at Calvary also lifts us up when we fall back into the hands of our sin or the powers of evil.

Questions:
(1) When is repetition a good thing? (See Phil. 3:1; 4:4; 2 Pet. 1:12-13.)

(2) How true is it that God's everlasting love is the theme which binds together old and new testaments?

(3) For what expressions of God's love do you give him thanks?

Psalm 137

Weeping by the Waters of Babylon

Here we are at the very heart of the sufferings of the people of
Judah in captivity as they *toiled day by day for their masters*.
The rivers of Babylon were the canals which irrigated the vast
plain between the Tigris and Euphrates, which the Jews may
even have been forced to help dig.

Verses 1-3: Too sad to sing
The psalm is set in a rest period during the long working day
when they *sat by* the canal they had been digging. But it was
not the hardness of the work and the bitterness of slavery for
which they *wept*, but their separation from *Zion* and the place
where they met God. 'Absence makes the heart grow fonder'.
This was worsened by the fact that Zion had been destroyed by
the very people for whom they were working.

To add insult to injury the same people *asked us for songs*!
Those who were ill-treating them, their captors and tormentors,
demanded songs of joy! Unquestionably they were merely
taunting them, rubbing their noses in it. So they utterly refused
to sing, but instead *hung their harps ... on the poplars*. Perhaps they
brought their *harps* with them to work to cheer each other up,
but certainly not to play and sing to entertain their captors.

Verses 4-6: Determined to remember
This situation had the beneficial effect of recovering their
loyalty to their *land* and their LORD. They were *his songs*, to be

sung to and for *him*. But they were away from the place where he heard them sung and *in a foreign land*, where other gods were worshipped. Not only that, but they were being asked to sing for the pleasure of their captors, not the glory of their LORD. *How can* they do this?

The effect of these thoughts on them was to produce a new longing for their old home. This goes to the extent of pronouncing a curse on themselves if they *forget Jerusalem*, if they do not *remember* her, if they do not regard her as their *highest joy*.

Verses 7-9: Longing for justice

From this they move on to curses on their enemies. Imprecatory songs seemed more appropriate than joyful ones. First, they call on God to take vengeance on the Edomites (v. 7). These people had concurred in Babylon's invasion, joined in the cruelty and looted the city after its destruction (Obad. 10–12). The prophet who predicted this prophesied that like things would happen to them (Obad.15). The people are now calling on God to *remember* and carry out this threat.

Next, an even more terrible curse is called down on the Babylonians themselves. Whereas verse 7 appeals to God to take notice and act, verse 8 directly accuses the chief perpetrator of this destruction: *O daughter of Babylon*. The words that follow sound horrendous to us, but they are simply the outworking of the 'lex talionis', the law of retribution which was at the heart of Old Testament justice, in order to restrain excess (Deut. 7:10; 32:35).

Slaughter of women and children was common practice among the heathen in their wars (2 Kings 8:12). The Babylonians had done such things to them: *what you have done to us* (cf. 2 Kings 25:7; Hosea 10:14), and Isaiah prophesied that they would be done to the Babylonians (Isa. 13:16). The people are concurring in God's sentence, which was to destroy the dynasty and nation of Babylon altogether. The Neo-Babylonian empire had a short history. It rose to power only twenty or so years before it conquered Judah and was overthrown at the end of Judah's captivity, giving it a life of less than a century.

However, the words of verse 8 seem to go beyond a call for justice, and the word *happy* sticks in the throat. It does not mean, however, that it was acceptable for the Medes and Persians to enjoy beating out the brains of little children. It means they had the privilege and blessing – the 'happiness' – of being God's instrument of judgment. As God had used Assyria to judge Israel (Isa. 10:5) and Babylon to judge Judah (Hab. 1:6), so he was raising up the Medes and Persians to judge Babylon.

The Bible makes no attempt to tone down man's cruelty to man or the severity of God's judgment on man's wickedness. The New Testament too speaks of judgment, though tends to postpone it until the last day. Meanwhile God shows great forbearance, because he has shown us another way of dealing with sin.He has punished it in his Son and offers forgiveness to all who will apply to him for it. Those who do this learn a different attitude from that which cries out for vengeance. This they leave with God, even though it may mean accepting persecution from their enemies. Yet they even find this a blessing (Matt. 5:10) and so pray for blessing on their persecutors (Matt. 5:44-45). Compare these verses with verse 8 of this psalm.

Question:
How does this psalm show we cannot get a complete picture of God and his ways from the Old Testament alone?

Psalm 138

Uninhibited Praise

David's psalm of praise and thanksgiving seems to have been motivated by some special deliverance in answer to prayer (v. 3). This may have been his final deliverance from Saul's persecution followed by his own accession to the throne. Alternatively it could have been a great victory during his reign. It was clearly a public occasion in the presence of the governing body (*gods* in v. 1 are probably rulers) and held in the temple (v. 2). Such is the greatness of the victory that he wants it published round the nations (v. 4).

Verses 1-3: David gives God all the praise
These verses tell us four things.

(1) Where David was when he sang this song – in Hebron (the capital before the capture of Jerusalem) *before the gods* (v. 1b), that is, the leaders of the tribes and families of Judah, the 'judges' (see Exod. 21:6; 22:8-9; Ps. 82:1); the word *gods* indicates the authority given them by God.

(2) The direction in which he was facing: *towards your holy temple*. The word HELAL means 'tent' and therefore refers to the Tabernacle, since the Temple was not yet thought of. At this time it appears to have been in Kiriath-Jearim, in the North of Judah near Gibeon (2 Sam. 6:2). David had either placed his throne facing North or turned his body to do so

while he sang. He was acknowledging both God's presence among them and his authority over them.

(3) How he was praising God: *with my whole heart* and voice (*sing*). This was the David who had cried to God from the pit of despair, to which there is a passing reference in verse 3, also to how God answered it by giving him courage to keep him going until the deliverance came. Now that was all over and he was entering on God's call to kingship, how full of love to God must his heart have been!

(4) What he was praising God for: his *love and faithfulness*, that is, his faithful love, his HESED. It was that which had kept him during his long trial (101:1) and made him a better man for it. It was that which had now brought these trials to an end and placed him on the throne. He takes no credit himself, for he had virtually given up on his nation when he had been driven into the arms of the Philistines. Nor had any man come to rescue him; it was the Lord's doing.The additional words of verse 2 have caused problems. NIV may be correct in rendering KAL *all things*, but older translations attach *all* to *your name:* 'you have exalted your word above all your name'. If correct, 'your name' would mean 'your self-revelation in creation and providence' (i.e. general revelation), while 'your word' means special revelation, that is, the revelation of his person and work, which he makes only to his own people. David had experienced God's personal service in being given a promise and seeing it kept.

Verses 4-5: David enlarges his vision
A God such as this deserved to be known and praised by more than Judah's judges. His Godhead, his deeds and *the words of (his) mouth* ought to be revealed to Israel's neighbours and their leaders, indeed to *all the kings of the earth*. He wants all people everywhere to join in *singing of the ways of the LORD*. A little country like Judah, or even all the twelve tribes, are insufficient to contain *the glory of the LORD*, which is *great* in the best sense of the word.

Although this is not a 'Messianic' psalm, this vision could not be realised until the coming of Christ to 'die for the Jewish nation and ... also for the scattered children of God, to bring them together and make them one' (John 11:51-52). Although in the passage in John's Gospel the high priest probably had in mind only 'the Jews of the Dispersion', when John calls it 'prophesying' he is making it refer to the universal preaching of the gospel, which Christ himself later commissioned (Matt. 28:19-20).

Verses 6-8: David is confident about the future
David has learned vital lessons from his long trial.

(1) Who it is enjoys God's care and who it is that does not (v. 6). Although at times he had uttered rash words, he had been made *lowly* by his experiences. On the other hand, the *proud* such as Saul had been deprived of God's favour, and were only observed by him from a distance. So he has learned that you do not have to attain worldly greatness to get near him; rather the opposite! (See Isa. 66:1-2; 1 Pet. 5:5.)

(2) What kind of life lay ahead of him (v. 7). His troubles are not over; in a sense they are just beginning, and he expects to *walk in the midst of troubles*. But he also expects that God will continue to help him in his troubles and to oppose whoever opposes him. For this is the original covenant promise (Gen. 12:3).

(3) That the God who begins a work continues it until it is complete (v. 8). This thought had enabled him to get by in his extremity (57:2, which uses the same word, GIMER, here translated as 'fulfils'). Indeed, God **must** complete it, for *his HESED endures for ever* – he is compelled by his nature. But he does it through prayer, as David's concluding words show.

Questions:
(1) Look again at verses 1-3 and separate what belongs to that historical occasion from what is of abiding application.

(2) Although we live in the days of the universal preaching of the gospel, how international is our thinking, praying and vision (vv. 4-5)? Are we too conditioned by the steep decline of Christianity in our own nation?

(3) What do you EXPECT from life, and what do you EXPECT correspondingly from God? (See John 16:33; Phil. 1:6.)

Psalm 139

The Searching Eye of God

This is one of David's most intensely personal meditations on his relationship with God. His feelings are somewhat mixed. On one hand he feels constricted by God's call (v. 5); but on the other he derives great comfort from the thought that he cannot get away from God (vv. 17-18). Also, his consciousness of the wickedness of his enemies (vv. 19-22) is balanced by his awareness of his own sinfulness.

Verses 1-16 are perhaps the fullest treatment of **God's omniscience** in Scripture. He knows our body's every movement – *going out and ... lying down* cover all our waking and sleeping hours, and every state active and passive (vv. 2-3). He even knows the unexpressed thoughts of our minds (v. 4). So complete is his knowledge that there is no hiding place from him (vv. 5-10), nor is there any time or condition from which he can be shut out. This is not because God has selected David to follow him around, but because he is *Spirit* (v. 7). The nature of spirit is that it is ubiquitous – everywhere and always. Omniscience results from omnipresence. It is a property of God alone (v. 6). Even the womb is accessible to him (vv. 13-16), which does not make God merely an X-ray or laser scanner, but is true because he has already foreordained what shall be (v. 16b). David's view of God and man is that each embryo or foetus is **made** by God, and even before that its subsequent life is foreknown (Jer. 1:5; Eph. 1:11; 2:10).

Verses 17-18. How does he view this? Is God a Big Brother, waiting to jump on his slightest mistake? This would evoke feelings of fear and anxiety, whereas David says God's *thoughts* of him are *precious*. He is glad that he is always in the mind of God – every second and moment, which when added together *outnumber the grains of sand*. He is encouraged to know that when he *awakes* from unconsciousness he knows he will continue in God's *thoughts* all day.

Verses 19-22. This is the difference between the righteous man and the wicked. The thought that God knows him so perfectly would be terrifying to *the wicked* if he believed or realized it; it would fill him with shame. But for the righteous man, such as David, it makes him even more determined to avoid the company of the ungodly who are unconscious of God's awareness of them and live as they will. David is resolved he will not associate with them lest he share their condemnation. He is still of the same mind as in Psalm 1. Here we have an example of what is a feature of some psalms – the 'imprecation' or curse. It is best seen as David speaking as a prophet of God pronouncing God's curse on the wicked. See the comments in the Introduction (Vol. I, p. 18).

Verses 23-24. This does not mean David sees himself as superior to these people. He knows that but for God's grace he would be as they. Nor can he trust himself to continue in this way. So he opens himself to God's continual searching, testing, correcting and leading. Such were his thoughts as (it would appear from vv. 11-12) night came on, when the sun was down but before the moon and stars came out.

Although originally composed for his own benefit and God's glory, he apparently issued this psalm for the director to use in public worship.

Questions:
(1) How conscious are you of the all-seeing eye of God upon you when not engaged in private devotions or public worship?

(2) If this happened more would it encourage you or make you ashamed and afraid?

(3) How can we cultivate 'The practice of the presence of God'?

Psalm 140

From Trembling to Trust

D avid is here suffering under the conspiracies and threats of his enemies. The similarity of the language to that of 59 make it likely that it comes from the time when he is beginning to go on the run from Saul. At this point he is looking, not only for a place of safe refuge, but for some spiritual counsel and support. Lacking this from any other source he finds confidence and assurance in prayer to God.

Verses 1-5: David cries to God for deliverance
This prayer is again expressed with great urgency and feeling: *rescue ... protect ... keep.* It is justified as before by the intensity of the opposition. His enemies are intent on *violence* not only against him personally but his supporters also, with whom they *stir up war every day* (v. 2). As a result of his success against the Philistines David had a large following (1 Sam. 18:6) and if he were murdered there would be a danger of civil war. Clearly Saul and his men were trying to alienate his followers from him, for until they can thrust their swords into his body they are sharpening their tongues (v. 3), that is, conducting a hate campaign against him. This metaphor for character assassination, plus the other two used here: poison (v. 3) and the snares of hunters (vv. 4-5), have been used in other psalms (59:7; 64:3-5). All the psalms from this period speak of a conspiracy against him.

Verses 6-8: David expresses his confidence in God
The note of desperation gives way to a spirit of confidence, which enables him to make specific requests rather than utter general cries. God had already proved himself as his God (v. 6a), his *strong deliverer*, and he had been to him like a helmet and shield (v. 7). This encourages him to persist in prayer, asking God to frustrate their plans (v. 8).

Verses 9-11: David's confidence turns to boldness
Having regained his assurance of God's personal care and protection, he can turn his thoughts to his enemies and spell out exactly how God should deal with them. The problem thrown up by these 'cursing' passages has been discussed in the Introduction (Vol. I, p. 18), to which you are referred. Here we can see how David arrives at this point. He is being maliciously and unjustly slandered, vilified and pursued for his life; but he commits his cause to God who restores the assurance of his personal protection. It is this which gives him the right to speak in God's name and prophetically pronounce **his** curses on his enemies.

Verses 12-13: David universalises his prayer
This prophetic note enables him to take on the cause of all the oppressed righteous. The battle he is engaged in is a microcosm of the whole conflict between good and evil which began at the Fall (Gen. 3:15) and will continue until the final defeat of evil at the end of the world (Rev. 20:14-15).

Questions:
(1) How is David's experience also a prophecy of the ministry of Christ? (See Matt. 4:1-11; Col. 2:15.)
    (2) What does this psalm teach you about the Christian's warfare? (See 2 Cor. 10:1-5.)

Psalm 141

Watch My Mouth

David continues to suffer at the hands of evildoers and continues to take it to God in prayer. Here he has moved on a little from 140 as he prays not only for God's restraint on his enemies but on himself, lest he should speak rashly and bring dishonour on God (v. 3).

Verses 1-2: David prays about his prayer
David is still putting his case in the Lord's hands. He realizes his prayer of 140 has only given him temporary respite and he still looks for full deliverance. This explains the suggestion we get here that David felt his prayer was going unheard: *Hear my voice* (v. 1). To this he adds a further reason why God should answer *quickly*. When the evening sacrifice is offered mingled with incense (v. 2, cf. Exod. 29:41; 30:8), God delights in it. Perhaps he had seen Samuel performing this rite at Ramah. 'Is not my prayer as sweet to you?' David seems to be saying. 'Will not you show your delight in it by a quick answer?'

Verses 3-5a: David examines his life
He continues in this introspective mood. Is God holding back because something is wrong with his prayers or in his life? Has he spoken rashly to God or man (v. 3)? Is there something deep down in his heart that is secretly drawing him to yield

to his enemies (v. 4)? Are his enemies trying another method – luring him with his *delicacies* back to the royal table in order to get David into their hands? David must have been living frugally and therefore was vulnerable to this. There was a danger that the resolution he made earlier (Ps. 1) and which he had kept till now would be broken. Or is he being obstinate (v. 5)? Is he being advised to take another course but refusing? Clearly he is willing to put any of this right.

Verses 5b-7: David reasserts God's curse
The result of the self-examination has been to clear his conscience and restore his boldness. Again he speaks as God's prophet, pronouncing his curse on his enemies (v. 5, cf. Ps. 35:4-8; 140:9-11 and see the Introduction [Vol. I, p. 18]). Since these people were the government (*rulers*, v. 6), they deserved a spectacular overthrow – something so drastic they would be forced to admit David's protestations of innocence were true. The end they deserved is that their bodies should remain unburied, so that their bones would lie on the ground like the earth the ploughman has turned over and be exposed to the light of day (v. 7). Then all would see they were cursed of God, for the supreme punishment and greatest shame in the ancient world was to be refused burial (Deut. 21:22-23; Jer. 14:16).

Verses 8-10: David reaffirms his confidence in God
Coming back to his immediate situation, he still needs God's protection (vv. 8-9). The realization that he is in the hands of the *Sovereign* Lord gives him assurance. The covenant God will not refuse refuge to a genuine asylum seeker! He will not let David die. He will save his judgments for his enemies (v. 10) by giving them so much rope they will hang themselves, while he passes by *in safety*.

Questions:
(1) To what extent is our praying affected by our state of mind or behaviour? (See Ps. 66:17-20; Heb. 9:14.)

(2) Verse 5a gives an opportunity to reconsider the Bible's teaching on receiving criticism (Prov 9:8-9; 19:25; 25:12; Eccles. 7:5). What makes it difficult for us to be like David in this? (See Prov. 16:32; Matt. 5:5.)

(3) Verses 8-10: does our problem with criticism explain why we lack the freedom with God David enjoyed here?

Psalm 142

David's Tight Corner

This psalm was David's *Prayer ... in the cave* (title) – probably not Adullam, but a cave in En Gedi where he was hiding, knowing that Saul and his men were approaching. The dramatic story is told in 1 Samuel 24:3-7. David and a few of his followers are sheltering in the back of the cave – the very cave into which Saul comes 'to relieve himself'. He may afterwards have lain down to rest, even gone to sleep, and since he was alone and unguarded David was able to creep up behind him and cut off a piece of his robe. His men wanted him to go further and cut off his head, since the situation seemed providential. It was indeed, but David interpreted the providence differently; to him it was his God-given opportunity to prove his innocence.

That is, however, more the subject of 57. Psalm 142 expresses his initial fear on finding himself apparently at the mercy of Saul – in *prison* (v. 7). In this dire strait he calls on God again; the title indicates it is chiefly *a prayer*.

Although short and one of the less well-known psalms, David clearly saw it as containing an important message and called it a *Maskil* (see on 54).

Verses 1-2: His Plea
The urgency of his prayer is seen in the balance and repetition in verse 1, which is not brought out by NIV, but reads literally:

with my voice to the LORD *I will cry, with my voice to the* LORD *I will supplicate*. The word translated *complaint* lacks the petulance and self-righteousness it denotes in our usage and simply refers to the troubled thoughts this latest crisis was producing in him. In fact, he has a sense of God's nearness: *before him*, and of his *mercy*, which is part of the meaning of *supplicate*.

Verses 3-4: His Plight
For his part he has given up hope (v. 3a), except in the fact that *God (knows) my way*, that is, a way by which I can escape. Certainly no one else knows; he himself seems to feel he has come to the wrong place – *the path* he has chosen into the cave has only led him into *a snare*, since he cannot get out with Saul there in the entrance. Nor is there anyone else who can help him (v. 4) – his few followers are in the same situation. The majority of his tribe and nation care nothing *for (his) life* and are not about to send a rescue party.

Verses 5-7a: His Prayer
In his *desperate need* he specifies the *cry* he began in verse 1. Neither he nor anyone else had the answer – he was shut up to God alone as his *refuge* and *portion*, meaning God is 'all I have'. So he asks for *rescue* from his pursuers and release from this place which had now become his *prison*. But his closeness to God keeps him from thinking only of his own safety and comfort. Indeed he probably blames himself for getting into this situation; therefore if he gets out of it God will receive the praise (v. 7a).

Verse 7b: His Prospect
Since he is God's chosen leader, God's glory is tied up with his own future. It is in the light of this that we must understand his vision of himself here - surrounded, no longer by enemies, but by *the righteous*, since this will be due to God's *goodness*. Indeed there may be a glimpse of his future coronation here, for *gather about* comes from the same root as 'crown'. As so often in the psalms, a desperate cry for help ends up in a mood of glorious hope.

Questions:
(1) Since our enemies are more spiritual ones, like temptation, can you see here an illustration of 1 Corinthians 10:13?

(2) How is this incident a good example of God answering prayer 'above all we ask or think' (Eph. 3:20)?

Psalm 143

The Struggle to Stay Confident

That this psalm comes from the same occasion as 140 is evident from its general tone: David is crying to God to save him from his enemies who are out to kill him (v. 3); and it has a similar progression of thought – from virtual despair (v. 4) to confidence that God's nature as righteous, faithful and loving means he will certainly take up David's cause (vv. 11-12).

However, we should take into account the fact that, having reached the assurance of 140:12-13, he is now back in the depths of despair. Evidently he is finding it difficult to sustain that level of confidence. But is that not something we all find – even we who have the knowledge of Christ and the ministry of his Spirit? We shall take this up in the **Question** section, but we shall also find, as we work through the psalm, that through this experience David is led to seek God for himself not just for his ability to get him out of trouble (v. 6).

Verses 1-3: David complains about his situation

In spite of the confidence he expressed at the end of 140 that God would deliver him, he continues to be in great danger (v. 3). This time he speaks in the singular: *the enemy*, referring to Saul, for he knows that if Saul were stopped, his men would call off the chase. As it is, he feels he is as good as *dead*: phrases

like *the ground ... darkness ... long dead* describe his present state
in hiding as a living death, and even that will not continue
indefinitely. Worse, he feels God is not even answering his
cries and he must plead with him to *hear ... listen* (v. 1). Perhaps
he has been praying wrongly? So he puts the emphasis on
God's *faithfulness and righteousness* and disclaims any right to
his consideration; indeed quite the reverse – *judgment* is what
he could expect if God were to deal with him in strict justice
(v. 2).

Verses 4-6: David reacts to his situation

He has completely lost heart and is near total despair (v. 4).
Then a chink of light appears in the thought of what God has
done before (v. 5). *The days of long ago* does not imply that
the psalm comes from late in his life; he is referring to the
stories of God delivering his servants in past days, stories
that may have been in the process of composition at that very
time, perhaps by Samuel with whom he was staying. Maybe
Samuel himself was encouraging David with these tales?
Whatever the cause, a change comes into his approach from
this point: he is thinking less of the nearness of his enemies
than of his distance from God. So now he begins to seek the
Lord **for himself**, not for what he can do for him (v. 6). The
music observes a pause for meditation on this: *SELAH*.

Verses 7-9: David prays for immediate deliverance

His change of tack in verses 5-6 does not mean he is no longer
bothered by his danger. What it does is to give him a new
confidence in his prayer. So much so that he is emboldened
to ask for it to happen *quickly* (v. 7) Moreover he sees it as the
personal act of a loving Lord, and from him he could expect
a *word* that he was safe, and that as soon as *the morning*. This
would come not from a human messenger but from the mouth
of God himself, a message that spoke of *your unfailing love*
(v. 8). His dependence is now total – he is not making plans
for the future but looking to God to *show me the way I should
go*. His plea for *rescue* is therefore based on his new-found
relationship with God (v. 9).

Verses 10-12: David prays for his future career

Now that he is assured of rescue he is able to look ahead to his future life. He rededicates himself to God's *will* and therefore prays for his *good Spirit* (how full of warmth is that expression!) to *lead* him, so that he may have a less turbulent existence (v. 10). In this spirit he returns to his immediate situation and prays again for it to end, but now he pleads God's *name* ... *righteousness* (v. 11) and *unfailing love* and presents his petition as his *servant* (v. 12)

Questions:

Why do we (Christians) find it difficult to sustain our confidence in God?

(1) Is it because this confidence soon becomes self-confidence or over-confidence? (See Matt. 14:25-31.)

(2) Or is it because God is reminding us that we are still sinners dependent on his grace alone? (See v. 2; cf. Ps. 130:3.)

(3) Or is it to encourage us to desire God for himself alone? (See v. 6; Luke 10:20.)

Psalm 144

War and Peace

David is here celebrating victory in battle: victory as *King*, (v. 10), and victory over *foreigners*, (v. 11). Quite likely the enemies here were the Philistines, against whom David fought a number of wars.

Verses 1-4: God has trained David for war
If David had any skill in battle it had come from God's training and proved his faithfulness (*my Rock*) and love (*my loving God*), which expression is one word, CHASDI, literally 'my steadfast love', the OT precursor to the great NT truth that 'God is love' (1 John 4:16). That this does not make God a 'soft touch' is clear from the warrior language applied to him here: *fortress ... stronghold ... shield*. God does not start wars, but if they happen he will come in on the side of the righteous. But David is not presuming on this: even the righteous *man is like a breath ... a fleeting shadow*. Why should God bother to *care for him* or even *think of him*? David had this thought while minding his sheep under the canopy of the stars (Ps. 8:3-4). A very different experience here raises the same question: why should a holy God fight for sinful man?

The answer lies in the next section.

Verses 5-8: David needs God to fight for him
Because God has trained him to fight, this does not mean he can do so on his own. The God who had intervened miraculously

will be needed again soon for the victory over the Philistines did not end the war, since other nations were involved in it: (83:5-8). But with the assurance that God was on his side (vv. 1-2) even though he is unworthy of this, David can call on him to 'bring out his big guns' against this conspiracy. He had already sent his angelic army; now let him employ the forces of nature which were at his disposal in order to rescue David and his people *from the hands of foreigners*. For they were 'foreign', not merely to Israel but to God, since they worship other gods. If it is asked 'why did not David make peace with them?' the answer is that he could not trust them to keep the terms of any agreement. For those who worship 'lies' (Isa. 44:20; Rom. 1:25) will be liars in their thoughts and words (v. 8). While this does not mean that unbelievers never speak the truth, it does mean they are likely to lie if it suits them. Truth is not just a matter of verbal accuracy but knowing him who is the Truth (Rom. 1:25; John 14:6). Truth begins 'in the inner parts' (Ps. 51:6)

Verses 9-11: David's feelings fluctuate
These verses reflect the fluctuating fortunes of Israel at this time. At one moment they are singing victory songs (vv. 9-10), and next moment they are crying to God to rescue them from a renewed attack (v. 11). Verse 9 is a virtual repeat of 33:2-3, uttered on their previous victory over the Philistines. A new victory deserves a new song! The church cannot simply go on singing the same old hymns for ever: new blessings call for new songs to keep worship fresh. The great revivals of the church always lead to a fresh outburst of hymn composition. But the grounds of the appeal of verse 11 are the same as before: their enemies are *foreigners* whose words cannot be trusted.

Verses 12-15: David's vision of peace
But the main ground for calling on God for victory is so that they might do his will and enjoy his promises. So David paints a picture of life in the land, which exactly matches what God had promised when he entered into covenant with them: see Deuteronomy 28:3-8. It was this for which David was fighting

and praying, not his personal prestige nor an expanding empire. Under a Philistine yoke they would know none of these things. Above all, they would not enjoy the supreme blessing of being a *people whose God is the Lord* (v. 15).

Towards the end of his life David looked back over his many battles and their ensuing victories when he wrote 18. In that psalm he re-used a number of phrases that he first composed for this psalm, for example: Psalm 18, verses 2, 9-14, 30-35. Verbs in the imperative in 144 (because they are prayers) are used in the past tense in 18 (because they are thanksgivings). What a blessed life it is when we can say 'Do this for us, Lord' and later 'You have done it'!

Questions:
(1) What do you think of the 'versicle and response' in the Book of Common Prayer which goes 'Give peace in our time, O Lord ... Because there is none other that fighteth for us but only thou, O God'? Should it (or some similar form of words) still be used in the church?

(2) How do verses 9-11 apply to the 'up and down' experiences of Christians? (See Gal. 5:16-17 and in Rom. 8 compare v. 36 with v. 37.)

(3) What does 'the peace of God' mean under the new covenant? (See Phil. 4:6-7.)

Psalm 145

How to Praise God

David is so full of praise here that the psalm carries an
unusual title: *praise of David*, a term not used in any other
title. See also verse 21. David certainly 'pulls out all the stops'
here, both in the extravagant language he uses of God and his
appeal to all creatures to join in the praise. This arises from
his exalted view of God as universal King and Provider of all
his creatures.

Like 111 and 112 this is an 'acrostic' psalm (see introduction
to 111). In most Hebrew manuscripts a verse beginning with
NUN ('N') is wanting, However, one Hebrew manuscript, the
Greek and Syriac versions and the Dead Sea Scrolls contain
such a verse and place it between verses 13 and 14, where it
appears in the NIV. Some do not accept its authenticity since it
has a strong resemblance to verse 17; they think the genuine
verse is either lost or was never written. As we shall see,
however, it fits well into the train of thought.

Verses 1-2: Exuberant praise
David is summoning up all the terms and phrases he can think
of to express his feelings about *God*: terms like *exalt ... praise*
(or 'bless') twice ... *extol*. So important is it for him to praise
God that he makes it a firm resolution: *I will* three times. This
is his chief concern in life, both in the long term: *for ever and*

ever (twice) and the short: *every day*. David's God is so great in his eyes that he alone deserves the title *King;* before him David is just an ordinary subject.

Verses 3-7: Reasonable praise

This is not fanaticism or emotionalism; there are solid reasons for it. God is *most worthy of praise* because he is not just *great* in the way some people are called 'great', but in a manner far beyond this: *his greatness no one can fathom* (v. 3). So it is not enough for David and those gathered at the feast to acknowledge him, his *greatness* must be proclaimed in every *generation*. Therefore the rising *generation* must be told of his *works and mighty acts* (v. 4).

To drive this home David uses some colourful language: God's *majesty (is) glorious* and his *works (are) wonderful* (v. 5); their *power (is) awesome* and his *deeds (are) great* (v. 6). They tell of a God of *abundant goodness* combined with *righteousness* (v. 7). There is a lovely poetic balance in verses 5-6 between what *they* (other generations) do and what David himself (*I*) does: *they will speak* and *I will meditate; they will tell* and *I will proclaim*. This is not to be pressed to make a rigid division of labour; it is a purely poetic way of expressing what God deserves from all.

Verses 8-13a: Universal praise

This section develops logically from the previous one. Why this insistence on everyone 'telling' everyone of the works of God? Because he is everyone's Sovereign and everyone's Provider. This is based on his character as *gracious and compassionate, slow to anger and rich in love*. This was how he described himself to Moses in answer to his request to 'see his glory' (Exod. 34:6). God was indeed angry at the time and had good reason to be, for those who had confronted him in his awesome majesty at Sinai and had sworn they would 'have no other gods but' him were now worshipping a golden calf! But as David sang in 103 when he used similar phraseology, 'he will not harbour his anger for ever' (103:8-16).

So while 'his wrath is being revealed from heaven against all the godlessness and wickedness of men' (Rom. 1:18), there is still compassion underlying it. Indeed there is love in wrath itself, for part of the office of love is to destroy all that harms the beloved. Ultimately this is revealed in the provision of his Son to redeem from evil (John 3:16). But here it is experienced in his universal rule or kingdom (v. 11). So the word he spoke to Moses about that generation of Israel is now extended: *the LORD is good to all, he has compassion on all he has made* (v. 9). Gentiles and Israelites alike acknowledge it (vv. 10-13). This might appear 'over the top', yet the greatest potentate of his day, Nebuchadnezzar of Babylon, came to utter these same words in Daniel 4:34! Nor is that a one-off: Daniel's visions and prophecies speak of a succession of empires rising and falling while the 'kingdom the God of heaven will set up ... will never be destroyed'.

Verses 13b-16: Thankful praise

The thought is developed further here. Not all sovereigns care for their subjects; many exploit them to satisfy their own pride and greed. God uses his sovereignty differently. To start with he bore their needs in mind when he created them and gave specific *promises* to this effect. Because *he is loving towards all he has made, the LORD is faithful to all his promises* (v. 13b). He has a particular concern for the unfortunate (v. 14), with whom most cannot be bothered because they are too busy looking after themselves.

But he neglects none. He knows they depend on him, that *the eyes of all look to you* for their *food* (v. 15). He is not tight-fisted with what he has made but *opens (his) hand (to) satisfy the desires of every living thing* (v. 16). In saying all this David is really giving God thanks for it on behalf of all creatures.

Verses 17-20: Special praise

Because God is universal King and benefactor, this does not mean there is no distinction between believers and unbelievers, between those who worship him and those who do not. While everything he does is just and fair, done in love to *all he has made* (v. 17), he has special favours for those who *call upon him in truth* (v. 18). These are the ones who consciously praise him and earnestly *cry* to him when in trouble, because they *fear* him - they stand in awe of his majesty and admire his greatness and goodness. He *hears their cry, fulfils their desires (and) saves them* from their troubles (v. 19). This *fear* does not mean they see him as distant and unapproachable, for he is *near* them (v. 18), so that they feel a *love (for) him*. Nor does he disregard this affectionate trust, but *watches over* them (v. 20). But *the wicked*, who ignore him in favour of some other deity or none at all, and therefore live as if they were accountable to none, *he will destroy*, if not sooner, then later. Nor is this inconsistent with his love, indeed it is an expression of it, for their wickedness causes pain to those who love him and are objects of his special care.

Verse 21: Total praise
David returns to his own personal praise, with which he began (v. 1) and in so doing sums up the psalm and its two aims: that the *mouth* of David himself should *speak in praise of the LORD*, for as king he must be an example to God's people; so that the whole creation over which God rules and for which he provides should *praise his name for ever*.

Questions:
(1) Is it right to use the term 'great' of any other than God? If so, in what sense? (Gen. 48:19; 2 Kings 5:1; Job 32:9 (NIV mg); Eccles. 2:9; 9:14; Dan. 2:48; Luke 1:15; 22:24-30.

   (2) Can you prove the truth of verse 13a from history and the present-day world?

   (3) Are you clear on the distinction between God's general and particular love? (For his general love see Matt. 5:43-45; John 3:16 and for his particular love see Eph. 2:4-9.)

Psalm 146

Better than Princes

This is the first of five psalms beginning *praise the Lord* or 'Hallelujah', which have been placed together, irrespective of their date of composition, to bring the Psalter to a rousing conclusion.

Verses 1-2: A call to praise
Many see a liturgical structure here, with the priest calling for *praise* (v. 1a), and each individual responding (vv. 1b-2), though some place verses 1b-2 in the mouth of a precentor responding on behalf of the congregation.

Be that as it may, the response goes beyond the call, for he vows to *praise the Lord*, not just on this occasion, but *all my life*. This is so sincerely meant that it is repeated in verse 2 line 2. The words were the inspiration for Isaac Watts' great hymn 'I'll praise my Maker while I've breath'. He too saw something of a revival in the cause of Christ which gave him great hope for the future of his church. The psalmist here also sees this new spirit of praise as a sign of good times to come. So he expected the rest of his life to be one of praise and no longer of lamentation, as in 102.

Verses 3-4: A warning against trusting rulers
It is possible that the priest or Levite leading the service takes over again here. Observing the people's euphoria, he is

concerned lest they expect too much from *princes* and begin to *put (their) trust in* them. If this psalm dates from the return from exile, King Darius may have taken their part on this occasion, but he was not a man of God and could easily turn against them if he thought it advantageous. His motive for giving permission to build the temple may have come from the discovery of the decree of Cyrus (Ezra 1:2) which, like all the laws of the Medes and Persians, 'cannot be repealed' (Dan. 6:8).

There may also have been a reference here to their own monarchy. This they were not permitted to re-establish on their return to the land; in fact they were a subject people for much of the rest of their history. If that was making them concerned for their welfare, they should not let it, for *princes* were only *mortal men who cannot save.* How often their kings had led them to disaster! Even the best ones had found themselves cornered and had to cry to God to come to their rescue. There was the occasional exceptional reign when all went well, but being *mortal men* they die, *their spirit departs (and) they return to the ground.* These words echo the judgment on sinful Adam (Gen. 3:19); however high their position or great their strength and talents, they are still *men* who have come from *the ground* and will return to it. They cannot continue *their plans* from the grave and unless their successor takes them up they come to nothing.

Verses 5-10: A commendation of God's reign
In contrast to their own past kings and present foreign overlords, their true King, *the LORD, reigns for ever* (v. 10). That is not his only difference from human rulers; look what he does: all that princes are supposed to do but frequently neglect. His rule brings *help,* so that those under it are *blessed* and can have *hope* (v. 5). For he who is their God, *the God of Jacob* and of all his descendants, is also *the Maker of heaven and earth and everything in them.* He has a power shared by none – creator power. Moreover, as *the LORD* he has covenanted to use that power for the good of *Jacob,* and he *remains faithful* to that promise *for ever* (v. 6).

Look at his track record. They had been *oppressed* for their faith in God, but he *upheld their cause* (v. 7). They had been *hungry*, especially in recent times when their harvests had failed (Hag. 1:10-11), but he had given (them) *food*. They had been *prisoners* in Babylon, but he had set them *free*. How literally we should take *the* LORD *gives sight to the blind* (v. 8) is not clear; certainly in a mental sense they had not been able to see their way ahead – not only in Babylon but in the years since they had returned. There is also a hint here of the forthcoming ministry of Christ, as predicted by Isaiah (35:5; cf. Matt. 11:5); his healing of the blind was a sign that he had come to reveal God to those blinded by the lies of Satan (John 9).

We can see the next clauses in a similar way: his support for those *bowed down* by their burdens, and his *love* for the *righteous*. This general statement is particularised in verse 9 where those *righteous* ones who have no human helper are taken into his special care: *the alien ... the fatherless and the widow*. If *the wicked* try to exploit their weakness he *frustrates (their) ways*. All these are the duties of human rulers, but they rarely pay much attention to them.

Such a God, who does this, not spasmodically but *for ever ... through all generations* (v. 10), deserves life-long *praise*. Thus does the second part of the psalm give inspiration for fulfilling the opening vow (v. 2).

Questions:
(1) Comparing this psalm with 102, how does the spirit of praise under the gospel exceed that under the law? (See Phil. 4:4-7; 1 Thess. 5:16-18.)

(2) Instead of 'trusting' governments, what should Christians do? (See Rom. 13:1-7; 1 Tim. 2:1-2.)

(3) What evidence is there in the world today that God is still working on the lines of verses 7-9? Would you include 'the Welfare State' in this?

Psalm 147

Praise is Good and Pleasant

Verse 2 would seem to place this psalm after the return from Babylon, when God had *gathered the exiles of Israel* back to their land and was enabling them to rebuild the walls of Jerusalem. The reference to God as the creator (v. 6) and provider of his people may indicate that a harvest feast was being celebrated.

Verses 1-6: Thanks for this latest blessing

After the characteristic opening 'Hallelujah' (*Praise the* LORD), they express sheer delight in the act of singing *praises to our God* (v. 1). *Good ... and pleasant* or 'lovely and beautiful' are terms we tend to use of created things or works of man. The Bible reserves them for spiritual acts (29:2; 92:1; 135:3).

There is particular cause to *praise him* at this time because of all that has happened to bring them to what they were that day (vv. 2-3). God has gathered *the exiles* from captivity, he has built up *Jerusalem*: the temple, the houses and the walls, and now he has comforted them in their sorrow, not just over their sufferings, but over the sins that caused them.

But he is mostly to be praised for what he is in himself: *great ... and mighty in power* (v. 5). So *great* is he that he knows how many *stars* there are (v. 4). For he put them there and has a place for *each* one, in fact he gives *each* one a *name*. But he knows more than that – *his understanding has no limit.* There is word-play here, for *limit* is the same word as *number.* The *number* of the stars is still unknown by us, but there is a number and it is finite. This is not true of God's wisdom, which is infinite. This may also recall the promise to Abraham to make Israel as numerous as the stars (Gen. 15:5), giving this generation hope that their present small numbers would increase.

Yet this *great* God bothers with human beings, however *humble* (v. 6). In fact it is such he particularly favours, whereas *the wicked*, however powerful, famous or rich, *he casts ... to the ground.* It was no doubt with such sentiments that Nehemiah and the Levites had comforted the people after Ezra's reading of the Law. The Law (TORAH) is more than laws; it contains promises too. Had not Isaiah prophesied that these very things would come true after their return from captivity (Isa. 40:1-2; 61:1-6)? These passages may have formed the basis for this psalm.

Verses 7-11: Thanksgiving for his general care
There is more about which to *sing to the Lord* and for which to offer *thanksgiving*, with *music* and *on the harp* (v. 7). The greatness of God is not only visible by night in the stars, but by day in his other works: *the clouds* which bring *rain* which *makes grass grow* (v. 8), providing *food for the cattle* on the ground and *the ... ravens* in the air (v. 9). Even the *young* ones are in his care.

Verse 10 does not mean God takes no *pleasure ... in the strength of a horse* or no *delight in the legs of a man*, that is, in his power, since it was he who gave it them. Verse 11 clarifies the meaning: he *delights* more in their response to him and *his unfailing love.* Strength is something in which God far excels all, but attitudes like *fear*, that is, awe and reverence, along with *hope*, which accompanies trust, are unique to man. This is the response he is looking for, for the Hebrew word for *sing* in verse 7 is literally 'answer'. We cannot truly sing his praises and offer true *thanksgiving* without a vision concerning who he is and what he does.

Verses 12-20: Thanks for his mighty word

Here the response of *praise* and thanks reaches its climax (v. 12). He is calling on the people of *Jerusalem* in particular to *extol the Lord* because of the way they have experienced his great power and unfailing love. He has re-erected their defences, *the bars of (their) gates* (v. 13). True, Nehemiah organised the work and the people did it, but it was God who had rebuked and encouraged them when they were lazy. Moreover, it was he who put it into the heart of Cyrus to set them free, that of Darius to permit the rebuilding of the temple and that of Artaxerxes to sanction the re-erection of the walls. It was he too who kept their enemies at bay while they did the work. So now they were enjoying *peace* within their *borders* and plenty of nourishing food (v. 14), which was itself a change from the days when all lay in ruins and the fields were barren.

What is implied in verses 12-14 is explicit in verses 15-18 – that God does all this by his *word of command* (v. 15). God controls the elements so that they can change rapidly from those adverse conditions of *snow ... frost ... hail ... icy* blasts of wind, to gentle *breezes,* causing a thaw so that the *snow* melts and *the waters flow* again. That same God is the one who has changed the fortunes of his people, who are no longer enduring the *icy blast* of his disfavour but are now experiencing the soft warm *breezes* of his love.

But God's word does more than command, it communicates. All alike experience his power and goodness in creation and providence, but *he has revealed his word to Jacob* alone, and *his laws and decrees to Israel* and to *no other nation* (v. 19). The rest *do not know his laws* (vv. 19-20). We are back in Psalm 19 and David's early life, to the gift of God's two books: the book of nature and the book of revelation, or as Francis Bacon called them, 'the book of the world and the book of the word'. Through the word we can personally know this God of infinite might who exercises it in powerful providences and gracious works of love.

Questions:
(1) Do you find your devotional times and church services beautiful and satisfying, as David did (103:1) and Mary did (Luke 1:46)? If not what should you do? (See Eph. 5:18-19.)

(2) Does it ever occur to you that when we enjoy our times of worshipping God, he does too? (See John 4:24.)

(3) Does your use of God's word match the great privilege of being selected to know it (vv. 19-20)? Does your trust in it give you an expectation of the mighty things he can do through it (vv. 15-18)? (See Heb. 4:12.)

Psalm 148

Praise from Heaven and Earth

These closing psalms of praise are working up to a great climax in order to bring the whole collection to a close on a high note. Psalm 148 sets out the themes for the praise of God and 150 describes the musical accompaniment. The opening 'Hallelujah' (*Praise the* LORD) is addressed to God's whole creation – heavenly (vv. 1-6) and earthly (7-12).

Verses 1-6: The Praise of the Heavens
Everything in the heights above is called on to *praise the* LORD (v. 1).

(1) *His angels*, the inhabitants of his own abode, created first and sharing his spiritual nature and holiness, who together form the armies of God, *his heavenly hosts*. The Gentiles worshipped these, but his people are to emulate the angels and worship God (103:20).

(2) The occupants of space, which can be observed from earth: *sun, moon ... shining stars*. Whereas the Gentiles worshipped these too or looked on them as governors of their destinies, his people are to see them as created objects like themselves, which exist for his *praise*.

(3) The clouds above, *you waters above the skies* (v. 4). What applies to the *highest heavens*, where God and his angels dwell, applies equally to the rain clouds.

Though separated by distance and composition, all are to unite to *praise the name of the LORD* (v. 5) because of the way they came into existence, *created* by the command of God (cf. Ps. 33:9). Although he made so many bodies, he did not leave them to wander haphazardly around but *set them in place* (v. 6). There they must remain *for ever and ever* because the same word that created them governs them continually. The expressions *ever and ever and never* are clearly limited to the duration of the universe and do not mean these creatures are eternal.

If we wonder how inanimate objects can praise God as well as living beings, the answer is that things do not have to be alive and conscious to glorify God. Their creation from nothing, their size and number, the fact that they inspire **us** to praise, all mean that they have a part in the universal worship of God.

Verses 7-12: The Praise of the earth

The first line here: *Praise the LORD from the earth*, is echoing the opening words: *Praise the LORD from the heavens* (cf. Hos. 2:21-22). This reflects the harmony and unity of God's original creation, which, although it has broken down through sin, will be recovered through Christ (Eph. 1:10).

The pattern of this passage is the opposite of the first in that it begins at the bottom of the scale with *the sea creatures* in the *ocean depths* (v. 7). Then it moves on to the variations in the climate (v. 8), then to the dry land, *the mountains and hills* (v. 9) ... next to what grows on them: *fruit trees and cedars*, then their living occupants (v. 10). From here it moves up the scale of being to humanity, taking in first the 'great' of the earth (v. 11) and then the rest of us, classified by age and sex (v. 12).

Since all alike (even though all are not alike) are objects of God's creation and under his control, they all have a duty to *praise the name of the LORD* (v. 13). As with the inhabitants of the heavens, so with those of the earth, they fulfill this duty in accordance with their nature – some unconsciously because they lack consciousness, others, that is, humans, consciously. The cosmos finds its unity in *the name* of the one Creator whose *splendour is above the earth and the heavens*. Thus, while much of this psalm may represent Old Testament cosmology, the basic thought is still true, and is the opposite of the cosmology that sees the universe coming into being spontaneously and in a random way.

At the top of the scale of worshippers here are *his people* whom he *raised up*, at that time called *Israel*, whom he chose and who were therefore *close to his heart* (v. 14). It is unclear to what *a horn* applies. Some say it is the Davidic king, but that succession ended with the exile and was never renewed. Others therefore apply it to the Messiah, who would be their Strength, their King and their Deliverer. Yet others take *the praise of all his saints* as being in apposition to *a horn* and say the strength of God's people lies in their worship.

This psalm probably inspired 'The Song of the Three Children (or Servants)' in the Apocrypha, sometimes attached to Daniel 3 as being what the three young friends of Daniel were thought to have sung in the fiery furnace.

Questions:

(1) Does this psalm enlarge your idea of what it means for Christians and the church to be God's 'priests'? (See 1 Pet. 2:9; Rev. 1:5-6.)

(2) Does it make you feel more at one with the whole of God's creation?

(3) Turn to Romans 8:18-25 and see how the creation is united in another way. From there go to Ephesians 1:10 to see how this damage is repaired.

Psalm 149

Praising the God of Judgment

The reference to praising God and wielding a sword at the same time (v. 6) may be a hint that this psalm was composed in connection with the rebuilding of Jerusalem's walls, when they had to be on guard against their enemies even as they built (Neh. 4:7-23). The dominant note is their glorying in God as their great warrior-king.

Verses 1-5: A call to praise
After the opening *Praise the Lord!* or 'Hallelujah' which commences all these late psalms, they are exhorted to *sing a new song* (v. 1). They were enjoying fresh blessings, and fresh blessings call for fresh songs. The walls of Jerusalem were not only important practically for defence, but symbolised the protection of God (Zech. 2:5). The *new song* both here and in 96, includes the note of judgment, later taken up in Rev. 5:9; 14:3. God not only cares for his people but destroys their enemies. This they were celebrating by coming together in an *assembly*.

The chief reason to *rejoice* is that the Lord who is the *Maker* of his people is still *their King*, who has asserted himself over their hostile neighbours and even over the Persian monarch who had been moved to release them and encourage their rebuilding programme. That this was regarded as a great victory is seen in the enthusiastic celebration with *dancing* to the *music* of *tambourine and harp* (v. 3), as they had at the Red Sea (Exod. 15:11), the defeat of Ammon by Jephthah (Judg. 11:34) and the slaughter of Goliath (1 Sam. 18:6).

The Lord had revived his people (Ezra 9:8), raised them from the dead (Ezek. 37:12-14) and proved that he *takes delight in his people* (v. 4), in spite of their frequent sinful failures, for they had humbled themselves for their sins and were now enjoying his *salvation* in a fresh way. God had restored their *honour* in the sight of others (v. 5), so they had everything to *rejoice* in and to *sing for joy*. The reference to *their beds* or 'couches' conjures up a picture of an open air gathering at the wall where they were working, only breaking off for a while for a time of praise. Nehemiah had set up a shift system in which some went on working while others rested.

Verses 6-9: A prayer for judgment
The sudden transition from praising to cursing has created problems, especially as the two are juxtaposed in verse 6. Some have gloried in this and gone to war singing it, as in the Peasants' War of the sixteenth century, the Thirty Years' War of the seventeenth century and Parliament's punitive expedition against the Irish at the end of the Civil War. Some have explained it from the famous 'sword and trowel' passage in Nehemiah 4:16-18. While the wall was in ruins they were exposed to their enemies, so they had to work with an armed guard and even a weapon to hand.

However, verses 7-9 seem to go beyond self-defence to seeing themselves as carrying out the judgment of God *on the nations* (v. 7), as Joshua had on the Amorites, Saul on the Amalekites and David on the Ammonites and others, when *kings* were captured and slain (v. 8). This was God's declared will (v. 9), and it was a privilege, even a *glory*, to be chosen as God's instrument of judgment.

This scarcely fits the post-exilic situation when the Jews had no standing army, military leader or king. Nor is there any evidence that they did such things. During this period God was preparing them for a different, more spiritual approach to his and their enemies, when the Word would take the place of the sword (Zech. 9:9-10). The dancing here may be a kind of 'sabre dance' which gives God the glory of defeating his enemies in his own way and time. What he had done down the ages and most recently in the overthrow of the Babylonians he would do fully and finally when he came to 'judge the earth'. *Praise the LORD!*

Question:
What does this psalm teach us about:
   (1) Christian work? (See 1 Cor. 9:6-12; 2 Cor. 6:1; Gal. 6:9; 1 Thess. 5:12; 1 Tim. 5:17; Rev. 2:2.)
   (2) Christian warfare? (See 2 Cor. 10:3-5; Eph. 6:10-18; 1 Tim. 6:12; 2 Tim. 2:3; 4:7; Jude 3; Rev. 12:17.)

Psalm 150

Praise from the Highest to the Lowest

This psalm gathers up all that concerns the praise of God, all the themes that have combined to make up this great collection of songs. Thus it transcends a particular period of time and involves us all, forming a fitting conclusion to the whole collection. No others were to be added; as the spirit of prophecy ceased with the preaching of Malachi around this time, so the spirit of inspired psalmic composition ceased with the dedication of the walls of Jerusalem. The collection was large enough.

Verse 1: WHERE God is to be praised
After the characteristic 'Hallelujah' or *Praise the* LORD the psalm calls on the entire cosmos to praise God – from his Temple or *sanctuary* on earth to his abode in *the mighty heavens*, encompassing everything that comes between. What chiefly unites the parts of creation is the praise of the One who made it all at the beginning of time.

Verse 2: WHY God is to be praised
There must be a good motive for making the praise of God the chief occupation of all things. Here it is. First, *what he has done* and does, *his acts of power* which are unique, for he alone created, he alone sustains and rules, he alone judges and he

alone saves. Where even the mightiest of creatures fail he triumphs. Second, *who he is in himself – his surpassing greatness.* The claim to mighty *acts of power* is no idle one, for he is God, the being who transcends all others. What other conclusion can be drawn from those great acts?

Verses 3-5: HOW God is to be praised

In a word, with everything available. Reference is made to the chief musical instruments in use at that time. Other psalms use one or two of them: in the great festivals one or two are prominent, as *the trumpet* was in the year of jubilee and *the tambourine (and) dancing* in times of victory. Leupold thinks that 'as each instrument is named, it set in and joined the chorus of praise'. Possibly each had a solo passage and was then added to the whole, producing a crescendo effect, as in Benjamin Britten's 'Young Person's Guide to the Orchestra'.

For its time it must have been a most impressive and moving sound, but we must not forget that it was not a concert to entertain the people but an act of *praise* to God; every instrument is told to *praise him.* Music is a gift of God with an early origin (Gen. 4:21), given not only to bring us pleasure but to delight God, for it involves our whole being: mind, mouth, heart and even body when accompanied by *dancing.*

Verse 6: BY WHOM God is to be praised

Not everyone can play an instrument or dance, but all have a voice, *everything ... has breath* and should use it to *praise the* Lord. This extends the call from the people of Israel who are clearly in view in verses 3-5 to all people, and from all people to all living creatures. Psalm 148 includes them all and even extends its scope to the inanimate world. This was how things had been at the beginning, when everything functioned as it was intended to, and brought joy to its Creator. This is what the witness of God's people, both Israel of old and the Church now, is seeking to bring about universally. The twelve occurrences of the word *praise* ('Hallel') after the opening 'Hallelujah' may reflect the unity of the tribes of Israel and the whole Church in the praise of God. This is what will come to pass at the end, as John saw in his vision:

'Then I heard every creature in heaven and on earth and under the earth and on the sea, and all that is in them, singing: "To him who sits on the throne and to the Lamb be praise and honour and glory and power, for ever and ever!" ... AMEN' (Rev. 5:13-14).

APPENDIX

THE CHRONOLOGY OF THE PSALMS

Each psalm must have been written by an historical person at a particular time and in connection with a specific occasion. Many psalms have 'titles' which attribute a psalm to a certain author and some describe what occasioned it. In the case of those which do not do this, clues can be found within the psalm as to who wrote it and what prompted him, though this cannot be finally proved. Putting them all together enables us to place the psalms in roughly historical order.

The **value** of this approach is:

1. it makes working through this longest of all the books of the Bible more interesting, as it follows the story which underlies the Old Testament;
2. it helps our understanding of the Psalms, in the same way as knowing something of the authorship and background of the New Testament letters assists us in understanding the message of their authors;
3. it guides us in applying them to our personal lives and the condition of our Church and churches, since the situations which prompted the Psalms, both individual and corporate, recur continually. This will make them of greater spiritual and practical benefit.

It has to be acknowledged that many of the psalms, even some which attribute authorship to a particular person, do not tell us the occasion on which they were composed, nor do they appear in chronological order in our Bibles. This may seem to discourage this approach. However, there are reasons for the Bible's arrangement of the psalms which help us understand why they are not presented chronologically.

(1) They cover a period of about a thousand years, from the time of Moses to that of Ezra. Biblical writers were not so interested in historical order as we are, and in any case the editors may have assumed that the readers, or at least their teachers, were familiar with what occasioned each psalm.

(2) According to the first century Jewish historian Josephus, the psalms were collected together at various times by such as David, Jehoshaphat, Hezekiah and Ezra. These collections may well have been in chronological order, although there is no record of this.

(3) Their present arrangement was made by Jewish scholars before the time of Christ, who arranged the Psalms into five books, each of which is rounded off by a doxology: Psalms 41:13; 72:19; 89:52; 106:48; and 150 (the whole of which is a doxology and thus rounds off the whole collection).

It is impossible to be certain what prompted these scholars to make their arrangement. No doubt it was partly determined by how much they could get on to one scroll, as is the case with the Gospels. As for what they selected for each scroll, no doubt modern scholars would have done it differently. We are more interested in classification than they were. Quite likely they regarded each book as an anthology, in which a variety of subjects and situations could be included, so that each scroll would have a representative selection. Books, being handwritten and on expensive materials, were scarce and costly, so that a particular synagogue might only possess one scroll out of the five and would need a balance of subject matter. We have not only a complete Psalter but an entire Bible and much external information to help us see how they are put together.

Where there is classification it tends to be thematic (rather like a Hymn Book): psalms with similar themes are grouped together. For example, 93–100 exalt God in his sovereignty ('the Lord reigns'); 121–134 are the famous 'Songs of Ascents' for the use of pilgrims going up to the temple; and 73–84 are all attributed to Asaph as he struggled with the problem of the ascendancy of the wicked in his time. These are followed by a small collection from his colleagues 'the sons of Korah', Heman and Ethan.

Therefore, while it is valuable to read the psalms in their Biblical order so that we may enjoy a variety of experiences, there is much profit in seeing them against their background. As for the method of dating them, there are some which mention the authorship and occasion in the text itself, usually as a heading for the so-called 'titles' are part of the inspired text. For the remainder, they contain clues which can be related to the history of Israel as we have it in the historical books of the Bible (Genesis to Esther). Since some may fit more than one occasion, it is impossible to be dogmatic about their place in the history, and where this happens, the occasion which appears most likely has been chosen.

THE PERIOD OF MOSES
Psalm 90: The plague of poisonous snakes

The subtitle *A prayer of Moses the man of God* makes this the earliest psalm in the Psalter. It was not the only poem or song to come from his hand. The triumphal ode recorded in Exodus 15 is called 'The Song of Moses'. He wrote a further song to accompany the housing of the Book of the Law in the Ark of the Covenant (Deut. 31:30–32:44). His blessing of the tribes of Israel before his death (Deut. 33) is also in verse. There are other poetical fragments: the song they sang as they left their camp carrying the ark (Num. 14:26-45), the ode to the well at Beer (Num. 21:17-18), and the curse on Heshbon and Moab (Num. 21:26-30). Even parts of the Law itself take on a verse form (Deut. 27:14-26; 28:3-6, 16-19).

The psalm is entitled *A prayer* because it is all addressed to God. While most psalms are songs of praise, many are prayers, like this one. It was composed at a time when numbers of people were being struck dead as a judgment on their sins (vv. 5-8). Occasions when this happened include the people's complaint about their diet of manna (Num. 11:33), and their discouragement over the report of the spies (Num. 14:26-45). The one that fits best, however, is Numbers 21:4-7, when further murmuring over food provoked a plague of venomous snakes from God.

In Numbers 21:7 the people request Moses to pray for them, which he does. Psalm 90 is probably the prayer he prayed. Verses 3 and 5 refer to sudden death overtaking them; verse 7 indicates that this was a visitation on the whole nation, and verse 8 speaks of (literally) secret lustings, referring to their discontent with the manna and longing for food from Egypt (Num. 21:4-5).

It may be objected that the average life span of 70 to 80 years mentioned in verse 10 was not in force at that time. But the longevity of such as Moses, Aaron, Caleb and Joshua was exceptional and no doubt due to the nation's need of these great leaders for a long time, and in some cases it was a reward for their outstanding godliness (cf. 91:16). Most of the people must have lived less than 100 years. The probable meaning is that this average life span was brought in during the desert period and soon became universal. Later leaders such as Samuel, David and Solomon lived only 60 to 70 years.

Psalm 91: Healing from the plague

Although anonymous, there are good reasons for attributing this psalm to Moses. The Rabbis did so, although on the doubtful principle that no other author is stipulated until 101, which means that 82 to 100 are also from Moses! The Septuagint and Vulgate ascribe it to David on the occasion of his numbering the people (2 Sam. 24). The atmosphere of the psalm is, however, that of a nomadic life rather than the more settled times of David's kingdom.

The most likely occasion is the ending of the plague of venomous snakes, which occasioned 90. The spirit of murmuring had been put away and God was again leading them on their journey (Num. 21:10-15). Eventually they arrived at the well 'Beer' (Num. 21:16-18) where Moses composed an ode. There is good evidence for believing he wrote this psalm at that time:

- The spirit of murmuring had given way to the spirit of faith (vv. 1-2); Moses had prayed they would look to God as their *refuge and ... fortress* and now they were doing so.
- The memory of *the pestilence* was still vivid (vv. 3, 6) and possibly they feared its recurrence.
- They were exposed to the dangers of that area: fierce desert tribes like Amalek, Moab and Midian, who might launch raids *by night* or fire *arrows* from behind rocks *by day* (v. 5).
- They had seen *thousands* of their friends fall prey to *the plague* (v. 7).
- Other rigours of the nomadic life were continuing: *snares* and traps (v. 3), disease (v. 6), *disaster* (v. 10), boulders and rough ground (v. 12) and wild beasts (v. 13).

As well as these incidents there is the lesson Moses is trying to instil into them from their recent experience: to repent of their discontent and replace it with a spirit of confidence in God as the one who protects his people from all dangers – the note he strikes at the very outset (vv. 1-2).

THE PERIOD OF SAMUEL
Psalm 115: The victory at Mizpah

There appear to be no psalms from the period from Moses to Samuel, about 300 years. This does not mean there was no poetic or musical output during this time. *The Song of Deborah* (Judg. 5) and *The Song of Hannah* (1 Sam. 2) indicate that spiritual songs were being composed, but none qualified for use in the national liturgy. This may have been because, generally speaking, this was such a barren period that no one encouraged and promoted compositions to be used in the worship of God. The two mentioned above are both intensely personal.

Samuel, however, established colleges of prophets all over the land. These were not training colleges but societies where those with prophetic gifts could meet or even live together. Periodically they would go out to minister to the people. This ministry included music and singing (see 1 Chron. 25). Its influence was strong, as we can see from its powerful effect on Saul (1 Sam. 19:19-24).

One reason for placing 115 in the time of Samuel is that there is no reference to the monarchy, the house of David, the city of Jerusalem or its temple. If the psalm were a personal poem these facts would not be significant. However, it is clearly a great national ode: it is sung by the whole congregation (vv. 1-3) and addressed to the whole nation (vv. 9-11): the people (v. 9), the priests (v. 10) and probably the prophets (v. 11). It is quite likely that it was sung antiphonally, to give the impression of a great concourse led by a choir of priests and prophets. A great national occasion which does not refer to the throne, David, the temple and the city is unthinkable, so it must predate all these. This can only point to the time of Samuel. But precisely when?

The psalm celebrates a deliverance from calamity (v. 2) and a victory of God over idols (vv. 3-8), leading to a rededication of the nation to God (vv. 9-13) and an ascription of praise to him (vv. 14-18). The occasion that best fits this scenario is Samuel's gathering of the people at Mispah (1 Sam. 7:5-14).

It had been twenty years since the ark of the covenant had been recovered from the Philistines, but it was still at Kirjath Jearim under guard (1 Sam. 6:21–7:1). Since the Lord dwelt between the cherubim above the ark, this signified a breach between him and the people, due to their worship of Ashtaroth. So when they indicated they wanted to return to the Lord, Samuel called on them to put Ashtaroth away, which they did. But Ashtaroth was a Philistine deity, and the Philistines took this as an insult and came out against them. Samuel prayed, however, and God destroyed the Philistines with a great storm. To mark this Samuel set up a stone and called it 'Ebenezer', meaning 'Thus far the Lord has helped us'. This is the key to the psalm.

THE PERIOD OF DAVID

The majority of the psalms come from the time of David, in fact well over a hundred. Many come from the hand of David himself as the supreme poet and musician in all Scripture.

David's psalms cover the whole of his life and reign, beginning in his youth while he worked as a shepherd. Even the earliest psalms indicate that, notwithstanding his youth and lowly occupation, he was well educated. No doubt this was because Bethlehem, his home, was an important national and religious centre. The fact that it had 'elders' (1 Sam. 16:4) may indicate the existence of some kind of meeting place for worship and instruction. There may even have been a community of Levites and prophets. Since the death of Samuel's sons, Shiloh had fallen into disuse as the centre of worship, and sacrifices were offered to the Lord in the principal towns, of which Bethlehem was one (1 Sam. 16:2). This was why Samuel was able to say truthfully that he was going there to offer sacrifice (1 Sam. 16:2).

If sacrifice was offered, Levites must have been operating there, one of whose duties was the education of boys. Not only would they be taught the Hebrew language and the Law of Moses, but also music and poetry. The prophets may have helped in this, since composing songs for worship was part of their ministry (1 Chron. 25:2-5). David would be taught these skills and he quickly showed his proficiency in them. 1 Samuel 16:18 claims he had a reputation for playing the harp. The Septuagint says he made an 'organ', which then would simply mean 'pipes' played by mouth.

David used his gifts, at least at first, for purely private devotion. Being away from society most of the time, he occupied his mind with the contemplation of God and his ways. Since he had no one to whom to preach his thoughts apart from his sheep, he expressed them in poetry and music.

(1) His early pastoral life

There are six psalms from this period: 1, 26, 23, 19, 139 and 8. These cover the time prior to his anointing by Samuel, the time between that and his first visit to Saul's court, the time after his return from court up to the fight with Goliath, and his brief return home after the fight.

Psalm 1: David meditates by the river

This psalm was composed by one who was well aware of the difference between good and evil, between *the wicked* and *the righteous* and between the word of God and *the way of sinners*. He is one who has meditated on this as he has observed what was happening in the natural world. David was such a one. Although anonymous, it well fits his early life as a shepherd.

He would often sit beside *streams of water* while his sheep drank from them. He would notice the *tree planted* by the stream and see how healthy it was compared with one on dry ground struggling to keep its *leaf* from withering; he would see this as a picture of the difference between the godly and the ungodly. In the fields he would see the corn being harvested: the good ears stored and the *chaff* blown away by the *wind*. From this he would draw the lesson of God's judgment on the wicked. These impressions that he formed at an early age were with him all his life.

Psalm 26: David meditates on the Sabbath

This psalm is attributed to David and has similarities with 1, for he is still conscious of the difference between the righteous and the wicked, and still clear about which company to choose (vv. 4-5, cf. Ps. 1:1). He appears to be examining himself on this prior to going up to the *house* of God (vv. 6-8), which would be his local meeting place (see Introduction to 'The Period of David'). This would therefore probably be composed on or for the sabbath day. There and then he prays for grace to keep his resolutions (vv. 9-12).

Psalm 23: David shepherds his sheep

This psalm is ascribed to David and clearly belongs to his early pastoral life. But whereas in the two previous psalms he is resting and contemplating, here he is working. In these six verses he gives us a full picture of the shepherd's daily round: walking, resting, feeding, facing danger, celebrating and returning home.

It may be possible to date the psalm more precisely to the time of his anointing by Samuel (1 Sam. 16:1-12), alluded to in verse 5. If so, David seems to have interpreted it spiritually, not realising its political significance until later. It enlarged his view of God, who was not generally thought of as Shepherd of his people at this time, though later it was to become perhaps the most popular metaphor for him: (28:9; 74:1; 77:20; 78:52; 79:13; 80:1; 95:7; 100:3; Isa. 40:11; Jer. 23:3-4; Ezek. 34:11-21; Micah 5:4). This is probably because the Holy Spirit had Christ in view, as he himself confirmed by his discourse in John 10. Here we see David showing he was no ordinary worshipper, but a prophet too.

Psalm 19: A Noontide Meditation

In these early psalms from David's pastoral period, we see that, although shepherding was a routine task, he gained a rich and varied experience from it. This was because he brought his love for the Lord and his knowledge of his word to bear daily upon his work. Sitting by the river-side opened one line of thought (Ps. 1), spending a sabbath in public worship opened another (26), and the daily round with the sheep yet another (23). Here he is under the open sky with the sun at its zenith, for he is more conscious here of the sun than of anything else. It gives him some profitable thoughts. Later we shall see him as night comes on (139) and then under the stars (8).

Psalm 139: David meditates at nightfall

In the previous psalm David was exulting in the God who has revealed his glory in the heavens to all, but is known more intimately by those who perceive him in his Word. Towards the end he realised that this same God knows **him** and that his Word is not only a window through which to behold God, but a mirror in which to see himself as God sees him (cf. James 1:22, 25).

Now night is coming on (vv. 11-12). This happens earlier and more quickly in the Holy Land than it does here, so that a shepherd will often still be out with his flock at nightfall. But his prayer of 19:12-14 is still with him: that he will conquer the *errors* the Word has exposed – the *hidden faults* and *wilful sins* – and that he will think and speak in a way *pleasing (in the sight of the LORD)*.

Just as the noon sun had suggested one line of thinking, so the approach of darkness suggests another. God is the Lord of the night as he is of the day. As 'nothing is hid from the heat' of the sun (19:6), so nothing can be hidden from the God to whom *darkness is as light* (v. 12).

Psalm 8: David under the stars

The setting of this psalm is still the great outdoors, and best fits David's time as a shepherd, as the reference to *flocks and herds* (v. 7) indicates. This occupation frequently involved remaining outside through the night (cf. Luke 2:8) and this appears to have been the case here, for David is contemplating *the moon and stars*, as he contemplated the sun in 19. From this experience he drew some profound thoughts.

(2) David's Life at Saul's Court

David's solitary life as a shepherd was temporarily interrupted when he came to the attention of Saul's courtiers (1 Sam. 16:14-23). Saul was in a state of depression resulting from his split from Samuel and his rejection by God for his failure to trust him enough to obey his Word (1 Sam. 15). This laid him open to evil spirits, a condition for which no cure could be found. Lacking our modern drugs the ancients used the therapeutic effects of music to treat such conditions. While this did not cure the malady, it kept it under control. David's skill, both in composition and performance, had become well-known and he was summoned to sing and play for Saul. How useful would those early psalms prove now! Whether he also composed fresh ones or used those of others as well we do not know, but in any case his ministry ended abruptly with a fresh Philistine invasion (1 Sam. 17:1-3), upon which David returned to Bethlehem and his sheep (1 Sam. 17:15).

How long the war had been on before the fight with Goliath is not clear. It may have been a considerable time since, when Saul saw David, he appears not to have recognised him (1 Sam. 17:55-58). However, David was not much older when he fought Goliath (1 Sam. 17:33), so it may be that Saul's depression had made him totally unaware of David himself and only conscious of his music. Some think 1 Samuel 16:14-23 should be placed after chapter 17 since it resulted in David's appointment as armour-bearer (v. 21), who would be expected to go out to war with Saul. In any case this would not solve the problem since in 1 Samuel 16:14-20 he appears to be unknown to Saul.

Whatever the explanation, the fight with Goliath brought David back to court life on a permanent basis (1 Sam. 18:4-5). When David became the favourite, not only of Jonathan, Saul's son and heir, but also of the people, due to his success against the Philistines, Saul became jealous and used cunning stratagems to get him killed in battle. One was to offer to make him his son-in-law, first by marriage to Merab the elder daughter, then, when he changed his mind, to Michal

(1 Sam. 18:8-30). This was a great opportunity for more fame and power, but the price was a hundred Philistine foreskins. This would expose David to great danger of his life.

During this period he expressed his experiences and his feelings in the following psalms.

Psalm 35: Saul's first plot
David is conscious here of being in great danger of his life, a state of mind he would be in after Saul's attempt to kill him (1 Sam. 18:10-11). He realises this was not just a passing fit of anger but a settled determination due to jealousy.

Psalm 64: David goes into hiding
Saul's plot to have David killed at the hands of the Philistines failed and his marriage to Michal duly took place (1 Sam. 18:26-27). Her love for David brought more division into Saul's family, which increased Saul's hatred for David, a hatred compounded of fear and jealousy (1 Sam. 18:28-30). There is no greater hatred than that which is born of these two emotions. Saul's next move is for a more direct assault on David, and he enlists the whole court, particularly his son Jonathan, to participate in his plot. Apparently the depth of Jonathan's friendship with David is not known to Saul at this time and he still thinks Jonathan is loyal to him. But Jonathan's sympathies are with David and he arranges a secret meeting with him to warn him of his danger (1 Sam. 19:1-7). While Jonathan obtains more information about Saul's intentions and instructions, David goes into hiding. This psalm well expresses his thoughts and prayers at this time.

Psalm 36: David's thoughts while in hiding
While David waited in hiding, Jonathan was attempting to bring about a reconciliation between him and Saul (1 Sam. 19:4-5). This psalm well expresses the thoughts he would have expressed and the prayers he would have uttered at such a time.

Psalm 12: Saul again strikes at David
Jonathan's attempt to reconcile his father to David was successful (1 Sam. 19:4-7) , David returned to court 'and was

with him as before', probably meaning he played and sang to him (1 Sam. 19:9). But when the Philistines again came against Israel and David repulsed them (1 Sam. 19:8), Saul's jealousy was aroused afresh. His anger was now so great that even while David was playing music to him, Saul tried to murder him with his javelin. But David saw what was happening and escaped in time, going into hiding again. This experience is reflected in the near despair of the opening verses, due to the treachery of which he was victim (vv. 3-4), leading to his hope in God alone.

Psalm 59: David under siege
See the introduction to the comments in the main text.

Psalm 140: David flees to Samuel
The story of how David's deliverance from Saul's men (59) was answered through Michal is told in 1 Samuel 19:11-17. While she was covering for him with a subterfuge and delaying their pursuit of him, David was making the fairly short journey from Gibeah to Ramah to find refuge with Samuel.

Clearly he is looking not merely for physical safety but for some spiritual counsel and support, and an atmosphere in which he could give himself to prayer. This psalm and 143 are prayers he might have prayed on this occasion. Although this does not feature in the title, the close similarity of these psalms to 64, 12, 36 and 59, make it probable they belong to this period. They have similar descriptions of his enemies as liars and conspirators set on murdering him, similar cries to God for deliverance, and they end on a similar note of confidence.

Psalm 143
David is still conscious, as he was in 140, of the threat from his enemies, in fact he is even more desperate. For further information see the introduction to the comments in the main text.

Psalm 141: David waits for Jonathan
David's prayer of 140 and 143 was answered in an unexpected way. First, he and Samuel moved from the latter's house (or the

Lord's shrine) to *Naioth at Ramah* (1 Sam. 19:18). Since *Naioth* means 'dwellings', this may have been a kind of college of 'the sons of the prophets' whom Samuel led. This would explain what happened next.

Saul heard of David's whereabouts and sent his men to capture him. On reaching the college they were confronted by a group of these prophets who were 'prophesying' under Samuel's direction (vv. 19-20). Since physically they would present no obstacle to the attackers, the Spirit of God took another course. He came upon the intruders and constrained them to take part in the 'prophesying'. This did not take the form of prediction or even preaching, but rather worship, usually called 'ecstatic prophecy'. This did not bring about any change in the state of or status of Saul's men, but simply deprived them of the will to take David by force.

Saul sent two more bands of men and the same thing happened (v. 21). Finally he went himself (vv. 22-24) and the same happened to him, but even more powerfully. His ecstasy was so intense that he stripped off his outer robe and lay half-naked all night – a true case of being 'slain in the Spirit!'.

It is unlikely that David showed his face to Saul and his men at Naioth. He well knew that this ecstasy was a temporary phenomenon and that when it lifted Saul would be as before, if not worse. So he left there and met up with Jonathan again. The story of their meeting is recounted in 1 Samuel 20:1-23, the main point for our purpose being that Jonathan agreed to David's request to make a further attempt at a reconciliation with Saul. While awaiting the result of this, David hid in a field (v. 24) and this psalm reflects his meditations on that occasion.

(3) David Goes Into Exile

While David waited in the field (1 Sam. 20:24) thinking and praying on the lines of Psalm 141, Jonathan was attempting a reconciliation with Saul. Far from succeeding, it only made matters worse, and Saul even hurled his spear at his own son (vv. 25-34)! Jonathan then returned to the field and gave the prearranged signal which told David that all hope of reconciliation was at an end (vv. 35-40). An emotional farewell took place along with a pledge of friendship reaching down to their respective descendants.

Psalm 131: On the road to Nob

David was now an outlaw and his long exile occupies the remainder of Saul's life and of the first book of Samuel. It is a period during which David expressed his thoughts and feelings in many psalms. We put 131 first because it appears to relate to a journey, being called *a song of ascents* or 'Marching Song'.[1] David is travelling from Gibeah, where Saul's court was, to Nob, the abode of the high priest Ahimelech and probably of the ark too. This was the nearest city to Saul's court. Here David would have at least temporary sanctuary. The shortness of the psalm fits the shortness of the journey. It also fits its spirit. David is no longer struggling for peace – he has it. The psalm shows how he came into it.

Psalm 52: David at Nob

See the introduction to the comments in the main text.

Psalm 120: From Nob to Gath

When David realised his whereabouts would quickly become known to Saul, he left Nob, not only for his own safety but that of the priests who might be compromised by his visit. The damage had already been done, however, as he was later to discover. Meanwhile, feeling he was not safe anywhere in Israel, he crossed the border into Philistine territory, the land of Israel's enemies (1 Sam. 21:10), over whom David had been winning victories. In fact he made for Gath, which was not only the seat of the king but the home of Goliath! What were his thoughts as he walked this road? Psalm 120 is *a song of ascents* or 'Marching Song', for use on a journey. Although the title does not tell us this, the text of the psalm well reflects his state of mind at this period.

Psalm 34: In Philistine territory

See the introduction to the comments in the main text.

---

1. In the Bible this psalm is placed with the other 'Songs of Ascent' (120–134). This does not mean they were all composed at the same time, for there is no reason why psalms composed earlier could not be used for an occasion other than one for which they were originally written. For further information see the Introduction to Psalm 120 in the main text.

Psalm 86: David hides in the forest

Forced to leave Gath, David and his men move into Judah, keeping well away from Saul's Gibeah. They find a cave in the mountains at Adullam near Bethlehem, which explains the visit of his family (1 Sam. 22:1-2). It would appear that they and others in that area were suffering under Saul's tyranny. While this influx increased David's followers to four hundred, he was still concerned for the safety of his parents and took them to Moab, probably travelling south of the Dead Sea to avoid the possibility of contact with Saul's men. There he found a stronghold ('Mizpah' means 'mountain height', 1 Sam. 22:3) where he could place his parents in the custody of the king of Moab.

At this point David received a word from God through the prophet Gad, who may have been one of his followers, escaping from Saul as David was; he certainly became one from this time, since he was with David during his reign (1 Chron. 21:9) and took part in writing the record of his life (1 Chron. 29:29). The word from God was that he should not remain in the 'stronghold' Mizpah, which might have been his plan, but return to Judah.

Since his use of Adullam had probably become known to Saul, he went on to an even more remote place – the mountain forest of Hereth, so remote its whereabouts are still unknown. It was here that he received news of the slaughter of the priests by Saul, as a result of his encounter with Doeg at Nob. The story is in 1 Samuel 22:6-25, and 86 probably expresses David's reactions to that news and to the situation this put him in. Its reference to the *attacking* of the *arrogant* (v. 14) and his appeals for mercy from God (vv. 1-4, 15-17) are appropriate to this period.

Psalm 40: David rescues Keilah

Between the Forest of Hereth where David was hiding and the Philistine land was the town of Keilah. A report reached David that it was under attack from the Philistines (1 Sam. 23:1-6). Although an outlaw, David as 'heir-apparent' felt some responsibility, but was uncertain whether his small band would be sufficient. He resolved only to go if God was with him, since then victory would not be in doubt, however great the odds. Now that Abiathar the priest was there with the ephod, David could quickly discover the Lord's will. The ephod was a priestly vestment containing the 'Urim and Thummim for making decisions' (Exod. 28:6-13, 23-30). The answer was affirmative, but since his men were fearful, he enquired again and received not only God's permission but his promise: 'I am going to give the Philistines into your hand'. This was how it worked out. Psalm 40 reflects the thoughts of a man who has waited on God for guidance and assurance and has received it.

Psalm 13: David escapes from Keilah

The story that provides the best background to this psalm is in 1 Samuel 23:7-13. After what he and his men had done for Keilah they might well have expected to remain there under the protection of the townspeople. This would have been a welcome change from hiding in caves and woods. It was not long before this hope was put to the test. Saul saw it as his opportunity to trap David. To this day it is easier to attack your enemy in his town than when he resorts to guerilla tactics and is scattered in the woods and hills.

For David to withstand this attack would require the co-operation of the people of Keilah. David realised he could not take this for granted and had Abiathar consult the ephod. The answer was clear: if he remained he would be given up to Saul. (It is interesting to compare this with Paul's experience in Acts 21:10-11). So in spite of the recent victory nothing has really changed for David. Now he had the added burden of disappointment over the ingratitude of the people he had saved. This explains the depths from which this psalm starts. Yet within a short span (only five verses in the Hebrew) how high he climbs!

Psalm 31: David takes to the hills

Forced out of Keilah, where could he and his followers go? His previous hide-outs were all known to Saul, who may already have posted men in them. So he moves further east to even more remote territory and wilder terrain (1 Sam. 23:24-25). 'The Desert of Ziph' lay in the Judean mountains towards the Dead Sea. Being high up he would be able to spot the approach of his enemies, and the rocky terrain would afford good cover. Most of all, to track anyone in that region was very difficult, as Saul found: 'Day after day Saul searched for him'.

But the most significant phrase is 'God did not give David into his hands'. It was not the place or his vigilance to which he owed his safety, but God's care. This is the theme of Psalm 31: it is the Lord in whom he has *taken refuge* (v. 1); God who is his *rock (and) fortress* (v. 3); *in the shelter of your presence* that he hides (v. 20). But he is having a great struggle to rest in this faith: He is in *great distress,* his eyes are *weak with sorrow* ... (vv. 9-13). Yet his faith comes out on top (vv. 23-24). For further comments see the introduction to the psalm in the main text.

Psalm 28: David is still hiding in the hills

1 Samuel 23:13 tells us that, in spite of the remoteness of his hide-out, David had to keep on the move, lest Saul should discover his whereabouts. This he was to do eventually anyway, thanks to the locals (1 Sam. 23:19). Meanwhile he was to have a visit from Jonathan (1 Sam. 23:16). These events are reflected in this psalm, in which David is still seeking to rest in God as his *Rock* (v. 1), who alone stands between him and *the pit.* Although he is far from *God's Most Holy Place* (v. 2), he can at least *lift up his hands* in that direction. He is in process of praying earnestly against his enemies (vv. 3-5) when it seems Jonathan arrives and encourages him, for the tone of the psalm changes to one of *praise* and confidence from verse 6.

Psalm 62: David is encouraged by Jonathan

David eventually found a new hide-out in the Ziph area: Horesh (1 Sam. 23:14-18). 'Horesh' means 'wood' which is how KJV translates it. Evidently it was a thickly wooded area, ideal for hiding. Although Saul was searching for him, David managed to get word to Jonathan, who came and encouraged him to persevere, assuring him all would work out well. It did, though not in the way Jonathan expected, for this was to be their last meeting. David was encouraged by Jonathan's words, but did not put his trust in them, as this psalm shows: *God alone* is his theme (vv. 2, 5, 6, 7). He shared his trust with the people (vv. 8-10), and concluded with a clear message from God (vv. 11-12).

Psalm 54: David is betrayed by the Ziphites
Since the title fixes the authorship and occasion, see the introduction to the comments in the main text.

Psalm 27: David's providential escape
The title attributes this psalm to David without specifying the occasion. Its similarity to the last but one (Ps. 62), however, indicates it belongs to this period. David there was focused on 'God alone' and was conscious of 'one thing' (Ps. 62:1-2, 5-6, 11). Psalm 27 was written in the same spirit (v. 4). The background is still the threat of his enemies, which was very real while he was in Ziphite territory. However, the sense of relief and exhilaration here show that the immediate danger, described in 1 Samuel 23:19-26 and reflected in Psalm 54, has been averted.

The story behind it therefore is 1 Samuel 23:26-29: 'Saul and his forces were closing in on David and his men'. But at that moment news arrived of a new Philistine invasion, so that Saul had to call off his pursuit, enabling David to move further east to En Gedi, near the Dead Sea. This was such a signal providence that the place was given a name (v. 28) which means 'Rock of Escapes'. Nor could David let the occasion pass without a celebratory psalm.

Psalm 22: David in the darkness
David has taken refuge among the rocks at En Gedi near the Dead Sea. An ancient city had once stood here called Hazazon Tamar (2 Chron. 20:2), which had fallen to Kedorlaomer in the times of the Amorite occupation (Gen. 14:7). It was an ideal refuge for David. On the one hand it was supplied with streams, palms and vines; and on the other it was perforated with caves. The only inhabitants were mountain goats and possibly deer.

Meanwhile, Saul had to abandon his pursuit of David to repel a further Philistine invasion. As soon as this was achieved he resumed his campaign against David, and with an increased force of 3000. The story of what happened next is told in 1 Samuel 24:1-2. David was not as safe as he thought; in fact he was in his tightest corner yet and felt like the goats and deer which inhabited that area. This may explain the title of the psalm's tune: *Doe (or hind) of the morning*. It is the lament of a hunted deer. It certainly explains the mood of the psalm: his sense of abandonment by God (vv. 1-2) and his fear of this huge force which *surrounded* him like a herd of mad bulls (v. 12). All he can do is to struggle in prayer for God's deliverance. His faith emerged triumphant, even though the threat was not removed.

Psalm 142: David's tight corner
As the authorship and occasion are specified in the title, see the introduction to the comments in the main text.

Psalm 57: David spares Saul's life
This is the second of the two psalms which relate to the incident with Saul in the cave: Psalm 142 expresses the intitial fear which Saul's presence there aroused; this one shows how David saw this as an act of God's providence to bring about a reconciliation rather than as an opportunity to kill the king. For further comments see the introduction to the psalm in the main text.

Psalm 11: David flees to the Philistines
After the incident in the cave, David continued to circulate in the desert area of Southern Judah. In spite of Saul's promises, David knew he could not trust him and must remain in hiding. Besides, the people no longer seemed to be on his side, although this may have been out of fear of Saul. Looking for food, David and his men found themselves in a district called Maon, where a certain Nabal had extensive land. The incident with him and his wife Abigail, recorded in 1 Samuel 25, does not appear to be reflected in the psalms. The big thing in David's life in this period was Saul's persecution, so it is not until the next incident with Saul that he composes a psalm.

After the confrontation with Nabal, David took refuge on a hill called Hakilah in a desert place still in Ziphite territory. Ziphite spies again inform on him. The temptation is too great for Saul and he again leads out his 3000 men against David (see 1 Sam. 26). As at En Gedi the tables are turned and David again has Saul at his mercy. Again David refuses the advice of his leaders and spares Saul. Again Saul admits his error and invites David back.

Again David is unconvinced of Saul's sincerity and hints he has thoughts of leaving the country altogether: 'they (my enemies) have driven me from my share in the Lord's inheritance and have said, 'Go, serve other gods" (1 Sam. 26:19).

But David's colleagues do not seem to agree and they question his decision and want him to stay in the mountains of Judah, as we see in this psalm (v. 1). But David puts his trust in God and goes ahead with his plan, putting himself at the mercy of Achish in Gath, along with his two wives and 600 men (1 Sam. 27:1-6). Being a large company they are allotted a whole town – Ziklag. Although David did this with a spirit near despair (27:1) it did give him the needed respite from Saul (27:4).

Psalm 56: David is rejected by the Philistines
The title attributes this psalm to David and specifies the occasion. For details of the background see the introduction to the comments in the main text.

Psalm 39: David in distress over Ziklag
Three days after being dismissed by the Philistine generals, David reached Ziklag, the town given by Achish for him and his party to use while living among the Philistines (1 Sam. 27:5-7). David returned to find it burned to the ground by the Amalekites, and the women and children, who had been left there unguarded, taken prisoner. His initial reaction was one of utter distress, described in 1 Samuel 30:1-6 and reflected in this psalm. David was so upset by this he had to ask God to prevent him from speaking rashly (vv. 1-2). When he did speak it was to deplore the shortness and uncertainty of life (vv. 4-6). He had left Ziklag a happy, thriving place; he returned to find it all death and destruction. Perhaps it was his fault; perhaps God was punishing him for going to the Philistines who worshipped other gods (vv. 7-11). If so, then perhaps God would have pity, at least on the innocent (vv. 12-13). What David did not realise, because his grief blinded him, was that his arrival was just in time to recover the captives, showing that his dispute with the Philistine generals had been in the providence of God.

(4) David's Reign in Hebron

While David was recovering the families captured by the Amalekites (see 1 Sam. 30; 1 Chron. 12:1-22), Saul and Israel were engaged in a fierce conflict with the Philistines (see 1 Sam. 31), the result of which was the deaths of Saul and Jonathan. The news was brought to David by an Amalekite (not 'flavour of the month' with David just then!) who claimed to have delivered the fatal blow on Saul and was treated in similar fashion by David (see 2 Sam. 1:1-16). David composed a funeral ode in honour of Saul and Jonathan (see 2 Sam. 1:17-27) which is not included in the Psalter, being unsuitable for singing to God.

Psalm 101: David's Coronation Ode

When all this was over, David sought the will of God (see 2 Sam. 2:1-4a) and was directed to go to Hebron. There he was joined by the entire army of Saul and proclaimed king, although only over Judah (see 1 Chron. 12:23-40). There was feasting and rejoicing, but David took it all very seriously, thinking it out and setting forth the principles on which he would seek to reign. Although couched in the form of a song of praise to God (v. 1), this psalm very clearly sets out the resolutions of one who has assumed a position of responsibility in the land. It therefore well fits the occasion of David's accession.

Psalm 138: David's Thanksgiving to God

In his Coronation Ode (101) David had thought out the principles on which he would govern the people of God. This largely private exercise is now followed by the more public one of thanking God, through whom he had emerged safely from those traumatic times and was now taking up the throne of Judah. The psalm expresses the thanks of one who had cried to God in great need and been heard (v. 3), which had been the story of David's life for many years past. Now that he is king he wants other kings to know the God who was so good to him (vv. 4-5). The closing verses aptly sum up what his experience had taught him, and the hope for the future this gave him.

Psalm 95: David calls on the people to praise God with him
Hebrews 4:2, following the Septuagint, attributes this psalm
to David, and, although there is no external evidence for
associating it with David's coronation at Hebron, it follows
well on the two previous psalms. It was clearly written for
a public occasion, one in which the leader is calling on all
assembled to share his joy in and thanksgiving to God. This is
no doubt what David would do after stating the principles on
which he proposed governing Israel (101) and expressing his
personal thanks to God (138). The theme of kingship is again
present (v. 3), for David is conscious that there is a greater King
above him, to whom he is accountable. But it is not sufficient
that the king should live in obedience to God; if they were to
enjoy God's promised blessing;, all must carefully heed what
God has said (vv. 7b-8), remembering the failures of their
forefathers (vv. 10-11).

(5) David's Reign in Jerusalem

David's seven-and-a-half year reign over Judah in Hebron was
also a seven-and-a-half year period of civil war between Judah
and Israel (see 2 Sam. 2:8–4:12). Saul's son Ishbosheth was set
up by Abner, Saul's general, as the puppet king of a virtual
military dictatorship under Abner. When they fell out and
Abner defected to David, Joab, David's chief general, became
jealous and suspicious and slew Abner. The two leading
'colonels' of Saul's army then slew Ishbosheth. Although this
sickened David, he saw it as God providentially opening the
way for him to become king over the twelve tribes and to reunite them as 'all Israel'. Their acclamation of him as king
is recounted in 2 Samuel 5:1-5, where the motive is seen to
be, not political necessity (as when Saul was chosen), but the
recognition that God had chosen him, and proved his choice
by giving him victories he never gave Saul.

Psalm 75: David takes the throne of Israel
This is one of eleven psalms attributed to Asaph, who was
to become one of David's chief musicians when tabernacle
worship was restored (see 1 Chron. 6:31-47, especially v. 39).
Clearly it expresses David's own thinking at this time. The
tune *Do not destroy* had already been used for Psalms 57–59

in circumstances that seemed more in keeping with such a theme. However, it does reflect the sense of foreboding that God's displeasure over the long family quarrel might cause a terrible judgment, like those which occurred in the times of the Exodus. This foreboding is tempered, however, by the additional title *A Song*, for there was much to celebrate. The psalm centres around the idea that God in his wisdom and sovereignty frequently removes one ruler and replaces him with another. It therefore well fits the occasion of David's accession to the throne of all Israel, following the unsettled times when the monarchy was disputed.

Psalm 80: David faces the Philistine attack

2 Samuel 5:6-15 describes the probable events leading up to this psalm. David's first task on becoming king of all Israel was to strengthen his position and that of the nation. Firstly, he captured Jerusalem in order to make it the political, military and religious centre of the nation. Secondly, he gained the help of friendly neighbouring nations like Tyre, who supplied him with materials and craftsmen for building his capital. Thirdly, he made a number of marriages in order to have a large family as a buttress against usurpers.

2 Samuel 5:17-21 shows how necessary was this unity and strength, for the Philistines were still hostile. They saw David as a threat to their interests and tried to take Jerusalem before he could fortify it. David had to retreat to one of his old mountain fortresses and await the guidance of God. In spite of his comparative weakness God's assurance was enough to give him a glorious victory in the valley of Rephaim near Jerusalem. This was commemorated by naming the spot 'Baal Perazim', which means 'the Lord who breaks out'.

This psalm of Asaph is the prayer of one enquiring of God, as David was doing in the times described in 2 Samuel 5. The God who dwells above the ark is being appealed to (v. 1). There had been losses at the hands of the Philistines, God's *vine* had been trampled down (vv. 8-13) because God was not fighting for the people. God is bidden to behold the desolation (vv. 14-16), come back and take their part, and *restore* them to his favour and their prosperity (vv. 17-19).

Psalm 33: Celebrating victory over the Philistines

If Psalm 80 concerns David's enquiry of the Lord about fighting the Philistines, this one concerns the victory that followed. It is clearly a joyful occasion (vv. 1-3), which testifies to both the sovereign power (vv. 6-9) and will (vv. 10-11) of God. The background is a military one (vv. 16-17) and fits well with the situation described in 2 Samuel 5:17-21: those who seek God's direction and enabling find an impending disaster turns into a spectacular triumph. However, the psalm is phrased in general terms so that it could be used on future similar occasions.

Psalm 83: David crushes the Philistines

A frequent practice in the ancient world was for a defeated nation to return with greater numbers, which was what happened after David's recent victory over the Philistines: see 2 Samuel 5:22-25. Often they brought in others by offering them a share of the spoil. Josephus writes of a confederacy of the Philistines with Syria and Phoenicia at this time. Psalm 83:6-8 indicates that several other nations joined them. The events recorded in 2 Samuel 23:8-39 probably occurred along with those recorded at the end of 2 Samuel 5, which is where 1 Chronicles 11:10-47 place them. If so, then the exploits of Benaiah against the Egyptians and Moabites show that those nations were also involved, at least by sending mercenaries.

It was probably because of the strength and size of this alliance that God forbade David attacking directly and instructed him to go behind Philistine lines (2 Sam. 5:23), a strategy which would appear to leave them cut off and the way to Jerusalem open. This would explain why David's men had to break through the Philistine lines to fetch water from Bethlehem (1 Chron. 11:16-19). It seemed a strange thing that God should lead them there, but it turned out to be a wise move. The valley there was full of balsam trees, a type of tree which picks up the slightest breath of wind. When the Canaanites heard this, they took it to be the sound of a mighty army marching against them. Indeed, that was what it was – the Lord's army, his host of angels 'gone out in front of you to strike the Philistine army' (2 Sam. 5:24).

This brought about a victory comparable with the defeat of the Canaanites by Deborah and Barak, and of the Midianites by Gideon (Ps. 83:9-12). It was commemorated in four psalms, of which 83 was probably the first, since it records the cry of David and the people to God when they found themselves up against these formidable forces (2 Sam. 5:23). This prayer was put into words suitable for public worship by Asaph.

Psalm 144: War and Peace

David is exulting in a recent victory which God has given him by teaching and enabling him to fight (vv. 1-2). This comes, not from the time of his conflict with Saul, but during his kingship over Israel (v. 10). It is clearly early days when there was still much to do to make the nation secure and prosperous (vv. 12-14). Also the danger of war from the surrounding nations is still very real (v. 11) and peace was a distant prospect. It is therefore not unlikely the psalm relates to the victory over the Philistines for which they had prayed in 83 and which is recounted in 2 Samuel 5:22-25.

Psalm 9: David celebrates the victory

Please see the introduction to the comments in the main text.

Psalm 2: David is reinstated as King in Jerusalem

Although not attributed to David here, the early church does so in Acts 4:25, and the reference to God's *Anointed One* (v. 2) installed as his *King on Zion* (v. 6) make him the most likely subject of the psalm. He is reflecting on an attempt made by neighbouring kings to overthrow him, which God has foiled (vv. 2-4). This would fit the defeat of the Philistine conspiracy which has been the subject of the last few psalms. It becomes the basis of a prophecy of Christ's reign over nations which were at this time hostile (vv. 7-9).

Psalm 98: David brings up the Ark of the Covenant

The tone of exultation in victory in this psalm is similar to that of 2 and makes it likely to have come from that time. 2 Samuel 6:1-11 records how, following this great victory, David turned his attention to establishing Jerusalem as his capital. His first task was not the defence, the housing, his own palace or even the temple, but bringing up the ark of the covenant, for it was here that the Lord dwelt (80:1). The first attempt at doing this ended in tragedy, as is recorded in 2 Samuel 6. However, until that disaster occurred, they were celebrating with great zeal, and the two psalms – 98 and 96 – fit this occasion very well.

Psalm 96: David brings the Ark to Jerusalem

For three months the ark remained where it was when the oxen stumbled, Uzzah touched it and was struck dead. The place was the house of one Obed-Edom who was 'blessed' by God during this time. This encouraged David to make another attempt to bring it to Jerusalem, as told in 2 Samuel 6:11-15. David had come to realise that on the first occasion they had tried to transport the ark in the wrong way – on a cart drawn by oxen instead of borne on poles by Levites. This he now put right (1 Chron. 15:1-15). When it succeeded, the joy of the people knew no bounds. There were great celebrations: sacrifices to God, feasts for the people and singing of psalms. 1 Chronicles 16:23-33 records that 96 was one of these.

Psalm 47: The Ark enters Jerusalem

The reference to God having *ascended* to his throne as King (v. 5) no doubt refers to the bringing of the ark into the city, as record-ed in 2 Samuel 6:17-19. The great acclamation of his universal sovereignty which accompanied this (vv. 1-4) is in keeping with the spirit of other psalms that date from this period.

Psalm 68: The Ark comes to rest

Clearly the ark is the subject of yet another psalm, for its presence among the people is vital as symbolising the presence of God. Originally it was carried before the people on their journey from Sinai across the desert to the promised land (vv. 7-10). Now it is being installed in its place in the Tabernacle (v. 18) accompanied by a great procession (vv. 24-25).

Psalm 15: Who may live with the God of the Ark?

Psalm 24:3 raised the question as to who may approach the ark which symbolised the presence of God the Holy One, to offer a sacrifice, gift or prayer. This psalm takes up that question and may therefore be regarded as dating from the time of the Ark's installation on Zion. In fact, it goes further than Psalm 24, for it talks of dwelling or living there (v. 1). Since even the priests did not do that literally, it may be seen as referring to fellowship with the God whose presence was revealed there.

Psalm 60: War breaks out again
Please see the introduction to the comments in the main text.

Psalm 108: Victory celebrations
The repetition of 60:5-12 in verses 6-13 of this psalm place it at the same time as 60. However, whereas in the first part of 60 things are very much in the balance, the opening of this psalm clearly breathes victory, putting it a stage further on in time. For more information please see the introduction to the comments in the main text.

Psalm 76: The Awesome God
There are several indications that this psalm was occasioned by the defeat of the Philistine confederacy recorded in 2 Samuel 8. In verses 1-2 God is said to have taken up his *dwelling place in Zion,* a reference to the recent removal of the ark to Jerusalem. Verse 4 refers to *light* emanating from God, that is, the 'Shekinah' glory that appeared over the ark. Verses 5-6 describe the decisive victory over Israel's enemies as an act of God himself. The call to the nations to serve God (vv. 11-12) is similar to 47:7-9, one of the psalms celebrating the setting up of the ark on Zion. In addition there is an interesting play on words in verse 10. *Men* is 'ADAM which has the same consonants as EDOM, one of the principal contenders in the recent war (2 Sam. 8:12); and *wrath* is HAMATH, virtually the same as the name of one of the Syrian tribes which came to acknowledge David as legitimate King (2 Sam. 8:9).

The story may have moved on a stage since 60 and 108. There Edom remained unconquered because of its 'fortified city' (Petra), but now even that was defeated.

Psalm 20: The King goes out to war

This psalm is a prayer for the people to pray as the king and his army set out for war. No doubt it was used regularly but the first occasion could have been the events of 2 Samuel 10 (1 Chron. 19). These occurred about the middle of David's forty-year reign. Since the decisive defeat of the Philistine confederacy early in this reign, Israel had been at peace with her neighbours, enabling David to organise the administration of the land by setting up various departments of state, as described in 2 Samuel 8:15-18. The incident concerning the Gibeonites in 2 Samuel 21:1-14, however, probably occurred during this period. The approximate time is shown by what happened in 2 Samuel 9. On the death of Saul, Jonathan's son Mephibosheth had been five years old (2 Sam. 4:4); now he was a grown man with a son (2 Sam. 9:12). So this must have been 15 to 20 years into David's reign, about 990 BC.

Notwithstanding this long period of peace, Israel's neighbours were by no means friendly to her. David had forgiven and forgotten the part played by Ammon in the war of 2 Samuel 8, but remembered how King Nahash had previously taken his side against Saul (2 Sam. 10:2). When Nahash died, David sent a delegation to express his sympathy with Nahash's son. However, this man regarded it as a pretext for spying, and David's men were grossly insulted. This led to war, in which Ammon hired Aramean mercenaries. Though Ammon was defeated by Joab and Abishai, the Arameans reinforced their army and took over the war. This led to David going out himself and taking command (2 Sam. 10:17). The people's united support for him was expressed by their coming together to commend him to God. For this David composed an ode, which was probably used whenever the king went out to war, so that it was placed in the collection of the *director of music* (title).

Psalm 93: The King returns victorious

As David went out leading his army against the Arameans (2 Sam. 10:17), the people committed him to their greater King, the Lord, in the words of Psalm 20. Now he has returned after a decisive victory, which was to keep this hostile nation quiet for many years to come (2 Sam. 10:18-19). But the real victor was not David but the One to whom they had committed him: God the absolute sovereign. The *seas* of war had been *lifted up* (v. 3) not just against David and Israel but against God himself, and it was he who had subdued them (v. 4)

Psalm 51: David sins and repents
Please see the introduction to the comments in the main text.

Psalm 32: David rejoices in God's forgiveness
Please see the introduction to the comments in the main text.

Psalm 21: David returns victorious
The sad lapse in David's life was rounded off by God's gift to him and Bathsheba of another son. They gave him the name 'Solomon', 'man of peace', marking David's reconciliation with God and his hope that the long wars were over and the rest of his reign would be peaceful. Although the hope would not come about until Solomon himself was king, God confirmed the reconciliation by sending word through Nathan that the child was to be called 'Jedidiah' (2 Sam. 12:24-25) – 'loved by the Lord'. Although for some reason this name was not used, it must have been a great assurance to them that the past had been put away and the marriage and family of David and Bathsheba, not to speak of his forthcoming reign, would be blessed by God.

So now political matters could be taken up again. Word came from Joab that the Ammonite capital Rabbah was about to fall and that if David wanted the honour of victory he should come immediately (2 Sam. 12:26-31). He did this and the Ammonites were decisively defeated. This is probably the victory being celebrated in 21, for although David wrote it for the people to use, it is strongly autobiographical. It begins with a recollection of his prayer to God to spare his life (v. 2), the prayer he had prayed in Psalm 51, when he might have found himself condemned to death as an adulterer and murderer. But God had done more than spared his life; he had reinstated him as king (v. 3) and given him a great victory (v. 5). In 20 the people had commended him to the Lord as he went off to war; here he has returned not only safely but victoriously, for which he and the people give thanks to God.

Psalm 18: David's special thanksgiving for the end of his wars

Please see the introduction to the comments in the main text.

Psalm 97: The Lord alone is King

That this psalm celebrates the same occasion as 18 is shown in the similar themes on which it touches: God's universal sovereignty (v. 1), demonstrated at the Red Sea and Sinai (vv. 2-6), his people's joy in him (vv. 8-9, 11-12) and his call to holiness (v. 10). It is considerably shorter than 18 and omits David's personal reminiscences. Indeed there is no claim to his authorship, so that it may have come from the hand of one of his musicians, perhaps for use at an annual celebration of the victory that marked the end of David's wars with his neighbours.

Psalm 92: Contemplating God's victory

Once peace was restored the people could return to their work and worship without fear of interruption. In Israel worship centred around *the Sabbath day*, which was not only for rest but 'a day of sacred assembly' (Lev. 23:3). Perhaps the psalm was composed for use on the first Sabbath after the defeat of Ammon, with its reference to the fall of Israel's enemies and the recovery of her power in verses 9-11. It was then added to the growing collection of psalms for use in regular public worship. So it is subtitled *a song for the Sabbath day* (it is better to omit the full-stop after *song* in the NIV).

Psalm 16: David faces trouble in family and nation

A period of comparative calm followed the end of David's wars with his neighbours (though the occasional skirmish with the Philistines recorded later in 2 Samuel 21:15-22 may have occurred during this period). This interlude afforded David the opportunity to organise society, and the final chapters of 2 Chronicles (from ch. 21) record how this was done for the government, the army and the priesthood. David also began to make preparations for a permanent temple.

This did not mean, however, that there was peace *within the nation*. The sad happenings of 2 Samuel 13 began the train of events which led to Absalom's rebellion and the division

this caused. This is reflected in this psalm, as can be seen
by comparing verse 3 with verse 4. In this situation David
is seeking to encourage the godly remnant of verse 3. This
explains the title *MIKTAM*, which literally means 'engraving'
or 'inscription', that is, some positive thoughts to be inscribed
on the memory to hold on to in turbulent times.

Psalm 25: David seeks God's wise guidance

Psalm 16 saw David coming to terms with his problems in
the family and nation. Both in his personal life and method
of governing he resolved to continue to stand where he had
stood at the time of his accession (v. 21). Only thus could he
count on God's help. Receiving assurance of this he was filled
with praise and confidence (vv. 1-2).

Now he begins to look ahead; he has no idea in himself how
to tackle the situation. When his *enemies* (v. 2) were foreigners
it was plain sailing. Now they are his subjects, even his own
children! So the emphasis of 25 is on the guidance of God who
alone can show him the best way to proceed. The reference to
the sins of my youth (v. 7) shows that the psalm comes from later
in David's life, and the mention of *his descendants* in verse 13
indicates that his family was on his mind at this time. This is
a time when his *enemies have increased* (v. 19), which must refer
to internal *enemies*, since he was having very little trouble with
external ones. But his concern is not just for himself but for
the nation, whose welfare under God was being threatened,
hence the closing prayer of verse 22.

For information on the structure of the psalm, see the
introduction to the comments in the main text.

Psalm 14: David's desperate appeal for God's intervention

David has been seeking to come to terms with the corruption
in his family and nation (16). In his bewilderment he has asked
God to show him how to handle this situation (25). But this
is not enough: the evil is so great and goes so deep he has not
the power to deal with it. If it is to be remedied God himself
must step in.

The language of the psalm is stronger than any he used
when he was up against external enemies. What could be

expected of them after all? But when the people of God were behaving like heathens, how could he do other than condemn them in the strongest terms? So powerful is this exposure of the human heart that Paul quotes it in support of his teaching on universal sinfulness, of Jew as well as Gentile (Rom. 3:10-12). The call for *salvation* to come (v. 7) is thus prophetic of the salvation of Christ, which Paul goes on to write about in Romans 3 and the following chapters.

Psalm 10: David wrestles with God over his non-intervention

Although not attributed to David, the language of this psalm is very characteristic of him, as is the situation. The title may simply have been lost. The sentiments of the psalm could have been uttered during Saul's persecution, but the reference to *the* Lord *is King* (v. 16) make it more likely it dates from David's reign. He was always conscious that his kingship represented God's, and that, in preserving him, God was preserving his own rule over the nation. This would mean that the *wicked man* who in his *arrogance ... hunts down the weak* (v. 2) is Absalom.

After Absalom had murdered Amnon for raping his sister Tamar he fled into exile (2 Sam. 13). Later he returned to Jerusalem and 'stole the hearts of the men of Israel' (2 Sam. 15:1-6). He could do this with ease because 'the men of Israel' had forsaken David's God and theirs and were no longer loyal to David (Ps. 16:4). They had become 'fools' who 'say in their hearts, 'there is no God'' (14:1). Also they despised and ill-treated those who did remain loyal (14:4). It is this situation over which David laments here and in which he calls on God to intervene.

(6) Absalom's Rebellion
Psalm 17: David pleads with God against his enemies

To help him steal the hearts of the men of Israel, Absalom launched a campaign of character-assassination against David (2 Sam. 15:1-6). This is what appears to lie behind this psalm, especially in verses 10-12. He has to do over again what he did when Saul and his men had vilified him: appeal to God to vindicate him (v. 2) and to keep his spirit from giving way to vengeful feelings (vv. 3-5).

Psalm 70: David's desperate cry to God

Please see the introduction to the comments in the main text. The reason for placing this psalm at the time of Absalom's rebellion is that it reveals a divided nation: there were those who were seeking David's life and desiring his ruin (vv. 2-3), which was in direct opposition to the will of God who had appointed him. But there were also those who were seeking that *God be exalted* (v. 4) and thus were standing with David. The scale of the rebellion had reduced him to a state of weakness (v. 5) in which he could only cry to God for *help* (vv. 1, 5).

Psalm 73: Why is God allowing this?

Please see the introduction to the comments in the main text. The background of this psalm is again wickedness among the people of God. If these had been Gentiles Asaph would hardly have been so overcome that he almost gave up his faith in the goodness of God. The only time during David's reign when wickedness was manifested on such a scale was the rebellion of Absalom.

Psalm 82: God will judge the judges

Please see the introduction to the comments in the main text. Asaph was a servant of David and would hardly be complaining of David's regime. We know that some of his highest officers, such as Ahithophel, went over to Absalom, and it seems to be these Asaph was condemning.

Psalm 58: David denounces the rulers of Israel

The theme and tone of this psalm are so similar to 82 that it is likely to refer to the same occasion. David's condemnation is far more vehement than Asaph's, partly because those who were now governing corruptly had previously served under David, and partly because David had the gift of prophecy and was therefore denouncing them in God's name and by his Spirit.

Psalm 53: David prepares to flee the land

When David's troubles with Absalom first began, he wrote 14, almost identical with this one. His language then seemed exaggerated. To say there was 'none who does good' just because his own son was corrupt might seem exaggerated.

His words, however, were prophetic. Events were moving swiftly: Absalom had gained a large following in Israel through his criticisms of David and his glittering display of chariots and horses (2 Sam. 15:1-6). After four years he made his move. Under pretext of fulfilling a vow, he obtained leave to go to Hebron (2 Sam. 15:7-9). It was a shrewd decision, for there David had first held court before moving to Jerusalem to become king of all Israel. This may have left behind some resentment against David. There Absalom set up his standard and had himself proclaimed king. David's original words are now justified. This was his final declaration before fleeing the land.

Psalm 109: David's reaction to Ahithophel's defection

David's complaint here is that this assault on his character was not confined to those he had labelled his 'enemies', who had joined Absalom's rebellion. Some former friends had also gone over. The obvious one in mind was Ahithophel, David's chief advisor, who defected to Absalom (2 Sam. 15:31). It is to him David is referring in verse 4. The plural in verse 5 may mean that Ahithophel's junior staff had joined him.

David's reaction was swift: 'O Lord, turn Ahithophel's counsel into foolishness' (2 Sam. 15:31). What follows in 109:6-20 is the full text of his prayer. This is not bitter vindictiveness, but prophecy, as already seen in other imprecations of this kind. It is not immoral, but David handing over the situation to God to whom vengeance belongs (94:1). David's response is not retaliation but *prayer* (v. 4). Verses 21-29 show he is not vowing to pay these people back, for he knows how weak he is anyway. He is looking to God to deliver him and vindicate him in this way. There is no bitterness against God, only praise (vv. 30-31).

Psalm 55: David comes to terms with Ahithophel's defection

That David is still dwelling on the treachery of Ahithophel is clear from verses 13-14, 20-21. But whereas in 109 he was occupied almost exclusively with the attack on himself, he now sees its consequences for the nation. Ahithophel has become part of a violent revolution in Jerusalem which, unless God prevents it, will have disastrous results (vv. 9-11). This is what David now addresses in this carefully composed psalm, which may be what the term *Maskil* refers to here. He also specified the use of *stringed instruments*, which on their own without wind instruments would produce the plaintive tone appropriate to the subject of the psalm.

Psalm 94: David appeals to the honour of God
Although not attributed to David, this psalm fits the time of Absalom's rebellion and Ahithophel's defection, and logically follows the two previous psalms. While David still has in mind the hurt being caused to himself and the damage being done to the nation by these events, his chief thought is that the honour of God is being impugned. His appeal therefore here is to God, to act in such a way that his own honour will be vindicated as well as his servant's integrity.

Psalm 7: David finds refuge from his enemies in God
Please see the introduction to the comments in the main text. If this psalm is connected with the incident of Shimei, it shows that underneath his outwardly calm acceptance of it, David felt it deeply.

Psalm 3: The first night of the flight
Please see the introduction to the comments in the main text.

Psalm 4: David's evening meditation
Please see the introduction to the comments in the main text.

Psalm 5: The morning after
Please see the introduction to the comments in the main text.

Psalm 88: Heman in solitary confinement
When Ahithophel, who had been David's chief advisor, defected to Absalom, David had prayed that the Lord would 'turn Ahithophel's counsel into foolishness' (2 Sam. 15:31). Fuller versions of this prayer are in 109, 55 and 94. The long passage from 2 Samuel 16:15–17:32 tells how God answered it. This was through David's friend Hushai the Archite, whom David sent back to Jerusalem for this very purpose

(2 Sam. 15:32-27). When Absalom was seeking the best way of defeating David, he first consulted Ahithophel, who gave him some advice, which at the human level seemed sound, part of which he followed when he took over David's harem. A harem was not a royal brothel but more of a status symbol, since it largely comprised the daughters of prominent men and even foreign kings. In other words, Absalom was claiming supremacy in Israel.

The other part of Ahithophel's advice was to strike at David immediately while he and his men were 'weak and weary', which would end their resistance. This too was excellent advice but Absalom hesitated and sought a second opinion – from Hushai! Here is his opportunity. He must get Absalom to delay and give David time to regain his strength. But how to do so in a way Absalom would accept? By appealing to his vanity and ambition. So Hushai's advice was: gather a larger army from the whole nation and march out at the head of it. This gives Absalom a vision of himself as a great king and conqueror, which he finds more attractive than Ahithophel's plan. So he follows Hushai's advice, giving David's spies time to report this to him and enabling him to re-group.

But this was not all that was happening in Jerusalem. Other associates of David, wise men, had remained behind. But far from being admitted to Absalom's court, they were imprisoned as dangerous to the new regime. Among these was the author of this psalm, Heman, leader of the guild of musicians to which Asaph and Ethan belonged and which went under the name 'sons of Korah'. He may have been one of David's wise men, whose wisdom was only exceeded by Solomon himself (1 Kings 4:31). From his psalm it appears he had been placed in solitary confinement: he refers to himself as *set apart with the dead* (v. 3), thrown into *the lowest pit* (v. 6), separated from his *companions and loved ones* (v. 17), with only God to talk to. It was not only David who suffered from Absalom's rebellion; to remain loyal to David was a costly thing.

Psalm 6: David crosses the Jordan

Although Hushai's wisdom and Absalom's vanity have given David a little breathing space, Absalom soon mustered his forces and went in pursuit of him. This situation is reflected in the very low spirits David gives vent to here. Not only is he under threat from Absalom's superior forces, but is now on the other side of the Jordan, out of his kingdom altogether (2 Sam. 17:24). It was a hard time for David, but the Lord revived his spirits.

Psalms 42–43: On the first Sabbath away
Please see the introduction to the comments in the main text.

Psalm 41: David at Mahanaim
Crossing the Jordan brought David into the land of Gilead, where he was met by the three chief men of the land (2 Sam. 17:27-29). Gilead had formerly been Ammonite territory, which explains the presence of Shobi from Rabbah in Ammon, who was probably successor to Hanun. In his time David had fought and defeated the Ammonites in retaliation for the insult to his ambassadors (2 Sam. 10). The new king was anxious to make amends and joined the two local chiefs of the tribes of Ephraim and Manasseh who had occupied Gilead from the time of the conquest. Together they brought provisions for David's retreating army. This was a great encouragement to David and his men at a time when their souls were downcast within them (42:5, 11).

He saw the hand of God in this and praised him in 41, which fits this situation well. He was being served by those who had *regard for the weak*, whom he saw as God's instruments *to* deliver him *in times of trouble* (v. 1). And he *was* in *trouble*. His enemies were still speaking against him and wishing his death (v. 7). He is still smarting from the treachery of Ahithophel (v. 9). But he accepts that this is all part of his punishment for his grievous sins (v. 4), as God had warned him (2 Sam. 12:7-12). If God did save him it would be sheer mercy (v. 10).

Psalm 69: David faces the rebel army
2 Samuel 18:1-4 suggests that the three leaders who provided hospitality for David and his followers at Mahanaim also brought their armies, for we now read of 'hundreds and thousands'. It is unlikely that David brought any troops, only

his 'officials', his 'household', a number of 'the people' and his personal bodyguard (2 Sam. 15:16-18). But even with these reinforcements his army would be no match for the one Absalom had now recruited from the whole land (2 Sam. 17:11). David knows he is outnumbered (v. 4), and his real feelings are expressed to God in this psalm.

Although God had reason to punish him (v. 5), Absalom and his followers did not (v. 4). The usurper was accusing the rightful king of usurping the throne! Ultimately what was at stake was God's name (v. 7), and his *house* (v. 9), for he knew Absalom could not be relied on to maintain the worship of God, much less build the long-desired temple. This helps explain the fierce imprecation of verses 22-28: it was God's curse on those who were in process of destroying the knowledge of God and obedience to him. Casting this burden on the Lord revives David's confidence that God will not let this happen, for the sake of his own glory (vv. 30-36).

Psalm 61: After the Victory
David wrote Psalms 3–4 as Absalom's army was on its way to fight him. When he wrote 61 things had moved on apace. We read in 2 Samuel 18:1-18 of how, in spite of inferior numbers, David's men gained the victory. Then we read on in 2 Samuel 18:29–19:4 of how David received the news of Absalom's death, killed by Joab in spite of David's orders to spare him. This is one of the most poignant passages in Scripture prior to Calvary, with which it has similarities. It reveals something of the heart of the Father as he abandoned his Son to the power of sin, death and the forces of evil. At the same time it shows how much greater is Christ than David. David could not 'die for' Absalom, but Christ has died for us. Finally, we read in 2 Samuel 19:5-8 of how Joab reproved David for his excessive grief, after which David emerged from hiding to receive his men at the gate of Mahanaim.

All this shows how mixed were David's feelings at this time: his joy in victory much tempered by the loss of his son. These mixed emotions are expressed in 61. David was writing *from the ends of the* land (not *the earth*, v. 2). He had found refuge in God during this exile (v. 3) but this did not

compare with being in his tabernacle (*tent*, v. 4), from which
he had been absent and to which he longed to return. Now
that the victory was won he could look forward to resuming
his rightful position as king, (v. 6), to dwell in God's *presence*
hereafter (v. 7), and promote his *praise* (v. 8). This was what he
had originally *vowed* to do, and what he would soon restore.

Psalm 63: David awaits his return to Jerusalem

2 Samuel 19 (from v. 9 to the end) tells of the arrangements
being made for the return of David to Jerusalem and his
restoration to the throne. A good deal of disputing took place
over this; meanwhile David was left in *the Desert of Judah*
(title), though on which side of the Jordan is not clear, since he
did not cross it until verse 39. He thus had plenty of time to
meditate and pray, the result of which was this psalm.

Clearly he is king at this time (v. 11), but away from the
sanctuary of God (v. 2) and longing to be there (v. 1). But
the tone is very different from 42–43 which also bewail his
absence. Then he was moving in the other direction, now he
is on his way home, expecting a swift restoration (vv. 4-5) and
freedom from his enemies (vv. 9-10, 11b).

Psalm 124: The homeward march

The leaders of Israel and Judah eventually came to an
agreement, enabling David and his men to cross the Jordan
and begin the return journey (2 Sam. 19:39-40). This they did
as victors in the battle, singing songs of triumph and rejoicing
as they marched home. Such a song did David compose for
them here, for it is entitled *A song of ascents* or 'Marching
Song'. It brings out the seriousness of the situation David and
his supporters had been in – of utter extinction (vv. 3-5), and
attributes their escape, not to their strength or strategy, but to
the favour of God who was *on our side* (vv. 1-2, 6-8).

Psalm 66: Celebrating David's return to Jerusalem

Please see the introduction to the comments in the main text.

Strangely, the historical account passes over David's arrival
in Jerusalem in half a sentence: 'when David returned to his
palace in Jerusalem' (2 Sam. 20:3)! The chapter is wholly given
to the rebellion of Sheba and the murder of Amasa by Joab.

No mention is made of celebrations. That there must have been one is evident from the insertion of 18 into the historical narrative (2 Sam. 22). Possibly this came after Sheba's rebellion had been quashed, whereas 66 was sung at the thanksgiving service held immediately after David's return.

It speaks of the awful position they had been in (vv. 10-12) and of a divine rescue comparable to the crossing of the Red Sea under Moses or the Jordan under Joshua (v. 6). Perhaps David recalled that event as he crossed the Jordan to return home. Had he not done so, and the throne been occupied by Absalom, Israel's subsequent history would have been very different. So the comparison was no exaggeration. Neither was the uninhibited rejoicing to which they gave vent (vv. 1-3). They are now coming into the *temple* (or tabernacle) from which they had been banished (vv. 13-15). He even sees it as a witness to other nations (vv. 4, 7), as well as an encouragement to the people of God of his gracious sovereignty (vv. 16-20).

Psalm 118: David reigns supreme

When David returned to Jerusalem after the defeat of Absalom, his troubles were not over. The resentment of the tribe of Benjamin over their loss of the kingship (under Saul) to the tribe of Judah (under David) had long been smouldering. Now it bursts into flame and finds a leader in Sheba, who is followed, not only by Benjamin but the other ten tribes, who unite against David and Judah. The story of this rebellion is told in 2 Samuel 20: Sheba appears to have travelled from Benjamin in the south right through the land mustering support, until he reached a city of Naphtali in the far north. The city was besieged by Joab and the army, who lifted the siege when the head of Sheba was thrown to them over the city wall.

Although this dispute was to recur in the time of David's grandson Rehoboam, for the time being his throne was secure at last and a great thanksgiving service took place, at which this psalm appears to have had pride of place. Although anonymous, it fits both David's style and this occasion. It celebrates his many military victories (vv. 10-16), and is centred around a procession which the king leads up to the city gates

(vv. 19-20), symbolising his return, not only from his foreign wars, but his battle with Absalom and Sheba's rebellion. It is arguably the most triumphant psalm in the whole collection and clearly marks a great occasion.

In verses 1-8 David appears to be leading the praise outside the city gates, recalling the time when he had been excluded from it. In verse 19 he re-enters the city, signifying his longed-for return.

(7) The Close of David's Reign
Psalm 38: David's grievous sickness
Please see the introduction to the comments in the main text.

Psalm 30: David's recovery
Please see the introduction to the comments in the main text.

Psalm 37: David the aged gives advice
Please see the introduction to the comments in the main text.

Psalm 71: David faces Adonijah's rebellion
Although it lacks a title, this psalm contains so many Davidic phrases and ideas, along with allusions to earlier psalms, that it is almost certainly by him. If David thought that, now he was old (vv. 9, 18), he would be left in peace to pursue his two great interests – the construction of the temple and the instruction of the next generation – he was sadly mistaken. For one thing he was forced to take to his bed with what appears to have been hypothermia (1 Kings 1:1-4). The proposed remedy might have been expected to get any man's blood flowing again, but it seems to have failed in this case!

But at this point another trouble came along in the shape of his son Adonijah, who made a bid for the throne and secured the support, not only of the priest Abiathar, but of the army general Joab, who provided him with a contingent of soldiers (1 Kings 1:5-7). It would therefore be to Adonijah and his supporters that David was referring when he spoke of his *enemies* (v. 9). But his long experience and many deliverances (vv. 5-6) gave him the confidence that God would again come to his aid (vv. 1-4, 17-21), so that much of the psalm consists of praise to God. Nor is he thinking only of himself, but of the message this would send to the rising generation (vv. 14-16, 24).

INTERLUDE: THE WORD AND WORSHIP OF GOD

In the case of a number of psalms, the author and circumstances of composition are of no particular importance and fit into almost any period. These are the ones that centre on the two great features of Old Testament religion: the Word and Worship of God.

The **Word of God** in its Old Testament form took shape over a long period of time and was gradually augmented. As this happened, the great teachers and prophets reflected on its uniqueness, importance and value, and set down their observations. No doubt David had a part in all this, even if he did not compose the whole of 119, which may have been compiled at a later date from a number of sources.

Public worship was the other great feature of Israel's life, with its daily and weekly offerings and the great annual festivals. Special psalms were composed by various authors for use at these, and were frequently augmented. Since this process certainly began in the time of David, it seems that the end of his reign is a convenient point at which to consider them before moving on to the psalms connected with his son and successors.

(1) Psalm 119: The Word of God
Please see the comments in the main text.

(2) The Worship of God
At Sinai God had laid down rules as to how he was to be approached in worship. At the heart of these were the great festivals which commemorated God's mighty acts on behalf of his people. They are listed and briefly described in Leviticus 23.

But worshipping God is more than following the procedures; it is a matter of expressing thankfulness and praise to him from the heart. Prior to the outpouring of the Holy Spirit by Christ on his ascension, his people needed words and music in which to express this praise, especially when they came together to celebrate God's mighty deeds.

So the Spirit of God moved gifted poets and musicians to compose songs for use at these festivals. Although the psalms themselves do not indicate this in their titles, there are clues that show their connection with particular festivals. This process began with David (to whom a number are attributed) and with the music school he established – 'the sons of Korah'. Josephus thought David used the peaceful period after the end of his wars for this purpose (Antiquities, Book VII, ch.xii, para. 3). Although not allowed to build the temple himself, David did all he could to prepare for it, not only in drawing up plans and collecting materials, but, along with others, in composing a collection of songs for use in it.

A. The Passover

Psalm 49
Passover night was the night in which Israel was 'redeemed' from bondage in Egypt, when the 'ransom' was paid in Egypt's first-born sons. The psalm centres around this theme (vv. 7-9). It also describes a dramatic overthrow of the rich and powerful (vv. 12-15), recalling the spoiling of the Egyptians followed by the destruction of Pharaoh and his army in the Red Sea.

Psalm 110
In 49 the emphasis was on the certainty of death for all alike ('high and low, rich and poor') and on the redemption from death to life which only God can provide. In 110 the emphasis is on the divine power which lies behind both the judgment and the salvation.

There is another way in which it moves us on from 49: it is more forward- than backward-looking. It is quoted or alluded to in the New Testament more frequently than any other Old Testament passage, and always in connection with the reign of Christ. So what is in view here is not so much Christ the 'passover sacrificed for us' as Christ the sacrificer, the King-Priest.

B. Psalms for Pentecost

The Passover was followed by seven 'days of unleavened bread', recalling their hasty departure from Egypt. On the fiftieth day after the Passover, that is, after seven weeks or 'a week of weeks' (hence the alternative title 'Feast of Weeks'), they took the first two loaves from the new wheat or barley and offered them to God (Lev. 23:15-22). Pentecost was thus to a great extent about celebrating the forthcoming harvest; this note is particularly strong in 65.

Since it was celebrated in the third month it also came to commemorate the giving of the law on Sinai, which took place in the third month after leaving Egypt. In later days the feast included the reading of the covenant and the law, and traces of this can be seen in 50. But the harvest theme is the most prominent one and looks on to its ultimate fulfilment in the Pentecost that followed Christ's ascension, when the first-fruits of the harvest of souls from all nations were brought to God. This is foreshadowed in the universality that characterises 65.

Psalm 65
Although ostensibly *a song* of thanksgiving for harvest, this *psalm of David*, given to *the director of music* for use in public worship, chiefly glories in the richness of God himself.

Psalm 99
In this anonymous psalm the commemoration of the giving of the law on Sinai (which became a feature of Pentecost) comes more into view, as verse 7 shows. But the strong universalist note continues, for the law of God is as relevant to the whole world as are the fruits of the earth, which was the theme of 65.

Psalm 114
This psalm celebrates the sovereignty of God over his natural creation through which he established Israel as his people and provided for them. Thus it was appropriate for Pentecost, especially as it contains a reference to Sinai (v. 6) and sounds the note of universality characteristic of Pentecost.

Psalm 50
Here the theme of universality appears again (v. 1), while Sinai, the covenant and the law become more prominent (vv. 5,

16-20). But chiefly, here is God coming among them to warn of the danger of abusing the services of worship, a danger which would be strongest at festival times such as this.

C. Psalms for the Feast of Trumpets

The seventh month, Tisri, corresponding to our September–October, was the highlight of the festal year. It was the first month of the civil year and believed to be the month when Creation took place. On the tenth day the great Day of Atonement was held, followed on the fifteenth by the Feast of Tabernacles.

It was therefore appropriate that the first day of this month should be marked by a feast at once joyful and solemn. This was the Feast of Trumpets, described in Leviticus 23:23-24 and Numbers 29:1-6 and it was so called because the worship and offerings were preceded by the blowing of rams' horns (81:3). This was an expression of joy in what God had done in both the distant and recent past, and at the same time a summons to prepare for what lay ahead later in that month.

It also coincided with the grape harvest, hence the word *Gittith* in the titles of 81 and 84 (cf. Ps. 8), which comes from 'Gath' and means 'wine-press'. It thus served as a thanksgiving for the provision of grapes for wine, which they would be making to store for the months ahead.

Psalm 81

This psalm was composed by *Asaph*, one of David's chief poets and musicians, and entrusted to *the director of music* for use at the Feast of Trumpets, as explicitly stated in verse 3.

Psalm 84

The reference to *gittith* in the title links this psalm with 81. As we have seen, *Gittith* means 'winepress', for the grape harvest coincided with the Feast of Trumpets. But the approach to the feast in this psalm is very different from that of 81.The writer, one *of the sons of Korah*, recollects his feelings when away from the house of God and thus from his presence. It is an 'absence makes the heart grow fonder' experience.

Psalm 29
The autumn rains which occurred in the seventh month (84:6) were frequently accompanied by violent thunderstorms. Perhaps the psalm was evoked by an experience, real or imaginary, of the sound of thunder drowning the sound of the trumpet. When God speaks he silences the voice of man.

D. A Psalm for the Day of Atonement
Psalm 130
Nine days after the Feast of Trumpets, on the tenth day of the seventh month, Israel observed the Day of Atonement. This was probably the high point of the year and included some unusual features. The high priest had to wear special white linen garments; two goats were used, one of which was sacrificed as a sin offering and the other released into the desert, and the high priest made his annual entrance into the holy of holies. The details are in Leviticus 16 and 23:26-32.

The psalm does not touch on the ritual as such, but rather deals with the way a person prepared himself for this day. The title *A Song of Ascents* refers to the journey of the worshippers to the shrine, and the psalm reflects the thoughts appropriate to the day. Leviticus 16:29, 31 refers to this preparation of heart in the words 'you must deny yourself' (NIV) or 'fast' (NIV mg). But the word is literally 'afflict yourselves' (ESV) or 'afflict your souls' (AV, NKJV). This is exactly what the psalmist is doing – probing *the depths* (v. 1) of his soul, facing the reality of his sinful state and finding forgiveness and redemption in God's promises.

E. Psalms for the Feast of Tabernacles
Tabernacles was the third of the three compulsory feasts (see Exod. 23:14-17) and one of the greatest. It occurred at harvest time and was therefore also called The Feast of Ingathering. When the land was at its most fruitful it was appropriate to remember how God gave it to them and what life was like before. So they are reminded of their time in the desert when they had no homes but were nomads living in tents.

They relived this period by dwelling in booths for eight days, hence the name 'Feast of Tabernacles' or 'Booths'. Full details are in Leviticus 23:33-44. It began and ended with solemnity but the greater part was rejoicing: in God's faithful provision in spite of their unfaithfulness to him; and in his great redemption. Every seventh year the Law was to be read at the feast to ensure that each generation would know it.

Psalm 78
As well as the Law, it was vital that all Israelites should know the main features of their history: how they became a free and sovereign people in a fruitful land of their own. So they did not just re-enact a part of this history, but were reminded of the whole of it. This brought out, not just God's faithfulness to them, but their unfaithfulness to him. God's grace triumphed even in this, however, since it resulted in the situation at the time this psalm was written by Asaph, that is, when the shrine was established on Zion and David was on the throne. This came about through the failure of the tribe of Joseph ('Ephraim', vv. 9, 67) to keep the people true to God and maintain his sanctuary when it was in their territory at Shiloh. God therefore transferred the kingship to Judah and David, and the sanctuary to Jerusalem and Zion.

Psalm 67
The Feast of Tabernacles included thanksgiving for the harvest and was also called 'The Feast of Ingathering' (Exod. 23:16), to be held 'after you have gathered the crops of the land' (Lev. 23:39). This psalm concentrates on the harvest theme (v. 6, which should read *the land HAS YIELDED its harvest*). But this is seen as a token of the total grace and blessing of God (v. 1), especially of his just rule (v. 4). Moreover, it has a vision of harvesting the nations to share in these blessings (vv. 2-5, 6b). The title uses several phrases to emphasise the joyful way these sentiments should be expressed.

Psalm 100
This 'psalm of thanksgiving' (title) appears to be an invitation to gather at the tabernacle or temple to offer joyful praises to God. Its exuberance – even shouting is encouraged (v. 1)! – which well befits the uninhibited singing that marked the Feast of Tabernacles.

Psalm 103

It would be tempting to link this psalm with David's repentance and forgiveness in the matter of Bathsheba and Uriah. He says much about God's fatherly pity for those who give way to their human weaknesses and fall into sin (vv. 7-13); indeed he puts God's forgiveness at the top of his list of *benefits* for which he praises him (v. 3). The notes of heart-searching and deep anguish which characterise the psalms connected with the Bathsheba incident (51 and 32), however, are absent here. Also, although he begins on the personal level, addressing his own *soul* in verses 1-5, he appears to be doing this as representative of the people for whom he is writing this psalm. So he quickly enlarges the scope to embrace the whole nation from verse 6 onwards.

So it is more likely to be a composition for the whole gathered people to use on a special occasion. It fits well with the Feast of Tabernacles with its recollection of the sins of Israel in the days of Moses when they crossed the desert. It has a strong stress on the covenant which was entered at Sinai and recalled in most of the major feasts. It makes some reference to harvest plenty in verse 5, while realising the transitory nature of such things (vv. 15-16). This leads him to re-affirm the people's trust in the God who is *from everlasting to everlasting* and has made an everlasting covenant with his people. Finally, it has similarities with 104 (a psalm very appropriate to harvest) especially in its opening and closing passages.

Psalm 104

Some versions have ascribed this anonymous psalm to David, and it is certainly similar to 103 both in the opening and closing words, and in its general atmosphere of rejoicing in God's transcendent being and mighty works. It beautifully complements 103, which is subjective, praising God for his personal care and forgiveness, whereas 104 is more objective, looking at his created works as they reveal how great and glorious he is. This makes it appropriate for the Feast of Tabernacles with its joy in the fruits of the earth. (Please see further comments in the introduction to this psalm in the main text.)

Psalm 111

This and the next psalm form a pair. Both begin 'Hallelujah' or *Praise the Lord*; both are 'acrostic', that is, they work their way through the 22-letter Hebrew alphabet, beginning each line with a different letter, in order. Each verse has two lines, except for verses 9-10 which have three. They are also paired as regards theme: 111 is on the goodness of God shown in 'the works of his hands', such as his provision of food, which links the desert journey with the harvest, celebrated particularly in the Feast of Tabernacles. Psalm 112 follows, bringing out how the man of God seeks to emulate him in generosity.

Psalm 112

This psalm is companion to 111 with its similar acrostic structure (see introduction to 111). It takes over where 111 leaves off, expounding what 'the fear of the Lord' (111:10) is. As 111 is about God's goodness, so 112 is about how someone who 'fears' God emulates him and thus is 'blessed'.

Psalm 117

This shortest of all the psalms is a fitting doxology to the previous pair, beginning and ending as it does with 'Hallelujah' or *Praise the Lord*. It calls on *all nations* to acknowledge the love and faithfulness of God to Israel, celebrated at the Feast of Tabernacles.

Psalm 145

This is the last of the psalms for the Feast of Tabernacles. Like the others, its theme is the great acts of God which bring out his goodness, righteousness and faithfulness to his promises. (Please see also the introductory comments on the psalm in the main text.)

F. Pilgrims' Songs

The feasts for which the preceding psalms were composed were held in Jerusalem on the hill of Zion. Most people lived outside Jerusalem and therefore had to make a journey if they were to attend the feast. Psalms 120–134 are a series of songs for use on these journey and are called *Songs of Ascents*. Although some may have been composed for other journeys (and are therefore considered in their appropriate places), they were put together in the psalter as suitable for the use of travellers to the feasts.

Psalm 121
Some of these *Songs of Ascents* are appropriate for the start of a journey, some for its course, and others for the arrival. This one is for use on the journey itself and therefore has a different preposition in the Title: *A Song FOR the ascents.*

Psalm 122
David, to whom the psalm is attributed, is seeking to express the feelings of those gathering with him for the feast. God has now brought his worshippers safely to his shrine, which they are on the point of entering as they sing this psalm. Fear of the hazards of the journey has given way to a sense of wonder at being in such a place as Jerusalem, and they pray for God's blessing to remain on it. Other songs which express similar sentiments are 48, 84 and 132.

Psalm 133
It is possible that *David* (title) originally composed this psalm to mark the reuniting of the tribes on his accession to the throne of 'all Israel and Judah' (2 Sam. 5:5); then, after the Tabernacle worship had been resumed in Jerusalem, he re-issued it as *A song of ascents*. It follows 122 well: the people have now entered the courts of the Lord for the festival service and are exulting in their unity in him, which becomes the theme of the psalm.

Psalm 134
In 121 the pilgrims were on their journey; in 122 they had arrived at their destination; 133 sees them at worship, and now in 134 the festival service has come to an end. What now?

THE PERIOD OF SOLOMON
Psalm 72: His Coronation Ode
This psalm, whether composed by David or Solomon, marks the latter's accession to the throne, which seems to have taken

place before David's death, when he was too old and ill to govern (1 Kings 1:38-40). See the introduction to the comments in the main text.

Psalm 127: His Coronation Oath
When Solomon's father, David, became king of all Israel, he made certain pledges to God about how he would reign, which he expressed in 101. Solomon appears to be doing the same here – resolving to do through God those things uppermost in his mind: building a 'house' for God; protecting the city of God, and raising up a family.

Psalm 128: Priest and People respond
This psalm appears to be a response to the previous one. Solomon has voiced his aims on becoming king, and now the priest and people express their agreement and pray that these aspirations may be realised through the blessing of God. There is a progression of thought from the individual (vv. 1-2) to the family (vv. 3-4) and to the nation (vv. 5-6).

Psalm 45: Solomon's wedding
Please see the introductory comments to the psalm in the main text.

Psalm 132: Solomon dedicates the Temple
The main achievement of Solomon's reign was the building of the temple in Jerusalem. 2 Chronicles 5–6 record the service of dedication and include verses 8-10 of this psalm in 2 Chronicles 6:41-42. Please see also the comments in the introduction to this psalm in the main text.

Psalm 135: The Response of Praise
Solomon's prayer at the dedication of the temple was preceded and followed by praise: 2 Chronicles 6:4-6 and 7:1-6. The psalm is one that may well have been used for this purpose, especially as the theme of God's choice which features in 2 Chronicles 6:4-6 is so prominent here (v. 4, cf. 132:13). To Solomon, the most amazing thing about the whole occasion was that this great God should choose a place and people

humanly insignificant in the world of that day for his own dwelling place (2 Chron. 6:18).

THE PERIOD OF REHOBOAM

Solomon's glorious reign ended somewhat ingloriously. His many political marriages brought peace with the neighbouring nations, but at a price. His wives brought their gods with them and turned the king's heart from the Lord. In his anger God declared that his descendants would lose the major part of the kingdom. Trouble began to stir at the close of his reign through the rebellious activity of Hadad, Rezon and Jeroboam. Thus, when Rehoboam succeeded to the throne, his foolish decision to make life even harder for the people than it had been under his father drove all but his own tribe Judah into the arms of Jeroboam.

Jeroboam had earlier taken refuge in Egypt, as had Hadad, who was in such favour with the Pharaoh that he gave him a member of the royal family in marriage. When Rehoboam tried to regain his lost territory by war, Pharaoh Shishak took the part of Jeroboam and broke the treaty he had made with Solomon on his first marriage to Pharaoh's daughter, brought his army against Jerusalem and plundered the temple, doing much damage in the process.

The whole story is recounted in 1 Kings 11–14 with some additional material in 2 Chronicles 12. The reactions of the godly in Judah are recorded in four psalms.

Psalm 74: Shishak's invasion and God's punishment

It is possible this is the same *Asaph* as he who wrote many psalms in the time of David. Otherwise it could be a son, or someone following his thought and style – a member of 'the school of Asaph'. Please see also the introductory comments in the main text.

Psalm 77: Shishak's invasion and the appeal to God's deeds

Asaph was so distressed by the troubles of his time that he poured out his heart to God in more than one psalm. This one is composed in co-operation with another of David's musicians – *Jeduthun* (1 Chron. 25:1-3) and has strong similarities with 74.

Psalm 79: Shishak's invasion and the reproach on God's name
Although the sentiments of 74 and 77 recur in this psalm, there is more stress here on prayer to God for deliverance from the invaders. *Asaph* is getting to grips with the situation, reasoning that God cannot let it go on and asking him to intervene on Israel's side.

Psalm 89: Shishak's invasion and the revocation of the covenant
Ethan had been one of Solomon's wise men (1 Kings 4:31), but this psalm may date from David's time, as he is now an old man (v. 47). His reactions to Shishak's invasion are expressed in this psalm. Please see also introductory comments in the main text.

THE REIGN OF JEHOSHAPHAT
Fifty years have passed since Rehoboam, and Judah has recovered from the devastation of Shishak's invasion, although the histories tell us little of how that took place. 2 Chronicles 12:12 simply says: 'Because Rehoboam humbled himself, the LORD's anger turned from him and he was not totally destroyed. Indeed there was some good in Judah'. The complete recovery was due in large measure to the two comparatively good reigns that followed. **Abijah** (2 Chron. 13) reigned for only three years and his aim was to reunite the twelve tribes. He went personally into 'the hill country of Epraim' and appealed to those under Jeroboam's jurisdiction to return to the Lord. But Jeroboam responded with an ambush, trapping Abijah and his men on Mount Zemaraim. The Lord intervened, 'routed Jeroboam, struck him down and he died'. But Abijah himself died soon after.

Asa reigned for forty-one years, and for the first ten enjoyed the peace won by his father. This enabled him to fortify Judah's defences, which stood them in good stead when the Ethiopians attacked (2 Chron. 14). Some progress was made in bringing the people of Israel back to the Lord (2 Chron. 15), but its king, Baasha, intervened and fortified Ramah, a border town. Sadly, Asa's faith wavered and he came to rely on Syria, with whom he made a treaty. He was rebuked by a prophet, whom he imprisoned, and his reign ended ignominiously (2 Chron. 16).

Jehoshaphat followed Asa's earlier policy, apart from a lapse when he became involved in Ahab's wars and narrowly escaped death. But he learned his lesson and put his efforts into strengthening his own country. His neighbours – Ammon, Moab and Edom – grew jealous, formed a confederacy and attacked. Jehoshaphat held his nerve, called for fasting and prayer, and even formed a choir! The confederacy broke up and the troops fled, leaving their booty (2 Chron. 20). The choir led them in praise on the spot, then Jehoshaphat organised a proper festival on returning to Jerusalem.

Psalm 46: Singing on the Battlefield

Although we cannot be certain which of the many wars of the kings this refers to, it must originally have been composed for one of these. The attributing of the battle and victory to God (v. 9) fits well with the words of the prophet Jahaziel in 2 Chronicles 20:15: 'The battle is not yours but God's'. The desolate scene which the army of Judah left behind (2 Chron. 20:24) is echoed in the reference to *desolations* in verse 8 of the psalm.

Alamoth means 'girls', indicating that it was led by the sopranos, whose high voices were best suited to the note of triumphant joy sounded here.

Psalm 125: Returning to the city

This *Song of ascents* or 'marching song', part of the corpus of psalms used by pilgrims to the temple feast, may have had its origin in the return of the army from their victory over the confederacy, celebrated in 46. That psalm gloried in God's choice of Jerusalem to be the city in which he dwelt (vv. 4-5). Psalm 125 begins at that point (v. 1): God has again demonstrated this from their recent victory.

Psalm 48: Within the walls of Jerusalem

This psalm takes us a stage further on from 125. The people are now depicted as entering the city and pausing to glory in it (vv. 1-8) before going into the temple to meditate on and marvel over their God himself (vv. 9-11), after which they leave to process around Mt. Zion (vv. 12-14). This *psalm of the sons of Korah* is a true *song* of praise.

THE REIGN OF HEZEKIAH

A century and a half have passed since Jehoshaphat celebrated the Lord's victory over the three-nation confederacy with three psalms. The Psalter was quite large now and psalms could be found for most occasions. Also, there was not much to celebrate during the reigns of Jehoshaphat's successors prior to Hezekiah. Jehoram and Ahaziah were both under the influence of Ahab of Israel. Joash reigned well until the death of Jehoiada the high priest, then he allowed idolatry to return. Amaziah and Uzziah recovered some of Judah's independence, but the former was assassinated and the latter became a leper. Jotham, although a good man, did nothing to reform the worship, and under Ahaz things deteriorated so much that Judah became involved in Syria's wars, which led to further trouble with Israel and the Philistines.

This was the situation when Hezekiah came to the throne (2 Chron. 28:19-25). His first task was to re-open the temple, purify it and restore the worship (2 Chron. 29). Next he held a great Passover, which even some from Israel attended (2 Chron. 30). He went on to purge the other cities of their idolatry (2 Chron. 31). Yet so endemic was Judah's sin that God permitted the Assyrians under Sennacherib to invade. But Hezekiah's faith held and God destroyed the Assyrian army (2 Chron. 32). Hezekiah became grievously sick, however, and was expecting to die, as Isaiah predicted. But his prayer was heard and Isaiah came back with another prophecy reversing the first (Isa. 38). The next two psalms can be seen as Hezekiah's thanksgiving after his recovery.

Psalm 116: Hezekiah thanks God for his recovery

The story of Hezekiah's sickness and recovery is told in 2 Kings 20, 2 Chronicles 32 and Isaiah 38. Following Hezekiah's prayer Isaiah predicted that he would 'go up to the temple of the Lord on the third day from now' (2 Kings 20:5). This psalm may be taken as Hezekiah's thanksgiving on that occasion, for the writer is *in the courts of the house of the Lord* to which he has

come to *sacrifice a thank-offering and fulfil (his) vows to the* LORD
(vv. 17-19). The fact that it is anonymous may mean he wrote
it himself.

Psalm 87: The Glories of the city of God

After Hezekiah's remarkable recovery from his fatal illness,
he was visited by ambassadors from Babylon, who came
with letters and gifts from their king, Merodach-Baladan,
congratulating him (2 Kings 20:12-13). Almost certainly,
however, they had an ulterior motive. Judah had achieved
a devastating victory over Assyria, Babylon's enemy and
conqueror. Nothing did more to open the way for Babylon's
supremacy over Assyria than this, especially if Judah allied
itself with Babylon against Assyria.

Isaiah rebuked Hezekiah for being too welcoming and
especially for showing the Babylonians the treasures of his
palace and kingdom. He foretold the future subjugation
of Judah to Babylon. If, however, this psalm belongs to this
incident, the writer sees another interpretation: their visit is
a token of an even further-off time when, not only Babylon,
but all Judah's foes, would unite with her in the worship of
God. This does not mean the psalmist is contradicting Isaiah's
words, only that what he foretold was not the end of the story.
The same tension exists in Isaiah's own prophecies. He who
predicted disaster for these nations in chapters 13–24 also
predicted their coming to Zion to worship God in 2:1-4. This
is the theme of this *psalm* or *song*.

THE BABYLONIAN CAPTIVITY

When Hezekiah was visited by Babylonian ambassadors to
congratulate him on his recovery from a serious illness, he
gave them rather too warm a welcome, for he showed them
the treasures of his palace and kingdom. He was rebuked
by Isaiah who prophesied 'the time will surely come when
everything in your palace ... will be carried off to Babylon ...
and some of your descendants will be taken away, and they
will become eunuchs in the palace of the king of Babylon'
(2 Kings 20:16-18).

At that time Babylon was a minor power and Assyria was
the dominant nation in the area, so that little weight was

given to Isaiah's words But the same prediction was made by Habakkuk, probably in the reign of Josiah some sixty years later, and was received with astonishment (Hab. 1:5-11). Then in 612 BC, shortly before Josiah's death, Nineveh fell, Babylon took over the Assyrian empire and went on to conquer Egypt. Judah was made tributary and under its last three kings the majority of the population went into captivity. Their sufferings and prayers are recorded in the next three psalms.

Psalm 123: Going to work in Babylon

This *song of ascents* or 'marching song' reflects the thoughts and feelings of the people as they went out day by day to work for the Babylonians, who made them slave labourers, as Egypt had done of old. Thus the warning issued by Moses that if they were faithless to their covenant with God, the Egyptian experience would be repeated tenfold (Deut. 28:48, 65-68), was fulfilled.

For faithless they had been. Apart from the reign of Josiah, there had been nothing but decline into sin – moral, social and religious – since the death of Hezekiah. So a hundred years later when God's patience was exhausted and they were deaf to their prophets, the Babylonians conquered them and they went into captivity. There they saw what an idolatrous society was really like, and they began to long after God again, as this psalm shows.

Psalm 137: Weeping by the waters of Babylon

Psalm 123 spoke of the slavery of the Jews in Babylon. Here are more details of this. The rivers of Babylon were the canals which irrigated the vast plain between the Tigris and Euphrates, which the Jews were forced to help dig.

Psalm 44: Recalling past glories

Please see the introductory comments to this psalm in the main text.

THE RETURN FROM CAPTIVITY

Jeremiah (25:12-13) foretold that the captivity in Babylon would last 70 years, and in 537 BC Cyrus, King of the Medes and Persians, conqueror of Babylon, issued his decree permitting the exiles to return (Ezra 1:1-4). So the dreams of the Jews came true and their sorrow was turned to singing. 50,000 returned under Sheshbazzar (Ezra 1) and began work on their new temple in order to resume the worship of the Lord.

Psalm 126: Facing hardships
Please see the introductory comments on the psalm in the main text.

Psalm 129: Celebrating freedom
This psalm may have been composed on the same occasion as 126 or at least around that time. Please see the introductory comments in the main body of the text.

Psalm 85: Praying for renewal
Please see the introductory comments on the psalm in the main text.

Psalm 136: Resuming the worship of God
The cries to God the Jews had uttered in their difficulties were not in vain; the altar was built and the offerings made on it (Ezra 3:1-6). This was probably the occasion for the special thanksgivings expressed in this psalm. For this the author drew on the refrain used at the dedication of Solomon's temple (2 Chron. 5:13: 'he is good, his love endures for ever'). If Solomon and his generation had cause to celebrate God's *goodness and love*, how much more did the returned exiles! They had endured the captivity and all the trouble that greeted them on their return home. Now they see what had enabled them to endure all this – God's everlasting love. So this refrain is repeated with every topic of thanksgiving throughout the psalm. Jeremiah had predicted that the time would come when they would sing these words (Jer. 33:11)! As was the practice on special occasions, the main acts of God's kindness from the beginning to the present time are brought together.

Psalm 102: Work on the Temple ceases
The altar has been restored, the worship of God resumed and the foundation of the temple laid. Next they set about the

building itself (Ezra 4). Their neighbours, who occupied what had been the northern kingdom ('Israel') and who later came to be called 'Samaritans', wanted to get in on the act, but were refused by the Jewish leaders. So instead these neighbours turned against them, hindered the work and eventually had it stopped altogether by order of the Emperor himself.

It is probably this scenario that lies behind 102. Verse 14 paints a picture of a scene in which the dust and rubble of the old building had not yet been removed from the site. This explains the *lament* (title) which forms the first part of the psalm. It is the *prayer of an* individual *afflicted man*, but no doubt one taking on himself the sorrow of the whole nation. It may also reflect the indifference of most of the people to the work of rebuilding, due to the king's ban, which caused them to turn their attention to their own houses, and for which Haggai reproached them (Hag. 1). This man feels he is alone in his concern for the house of God. Could it be Haggai himself or one close to him? But the title's wording is to encourage any *afflicted* person to *pour out his lament before the* LORD.

Psalm 146: The Temple building is resumed
The site of the temple remained a heap of rubble and dust down to 520 BC, when the work was resumed. This was due, not to a change of mind on the Emperor's part, but to a change of heart in the Jews through the preaching of Haggai and Zechariah (Ezra 5:1-2). A further complaint from Judah's neighbours was overruled by Darius who gave permission for the work to continue. This psalm reflects the joy and praise to God they expressed at this time. God had shown his authority over *princes* (v. 3) and his partiality towards the weak and afflicted (vv. 7-9).

Psalm 113: Continuing the work on the Temple
Please see the introductory comments to this psalm in the main text.

Psalm 105: Thanksgiving on the dedication of the Temple
It took four years to rebuild the temple: it was commenced in the second year of Darius (Ezra 4:24) and completed in his

sixth year (Ezra 6:15-18). Psalms 105–106 could well have been composed for and used on this occasion. The author draws heavily on Asaph's compositions for celebrating the recovery of the ark in David's time rather than the material used at the dedication of the first temple by Solomon. Thus 105:1-15 corresponds to 1 Chronicles 16:8-22 and Psalm 106:1, 47-48 to 1 Chronicles 16:34-36. This may have been because of the similarity of the situations prior to these events. Before the earlier occasion the ark had been in captivity, whereas 105 followed the time when the people had been in captivity.

This also helps explain the dominant themes of the two psalms. Psalm 105 links their recent deliverance with those interventions of God which had marked their earlier history; 106 dwells on the perversity of the people for which they had been sent into captivity. Thus 105 stresses God's faithfulness and 106 the people's unfaithfulness.

Psalm 106: Confessing the people's unfaithfulness
Please see the introduction to 105 and the introductory comments on the psalm in the main text.

Psalm 107: The first Passover in the second Temple
The dedication of the Temple took place in the month Adar, corresponding to our February. The next month was the first month when Passover was celebrated. Ezra 6:19-22 records this, the first Passover in the second Temple. That this psalm may have been composed for this occasion is indicated by the reference to sacrifice *thank-offerings* in verse 22. But the theme of the whole psalm is, like the Passover, God's deliverance, with the most recent deliverance – from captivity in Babylon – in the forefront (vv. 2-3).

Psalm 149: Working on the walls of Jerusalem
We now move on sixty years to the return of Ezra and another batch of exiles (Ezra 7). This had been a period of spiritual decline and Jews were even intermarrying with Gentiles. Ezra was authorised by the Persian King, Artaxerxes, to teach the law of God and impose it on the people, something quite remarkable, since it was very different from 'the laws of the Medes and Persians'.

Ezra with his teaching and leadership, probably supported by Malachi's preaching, achieved much reform of worship and behaviour, but the rebuilding programme was still in abeyance and the walls were still in ruins. So ten years later when Nehemiah heard of this, he obtained permission to return and supervise the rebuilding of the walls (Neh. 1). With their enemies still harassing them, Nehemiah had to arm the workers and set up a guard system (Neh. 4:7-23). This tension is reflected in the psalm (vv. 6-9), but the dominant note is praise: the building work was under way and the people in good heart. It is likely the celebration took place away from the temple, since *the tambourine* (v. 3), accompanying dancing, was not used in temple services.

Psalm 147: Thanksgiving for the completion of the walls
Nehemiah's organisation and the people's co-operation meant the walls were completed in fifty-two days (Neh. 6:15). Time for another celebration! Being the seventh month (Neh. 7:73–8:1) this would be the Feast of Tabernacles, probably the most joyous of all feasts (reflected in verses 1, 7, 12.) However, because Ezra was reading and preaching the Law, the people were mourning over their sins (Neh. 8:9). Nehemiah and the Levites encouraged them to be joyful, at which they went away to their private parties (Neh. 8:12) then came together for the Feast of Tabernacles (Neh. 8:13-18). This psalm combines themes appropriate to that feast – the mighty works of God (vv. 15-18) and the revelation of his law (vv. 19-20) – with thanksgivings for the completion of the wall (v. 2) assuring them of God's continued protection (vv. 12-14).

Thanksgivings on the Dedication of the walls
The celebrations for the completion of the walls, which coincided with the Feast of Tabernacles (149, 147), were not immediately followed by their dedication. Certain other things had to be done first, recorded in Neh. 9:1–12:26. First, the people came together and confessed the sins of the nation through its entire history, and God's mercy to them down the ages (Neh. 9). Then they renewed their covenant with God, the details of which are spelled out in Nehemiah 10–11. They pledged themselves not to intermarry any more with Gentiles, to keep the sabbath and

to give tithes and first-fruits. All this preceded the dedication of the walls, for even under the old covenant, relationship with God had priority over buildings and services.

The ceremony of the dedication of the walls is recorded in Nehemiah 12:27-43. It took the form of two processions with Ezra leading one party and Nehemiah the other, and included the singing of two psalms specially composed for the occasion: 148 and 150.

Psalm 148
Although this psalm does not specifically refer to this occasion, its wide-ranging scope makes it appropriate, particularly as, along with 150, it brings the whole collection to a close on a high note. Psalm 148 sets out the themes for the praise of God – that this great creating God (vv. 3-12) should have made Israel his own people (v. 14)! Psalm 150 describes the musical accompaniment. The opening 'Hallelujah' (*Praise the* LORD) is addressed to the whole creation – heavenly (vv. 1-6) and earthly (vv. 7-12).

Psalm 150
This psalm gathers up all that concerns the praise of God, not only for this auspicious occasion, which finalised the re-settlement of the Jews in their land, but for all occasions. Thus it transcends a particular period of time and involves us all, forming a fitting conclusion to the whole collection. No others were to be added; as the spirit of prophecy ceased with the preaching of Malachi around this time until it should be revived by the Messiah's immediate predecessor, John, so the spirit of inspired composition ceased with the dedication of the walls of Jerusalem until this too should be revived at the coming of the Messiah into the world. Until then the collection was large enough.

Subject Index

Scripture Index